CCDE v3 Practice Labs

Preparing for the Cisco Certified Design Expert Lab Exam

Martin J. Duggan, CCDE No. 2016::6

Cisco Press

CCDE v3 Practice Labs: Preparing for the Cisco Certified Design Expert Lab Exam

Martin J. Duggan

Copyright© 2023 Cisco Systems, Inc.

Cisco Press logo is a trademark of Cisco Systems, Inc.

Published by:
Cisco Press

ScoutAutomatedPrintCode

Library of Congress Control Number: 2022908151

ISBN-13: 978-0-13-749985-4

ISBN-10: 0-13-749985-X

Warning and Disclaimer

This book is designed to provide information about the Cisco Certified Design Expert Lab Exam. Every effort has been made to make this book as complete and as accurate as possible, but no warranty or fitness is implied.

The information is provided on an "as is" basis. The author, Cisco Press, and Cisco Systems, Inc. shall have neither liability nor responsibility to any person or entity with respect to any loss or damages arising from the information contained in this book or from the use of the discs or programs that may accompany it.

The opinions expressed in this book belong to the author and are not necessarily those of Cisco Systems, Inc.

Trademark Acknowledgments

All terms mentioned in this book that are known to be trademarks or service marks have been appropriately capitalized. Cisco Press or Cisco Systems, Inc., cannot attest to the accuracy of this information. Use of a term in this book should not be regarded as affecting the validity of any trademark or service mark.

Special Sales

For information about buying this title in bulk quantities, or for special sales opportunities (which may include electronic versions; custom cover designs; and content particular to your business, training goals, marketing focus, or branding interests), please contact our corporate sales department at corpsales@pearsoned.com or (800) 382-3419.

For government sales inquiries, please contact governmentsales@pearsoned.com.

For questions about sales outside the U.S., please contact intlcs@pearson.com.

Feedback Information

At Cisco Press, our goal is to create in-depth technical books of the highest quality and value. Each book is crafted with care and precision, undergoing rigorous development that involves the unique expertise of members from the professional technical community.

Readers' feedback is a natural continuation of this process. If you have any comments regarding how we could improve the quality of this book, or otherwise alter it to better suit your needs, you can contact us through email at feedback@ciscopress.com. Please make sure to include the book title and ISBN in your message.

We greatly appreciate your assistance.

Editor-in-Chief: Mark Taub	**Copy Editor:** Bart Reed
Alliances Manager, Cisco Press: Arezou Gol	**Technical Editor:** Daniel Dib
Director, ITP Product Management: Brett Bartow	**Editorial Assistant:** Cindy Teeters
Executive Editor: Nancy Davis	**Designer:** Chuti Prasertsith
Managing Editor: Sandra Schroeder	**Composition:** codeMantra
Development Editor: Christopher A. Cleveland	**Indexer:** Timothy Wright
Project Editor: Mandie Frank	**Proofreader:** Barbara Mack

‧ı‍|ı‍‧‍ı‍|ı‍‧
CISCO.

Americas Headquarters
Cisco Systems, Inc.
San Jose, CA

Asia Pacific Headquarters
Cisco Systems (USA) Pte. Ltd.
Singapore

Europe Headquarters
Cisco Systems International BV
Amsterdam, The Netherlands

Cisco has more than 200 offices worldwide. Addresses, phone numbers, and fax numbers are listed on the Cisco Website at **www.cisco.com/go/offices.**

CCDE, CCENT, Cisco Eos, Cisco HealthPresence, the Cisco logo, Cisco Lumin, Cisco Nexus, Cisco StadiumVision, Cisco TelePresence, Cisco WebEx, DCE, and Welcome to the Human Network are trademarks; Changing the Way We Work, Live, Play, and Learn and Cisco Store are service marks; and Access Registrar, Aironet, AsyncOS, Bringing the Meeting To You, Catalyst, CCDA, CCDP, CCIE, CCIP, CCNA, CCNP, CCSP, CCVP, Cisco, the Cisco Certified Internetwork Expert logo, Cisco IOS, Cisco Press, Cisco Systems, Cisco Systems Capital, the Cisco Systems logo, Cisco Unity, Collaboration Without Limitation, EtherFast, EtherSwitch, Event Center, Fast Step, Follow Me Browsing, FormShare, GigaDrive, HomeLink, Internet Quotient, IOS, iPhone, iQuick Study, IronPort, the IronPort logo, LightStream, Linksys, MediaTone, MeetingPlace, MeetingPlace Chime Sound, MGX, Networkers, Networking Academy, Network Registrar, PCNow, PIX, PowerPanels, ProConnect, ScriptShare, SenderBase, SMARTnet, Spectrum Expert, StackWise, The Fastest Way to Increase Your Internet Quotient, TransPath, WebEx, and the WebEx logo are registered trademarks of Cisco Systems, Inc. and/or its affiliates in the United States and certain other countries.

All other trademarks mentioned in this document or website are the property of their respective owners. The use of the word partner does not imply a partnership relationship between Cisco and any other company. (0812R)

Figure	Credits
Figure 3.1	elenvd/123RF
Figures 3.5–3.7, 3.14	Google

About the Author

Martin J. Duggan, CCDE#2016::6 and CCIE#7942, is a Principal Network Architect designing network solutions for global financial accounts at Systal Technology Solutions. He is one of Systal's key technical leadership resources, helping Systal to be a dynamic and innovative services integrator and provider that offers fast, agile, and tailored support to meet business aspirations and challenges. Martin gained his Routing & Switching CCIE in 2001 and has been passionate about Cisco qualifications and mentoring ever since. He wrote the *CCIE Routing & Switching Practice Labs* series for Cisco Press and was keen to do the same for the CCDE program after completing his CCDE. He resides in the UK, where he draws inspiration for his CCDE scenarios from his successful career in the communications industry.

Martin enjoys gliding, cycling, snowboarding, and karate when not designing networks, and he creates content for multiple Cisco exam tracks.

Follow Martin on Twitter @Martinccie7942

About the Technical Reviewer

Daniel Dib, CCIE #37149, CCDE #20160011, is a Senior Network Architect at Conscia. He works with designing scalable, modular, and highly available designs that meet business needs. Daniel has a background in implementation and operations and achieved his CCIE certification in 2012. In May 2016 he became the second person in Sweden to achieve the Cisco Certified Design Expert certification.

The last couple of years Daniel has been working mainly with SD-WAN and networking in public clouds such as AWS and Azure. He is an active part of the networking community and writes a blog at https://lostintransit.se. You can follow him on Twitter @danieldibswe

Dedication

This book goes out to my family. They are the reason I always seem to have a goal for something like writing this book or trying to keep a glider in the air for five hours. They always provide me with an incredible level of support, and I simply couldn't achieve my goals without them.

Jake, my favorite son, you are a joy to spend time with. I love that you are so interested in my books, and I think it's about time we wrote one together. It could be epic Lego builds, electric motorbike mayhem, karate for kids, or a gastro cookbook. I will let you choose, and we can have a lot of fun with the research!

James, my other favorite son, you've progressed from CCNA to CCNP so quickly, and I couldn't be prouder of your progress and watching you grow. I thoroughly enjoy our mentoring/banter sessions that always seem to be during a bike ride or game of *Call of Duty* (is that a coincidence or is it planned?). Regardless, you have an amazing career ahead of you, and I will be grateful if you can mentor me. We should write a pizza cookbook with Jake, though, before you disappear off on some exciting assignment.

Anna, my favorite daughter, you are the real architect of the family. I can't believe you are almost finished with your degree. It has been a journey, and I'm so proud you have persevered and have done so well. You are an amazing young lady and will be offered some incredible opportunities, so I can't wait to see how your career develops and your life unfolds. It's going to be great, and you fully deserve it.

I am blessed to have the three of you. When I'm on a mountain and I see you all hurtling through the snow under full control (Jake, semi-controlled), I am definitely in my happy place!

Charlotte, you've got some work to do on the skiing front, but you're perfect in every other way. I love the time we get together, whether it's the school run, having a coffee, cycling, or being my favorite co-pilot. I'm a happy and lucky man.

Mum and Dad, thanks for being there and for everything you do for our family.

Acknowledgments

I'd like to express my gratitude to the team at Cisco Press, especially Nancy Davis and Chris Cleveland, who have turned a vision into something real. They will either be taking the CCDE lab or a long holiday after this project. Thanks also to the technical reviewer, Daniel Dib. I was so fortunate to get you involved in this project and really value your contribution. It brought back memories of our original CCDE study group, our journey towards CCDE, and the CCIE lab content creation week in Brussels.

Russ White, Bruce Pinsky, and the original CCDE creators, thank you for producing an incredibly valuable certification. The design community has grown considerably because of your baby.

Elaine Lopes and Mark Holm, thank you for keeping the CCDE challenging, real world, current, and achievable. It's simply the best certification track a candidate could wish to pursue.

Mark Holm, I am also grateful for the Foreword you kindly provided.

Contents at a Glance

Reader Services

Register your copy at www.ciscopress.com/title/ISBN for convenient access to downloads, updates, and corrections as they become available. To start the registration process, go to www.ciscopress.com/register and log in or create an account*. Enter the product ISBN 9780137499854 and click Submit. When the process is complete, you will find any available bonus content under Registered Products.

*Be sure to check the box that you would like to hear from us to receive exclusive discounts on future editions of this product.

Contents

Foreword

The CCDE certification is regarded by many as the pinnacle of Cisco career certifications—a certification that many long-standing networking professionals who want to transition to an architectural role choose to pursue. Working on the border between the business and the network is an area that requires a different mindset than what is seen with typical networking-oriented certifications. On one side, you need to be well-versed in the many technologies found in networks, knowing what each technology can provide the business, either from a technical or business aspect. On the other side, you must also be able to determine what the business expects from the technical solution. Your task is essentially to translate all the stated requirements and constraints—whether they are of a technical, financial, or business-oriented nature—into a solution that meets them.

The CCDE Practical Exam is designed to mimic real life, so you are also likely to be asked to justify and/or explain the decisions you make, just like it often happens in real-life design situations. Design is not an exact science—often there are many ways to achieve the goals, and some proposed solutions may be more optimal than others. This is where you as a CCDE can make a difference.

Preparing for the CCDE Practical Exam is a daunting task that requires real-life job experience and study efforts. Just as important is adopting the required mindset and getting used to working under pressure. During the exam you will be faced with multiple scenarios, each of which you are expected to finish within a finite time limit. You will have to read the provided resources (diagrams, background information, strategies, emails asking for advice, etc.), analyze the current environment, and figure out what the goals are. All of this will provide you with the information required to be able to answer the questions. In doing this, it is important to keep time management in mind, as you must complete any given scenario within the time limit. One of the best ways to do this is through practice, practice, and practice. This is where this book comes into play; it is designed to allow you to get experience working your way through exam-like scenarios.

As you work through the practice scenarios, it is important to be honest with yourself. Maybe you found that you lacked a bit of knowledge in certain areas, or that you could improve on your speed. Include these aspects in your self-evaluation after each practice scenario to get an idea of where you are.

I wish you the best of luck in pursuing your CCDE certification!

Mark Holm
CCDE Exam Program Manager
CCIE #34763 (EI, DC, SP)
CCDE #20160020

Introduction: A License to Design

Design methodology isn't just focused on technology; an architect or designer also needs to focus on business priorities to bring true value to a solution. A design is often a compromise and has multiple constraints that are outside of the domain or scope of influence of an IT organization. To successfully deliver true value, a Cisco Certified Design Expert (CCDE) can be relied upon to assist organizations in seeing the bigger picture and interface between technical and business domains with their wealth of technical expertise and business acumen. Cisco's CCDE certification has recently been updated to v3 to enhance the skillset of expert-level designers and architects to ensure the technical solutions businesses demand are able to meet the business and technical requirements in this increasingly complex world in which we live. The CCDE certification has been running since 2007 with a steadily growing niche community.

In comparison, the CCIE certification has been running since 1993, with numbers now being issued beginning from upward of #60,000. Reading between the lines, does this mean the CCDE certification is not as desirable or is considerably harder to achieve than the CCIE? Fortunately, the answer is "no" on both counts. It is a highly desirable vendor-agnostic (up to v3) certification, and candidates who are not dedicated to network design find it challenging to demonstrate that they possess the qualities that the certification stipulates in order to be successful. CCIE exams are mature and very specific within each track. You are openly informed which equipment and code you will be presented with and have a wealth of training material available to purchase with very specific blueprints to follow. The exam questions are also well-defined, and you have the ability to double-check your practical tasks to validate your success as you progress through the exam (configure X in order to achieve Y, and so on).

In contrast, the CCDE certification tests candidates on their experience to prove their status and validate their technical and business experience. It's real world (what technology should customer X choose in order to satisfy requirement Y?). Passing the certification isn't a case of studying technology or "labbing out" how protocols interact. I generally explain to candidates that in order to be successful in the CCDE lab, you actually need to be operating as a CCDE in your role on a day-to-day basis already. You just need to convince the Cisco testing engine. You've typically already achieved a CCIE certification to cover the technical aspects you will find in the CCDE lab, and your technical and business engagement experience in your design role is really what is going to differentiate you in the lab exam to be successful.

One of the biggest problems in achieving a Cisco expert-level certification is not knowing what you don't know, so these labs are going to be the turning point in your preparation and will coach you in exam technique as well as design methodology. The labs presented in this book will help you focus on the "why," as opposed to the "how," which you may be more used to. This is absolutely crucial for the certification. Also, this is a first-class certification, and you have never seen anything like it previously, which is a credit to the creators. It was developed by the likes of Russ White and Bruce Pinsky, who have both been role models in my career and certification quest. Both are gurus, and having met them a number of times, I can tell you they are very nice chaps to boot.

The certification was developed as it became more and more apparent to the folks at Cisco that, even though they had been fundamental in assisting TAC by creating the CCIE program in order to implement and troubleshoot networks successfully, they actually didn't have an expert level of designers to ensure that networks were designed correctly from the outset. Can a network scale? Where is the fault domain? Is modularity required? If these design fundamentals are achieved from the offset, then the concept of firefighting shouldn't exist, and your IT team can be more productive while your customers will be content with stability and a network that can scale or divest without damaging the underlying business.

You need to effectively be "T" shaped in order to be successful with the CCDE certification. By this I mean, ideally, you should be operating currently as an IT architect and have a wide breadth of IT knowledge horizontally (high level and broad, covering many disciplines and fields, including business acumen) and depth of knowledge vertically (low level and specialized in a particular field; Layer 3 is a must). This is opposed to an IT specialist (think CCIE), who would typically be "I" shaped and primarily have the vertical knowledge and be an expert in his or her own field while lacking broader, wider knowledge.

A question that is posed to the CCDE community regularly is, Do I need to be a CCIE in order to become a CCDE? The answer that is generally given is "yes and no," or as Cisco prefers to say, "it depends." Having a CCIE is an advantage but entering the exam with a CCIE mindset is not going to help you attain the CCDE certification. You may focus too closely on small issues (sweating the small stuff) and miss the bigger picture of what is being requested from you. The previous CCDE certification track owner Elaine Lopes summed this up nicely by saying, "don't bring a knife to a gun fight!" Bring the right expertise and mindset to the exam, and you have a far higher chance of being successful. Achieving the CCDE certification is really about proving you have had the experience and possess the knowledge, experience, and intelligence to operate effectively with multiple business and technical constraints. Everyone I have met who has been working toward or who has passed the CCDE tells me they have grown considerably in their journey toward attaining the CCDE. Pass or fail, you are definitely going to learn new skills, grow your network, and enhance your career. Cisco states the following: "Unlike the CCIE, which focuses on low-level network design and implementation, the CCDE validates your ability to work in the world of key stakeholders. Your CCDE certification proves your proficiency in the art of soliciting and documenting true requirements and then translating them into a high-level design for a complete solution that delights your stakeholders. The result? The business gets solutions that meet their requirements, fit their budget and schedule, and address today's needs with a view to the future. You get all the glory. The CCDE enables you to design for the changing needs of a complex world."

What's New for CCDE v3?

A significant change to v3 is the delivery. The exam is now more aligned to a CCIE lab exam and administered and delivered in-house within Cisco, with identical pricing and scheduling to the CCIE lab. Initially up to six administrations of the exam are planned per calendar year, and results are delivered within 48 hours, which is a significant improvement over the legacy delivery. There is now an increased focus on business strategies and the resultant impact on designs, which can be challenging if a candidate is purely focused on technology in their day-to-day role. "Core" and "area of expertise" modules have now been introduced, which allow an expert in a specific field to leverage their experience in a final scenario, while the first three scenarios will be based around core competencies. Up until v3, the lab exam was purely vendor-agnostic, but Cisco-specific technologies may appear in area of expertise modules. At exam launch, the Area of Expertise options include the following:

- On-prem and Cloud Services
- Workforce Mobility
- Large-Scale Networks

What's Expected of Me in the Practical Exam?

You will need to show you can analyze design requirements based on real-world business scenarios and use this information to develop, implement, validate, and optimize network designs. You need to be skilled at reading comprehension, as you will be presented with a significant amount of background information that sets the scene of the scenario, information about the existing network, issues, and strategy, along with any relevant business information. You will have to find what is actually important from this information, which means skimming and taking notes or highlighting specific sections within the documents—points that could ultimately influence a design decision. Time is a big factor due to the quantity of information that grows as the scenario progresses, with new information in emails being presented to you. You will need to know what's relevant to your design decision and where that information is in order to locate it quickly when required. There could be sections of a network presented within the exam that you are not familiar with; as such, you will need to be able to abstract and see any technology you are not familiar with or considered non-core to the syllabus as a "black box." In other words, have a flow or connection to it but don't concern yourself about the complexity that lies inside.

Over the course of the eight-hour test, you will be presented with four separate scenarios (two before lunch and two after lunch). The first three scenarios will be based on core competencies, and the final will be the area of expertise module. Each scenario will include the following components:

- **Use cases:** Use cases are going to be the main theme of the scenario where you will be performing one of the following:

  - **Add technology/service:** Here you could be adding a new application to an existing network or new technology such as VoIP, Wi-Fi, and so on. You will need to determine what you need to do to support this addition, including implementation and how it could affect the existing infrastructure/services.

  - **Replace technology/service:** Here you could be replacing a legacy technology/service currently running in the network. You will need to determine what you need to do to support this replacement, including the implementation plan and how it could affect the existing infrastructure/services.

- **Merge/divest:** Here you could be merging or divesting businesses or departments and will need to determine how this can affect the legacy infrastructure and services.

- **Scaling:** Here you will need to consider the ability of the network to grow with planned growth levels and organic growth while still functioning correctly. Will modularity be required, for example?

- **Greenfield:** This is generally every architect's best-case scenario; however, implementation will need to be planned, and you will usually need to consider migrating traffic or applications and how your design will cater for this.

- **Design failure:** Here you are likely to be presented with a suboptimal network that has been designed poorly or has suffered from organic growth and is no longer functioning correctly. Your design will need to provide optimization and possibly introduce fault domains, scalability, and enhanced manageability. You could be asked to optimize and then redesign a network with all the necessary migration steps factored into your implementation plan.

- **Design lifecycle:** These are the actual questions you will be presented with. You will need to analyze, design, and create an implementation plan as well as validate and optimize throughout the scenario.

- **Technologies:** These are the technologies you will need to be proficient in so you can make a valid design decision based on requirements and constraints presented to you within the scenario. The supplied blueprint is the place to check which technologies you should be proficient in, but ultimately you need to be an expert in Layer 3 protocols to be successful.

Exam Technique

It took me a while to realize this, but I discovered I couldn't guarantee I would pass the exam based purely on my technical ability, business acumen, and experience. I have been fortunate enough to work in both service provider and enterprise fields in multiple disciplines, but the lab exam is intense, and it takes some strategy to guarantee success. Here are some pointers I learned from my journey that will help you:

- You have two scenarios in the morning and two in the afternoon, each are fixed at two hours; if you finish a scenario early you can move onto the next but there is no longer an option to borrow anytime from another. There are progress bars for each scenario showing you, as a percentage, how far through the scenario you are. Try not to be preoccupied by the two-hour time limit. It's going to take approximately 15 minutes at the beginning of each scenario to read the background information and make any relevant notes that could affect your design decisions. Therefore, it might look like you are running behind initially but absorbing the background information is a good investment of your time.

- You can highlight information in the background information/exhibits using different colors. This can be very useful to highlight specific constraints or information that will undoubtedly influence a design decision. Using different colors for different subject areas can be advantageous and speed up locating the information when required. Use the labs in this book to practice pulling out relevant information and have a scheme in mind if you plan to use the highlighter in the exam; maybe use blue for constraints, red for security requirements, or whatever allows you to go back and find relevant information efficiently.

- You will be supplied with plastic sheets on which to make notes during the exam. If you don't want to search through documents for valuable information, you may prefer to simply write down relevant facts and have them immediately at hand without searching through multiple documents and rereading highlighted text, for example. These notes can be hard to read though and put back into context, and they will take valuable time to actually write, so really try to limit the information you jot down here. The same is true for the notepad available within the desktop you are using.

- As in many Cisco exams, you can't go back in terms of questions (you can check exhibits and emails as often as you like, though). You may be presented with some information that states a customer made a specific design decision as a level set that may then influence an earlier decision you made. Don't worry if the decision didn't match your choice, as you may have made the right choice even if the customer went in another direction. Just carry on with the next question.

- You will get bombarded with new information, such as exhibits and emails. This can be hard to keep track of, but you need to read this information, as it is crucial and will affect your design decision. Make sure you don't have any exhibits minimized at the risk of not seeing the contents.

- Stay connected to the scenario; it will shift in direction and technology, but you need to stay engaged and look at the bigger picture rather than answer each question in a solitary manner. Remember, it's the same fictitious company going through a series of design challenges over a period of time.

- If you feel you don't have sufficient information to answer a question, you need to go back and look at your background information/exhibits. This is definitely not a guessing game; you are making informed decisions and not assumptions.

- Best practice is useful, but there may be a reason why you would do something differently in the exam. Have best practice in mind, but don't let it completely influence your design decision.

- You may be asked to fill in tables with missing information. These can be quite daunting. Just make sure you only fill in columns that are actually required. The instructions should be quite clear.

- You may be asked how you would implement a solution or migrate to a new one. If so, there will likely be multiple steps involved that you are required to place into a specific order. These can be seen as the hardest questions due to the number of variables, but typically there is only one way or a limited number of ways you can achieve the correct order, so practice in these labs and think about how you have delivered projects as part of your role. When you break it down to its simplest form, just be sure you don't add a step that "breaks something before it makes something"!

■ There is a comment button, and all comments are read by the team. The clock is still ticking, though, so you need to decide how important your comment is going to be. Exams are very well written and verified, so it is very unlikely you will spot an error. However, if you are confident you have seen an issue, it's worth making a quick comment.

■ Take a break between each scenario, unless you are seriously behind. You need to reset and tackle the next scenario as a completely new exam with a clear head.

■ Consider wearing noise suppressing headphones if your testing center has them available so you are not interrupted and can focus.

■ Russ White advises to focus on the "why" rather than "how."

■ If you go into the exam and tackle it as a CCIE, you will be leaving as a CCIE.

What Should I Study?

This is a question that is posed to everyone who is successful, and each one has a different take on it. Clearly you need to be proficient in the blueprint topics, but if there is one thing you should spend significant time on, I would say Layer 3. You need to know open standard routing protocols inside and out—which one would be suitable for a particular application and which one wouldn't, how it affects the design if you need to modify areas and zones, how to create failure domains and summarize, and so on. Unfortunately, there is no single book to read. Remember, Cisco expects you to be operating as an architect/designer and have multiple years of experience.

The following list should provide insight into where you should consider investing your study time:

■ **Cisco Live:** Attend the CCDE Tectorial to attempt an example lab during the session and search for design sessions, including areas of technology where you are your weakest. If you cannot attend in person, watch the videos to get the most from the recorded sessions (you will always learn more than you would by just reading the presentations).

■ **Cisco Press:** Look for design-based publications and architecture. Anything from Russ White and Definitive MPLS Network Designs is a must due to the way the author presents the networks in a similar manner to how the scenarios in the exam are presented with background information.

■ **Study groups:** Form your own study group or see if you can join an existing one in order to discuss technologies or work through labs you have purchased together. Also, you can discuss methodologies/technology choices, offer to discuss your area of expertise, and learn from others discussing theirs.

■ **Cisco-validated designs:** Read up on designs for different network zones, learn why a design is being recommended, and think about scalability, manageability, speeds and feeds, failure domains, and convergence.

■ **Unleashing CCDE:** Read blogs created by the CCDE team and CCDEs in the community. Aim to write one yourself when you have passed!

■ **Bootcamps:** If you still feel you aren't ready, there are legitimate vendors operating in this space. Ask the community for advice to see which may offer the best value for you based on your own background.

Remember, gaining the CCDE is a journey. It's going to take time, and you might not be successful initially.

Prerequisites

There are no formal prerequisites for taking the CCDE, but you should have a thorough understanding of the exam topics before taking the exam.

CCDE candidates are recommended to have five to seven years of experience with designing and architecting network solutions, as well as engaging in other related activities, such as pre-sales work.

You will need to pass the 400-007 CCDE written exam prior to attempting the CCDE lab exam. The written exam validates High-Level Design (HLD) aspects as well as business requirements within the context of enterprise network architecture. The exam is a two-hour, multiple-choice test with 90 to 110 questions that focus on core enterprise network architecture HLD aspects. The exam serves as a prerequisite for the CCDE practical exam and will continue to be available as a means of recertifying your expert-level and lower certifications. The exam is closed book, and no outside reference materials are allowed.

CCDE Practical Exam v3: Blueprints and Exam Weighting

1.0 Business Strategy Design (15%)

1.1 Impact on network design, implementation, and optimization using various customer project management methodologies (for instance, waterfall and agile)

1.2 Solutions based on business continuity and operational sustainability (for instance, RPO, ROI, CAPEX/OPEX cost analysis, and risk/reward)

2.0 Control, data, management plane and operational design (25%)

2.1 End-to-end IP traffic flow in a feature-rich network

2.2 Data, control, and management plane technologies

2.3 Centralized, decentralized, or hybrid control plane

2.4 Automation/orchestration design, integration, and on-going support for networks (for instance, interfacing with APIs, model-driven management, controller-based technologies, evolution to CI/CD framework)

2.5 Software-defined architecture and controller-based solution design (SD-WAN, overlay, underlay, and fabric)

3.0 Network Design (30%)

3.1 Resilient, scalable, and secure modular networks, covering both traditional and software-defined architectures, considering:

3.1.a Technical constraints and requirements

3.1.b Operational constraints and requirements

3.1.c Application behavior and needs

3.1.d Business requirements

3.1.e Implementation plans

3.1.f Migration and transformation

4.0 Service Design (15%)

4.1 Resilient, scalable, and secure modular network design based on constraints (for instance, technical, operational, application, and business constraints) to support applications on the IP network (for instance, voice, video, backups, data center replication, IoT, and storage)

4.2 Cloud/hybrid solutions based on business-critical operations

4.2.a Regulatory compliance

4.2.b Data governance (for instance, sovereignty, ownership, and locale)

4.2.c Service placement

4.2.d SaaS, PaaS, and IaaS

4.2.e Cloud connectivity (for instance, direct connect, cloud on ramp, MPLS direct connect, and WAN integration)

4.2.f Security

5.0 Security Design (15%)

5.1 Network security design and integration

5.1.a Segmentation

5.1.b Network access control

5.1.c Visibility

5.1.d Policy enforcement

5.1.e CIA triad

5.1.f Regulatory compliance (if provided the regulation)

CCDE Practical Exam v3: Core Technology List

The following is a list of technologies associated with both the CCDE v3 written exam and the CCDE v3 practical exam. Candidates are expected to have a deep understanding of these technologies. Each of these technologies may appear in any delivery of the exam.

1.0 Transport Technologies

1.1 Ethernet

1.2 CWDM/DWDM

1.3 Frame relay (migration only)

1.4 Cellular and broadband (as transport methods)

1.5 Wireless

1.6 Physical mediums, such as fiber and copper

2.0 Layer 2 Control Plane

2.1 Physical media considerations

    2.1.a Down detection

    2.1.b Interface convergence characteristics

2.2 Loop detection protocols and loop-free topology mechanisms

    2.2.a Spanning tree types

    2.2.b Spanning tree tuning techniques

    2.2.c Multipath

    2.2.d Switch clustering

2.3 Loop detection and mitigation

2.4 Multicast switching

    2.4.a IGMPv2, IGMPv3, MLDv1, MLDv2

    2.4.b IGMP/MLD Snooping

    2.4.c IGMP/MLD Querier

2.5 Fault isolation and resiliency

    2.5.a Fate sharing

    2.5.b Redundancy

    2.5.c Virtualization

    2.5.d Segmentation

3.0 Layer 3 Control Plane

3.1 Network hierarchy and topologies

   3.1.a Layers and their purposes in various environments

   3.1.b Network topology hiding

3.2 Unicast routing protocol operation (OSPF, EIGRP, ISIS, BGP, and RIP)

   3.2.a Neighbor relationships

   3.2.b Loop-free paths

   3.2.c Flooding domains

   3.2.d Scalability

   3.2.e Routing policy

   3.2.f Redistribution methods

3.3 Fast convergence techniques and mechanism

   3.3.a Protocols

   3.3.b Timers

   3.3.c Topologies

   3.3.d Loop-free alternates

3.4 Factors affecting convergence

   3.4.a Recursion

   3.4.b Micro-loops

3.5 Route aggregation

   3.5.a When to leak routes / avoid suboptimal routing

   3.5.b When to include more specific routes (up to and including host routes)

   3.5.c Aggregation location and techniques

3.6 Fault isolation and resiliency

   3.6.a Fate sharing

   3.6.b Redundancy

3.7 Metric-based traffic flow and modification

   3.7.a Metrics to modify traffic flow

   3.7.b Third-party next hop

3.8 Generic routing and addressing concepts

   3.8.a Policy-based routing

   3.8.b NAT

CCDE Practical Exam v3: On-Prem and Cloud Services Technology List

The technologies shown in this document are associated with the On-prem and Cloud Services *area of expertise* of the CCDE v3 practical exam. Candidates are expected to have a deep understanding of these technologies. Each of these technologies may appear in any delivery of the exam.

Note: The technologies listed here are in addition to the technologies listed in the CCDE Core Technology list.

1.0 Transport Technologies
1.1 Data Center Interconnect options
2.0 Layer 3 Control Plane
2.1 Inter-fabric connectivity, such as multipod, multisite
2.2 External connectivity for on-prem and cloud
2.3 Multi-cloud network architecture
3.0 Network Virtualization
3.1 Overlay
3.1.a Management plane
3.1.b Control plane
3.1.c Data plane (such as VXLAN, MPLS)
3.1.d Segmentation
3.1.e Policy
3.1.e.i Security
3.1.e.ii Topologies
3.1.e.iii Data center interconnect
3.1.e.iv Multiple site strategy
3.1.e.v Service insertion
3.2 Virtual Networking
4.0 Automation
4.7 Deployment models
4.7.a Bare metal
4.7.b VM
4.7.c Microservices
5.0 Data Center
5.1 Storage
5.1.a Physical topology
5.1.b QoS requirements
5.1.c FC and FCoE
5.1.c.i Zoning
5.1.c.ii Trunking

5.1.c.iii Link aggregation

5.1.c.iv Load balancing

5.1.d iSCSI

5.1.d.i Authentication

5.1.d.ii Multipathing

5.2 Application delivery

5.2.a Load balancer deployment modes

5.3 Compute

5.3.a UCS blade integration

5.3.b UCS rack server integration

5.3.c HyperFlex integration

5.4 Compute connectivity

5.4.a SAN/LAN uplinks

5.4.b Port modes

CCDE Practical Exam v3: Workforce Mobility Technology List

The technologies listed in this document are associated with the Workforce Mobility *area of expertise* of the CCDE v3 practical exam. Candidates are expected to have a deep understanding of these technologies. Each of these technologies may appear in any delivery of the exam.

Note: The technologies listed here are in addition to the technologies listed in the CCDE Core Technology list.

1.0 Security

1.1 Network control and identity management

1.1.a Cisco ISE

2.0 Wireless

2.1 Enterprise wireless network

2.1.a WLAN architectures

2.1.a.i Centralized

2.1.a.ii Distributed

2.1.b Roaming optimizations

2.1.c Mesh network architecture

2.6 mDNS

2.7 Location services and solutions

   2.7.a RTLS

   2.7.b DNA Spaces

   2.7.b.i Analytics

2.8 Automation, Assurance, Insights, and Telemetry (Legacy and DNAc)

   2.8.a AVC/NetFlow

   2.8.b DNAc

CCDE Practical Exam v3.0: Large-Scale Networks Technology List

The technologies shown in this document are associated with the Large-Scale Networks *area of expertise* of the CCDE v3 practical exam. Candidates are expected to have a deep understanding of these technologies. Each of these technologies may appear in any delivery of the exam.

Note: The technologies listed here are in addition to the technologies listed in the CCDE Core Technology list.

1.0 Transport Technologies

1.1 Carrier Ethernet

1.2 Ring-based (such as SONET/SDH, OTU)

1.3 Frame relay (migration only)

1.4 Wireless (including satellite links, microwave links)

1.5 Optical

2.0 Layer 2 Control Plane

2.1 Loop detection protocols and loop-free topology mechanisms

   2.1.a REP

2.2 Transport mechanisms and their interaction with routing protocols over different link types

3.0 Layer 3 Control Plane

3.1 Factors affecting convergence

   3.1.a Transport

3.2 Generic routing and addressing concepts

   3.2.a Large-scale NAT

CCDE Practical Exam v3.0: Business Information

The CCDE candidate needs to possess some business acumen. Typically, a CCDE will be an interface to the customer CTO and business leaders, translating business requirements into technical solutions. If this area is new to you, I would suggest you investigate the following business areas at high level:

- Values

- Strategy

- Vision

- Mission

- Objectives

- Goals

- Operations

- Value Proposition

- Return on Investment (ROI)

- Business Innovation

- Business Disruption

- Total Cost of Ownership (TCO)

- Capital Expenditure (CAPEX)

- Operational Expenditure (OPEX)

The Labs Presented in This Book

Treat the following three labs as if you were taking the real exam. Aim to get them completed individually within the two-hour limit, but don't worry if they run longer, as they are arguably slightly more difficult than the real exam (this is part of my "train hard and race easy" methodology). The most important thing to consider is that you will gain the maximum value from each lab by taking it after you feel you have completed your study plan. Quite simply, you need to put everything into practice that you have learned. Reference the technology and exam technique to see if you are ready to take the real exam. If you identify some specific areas of technology you may be weaker in, go back and study them prior to taking the real exam. Don't be tempted to work through the debrief to see what was expected of you from each lab until you have actually taken the lab under exam conditions. Labs are extremely difficult and time consuming to create to ensure reality, complexity, and flow. There are very few on the market, so you will need to maximize the benefit of each lab you take.

Consider highlighting the relevant text in the actual book using multiple colors or making a separate note of requirements, constraints, or general information you feel may be of value in order to make an informed design decision. Due to the printing of the book, you might be able to see a subsequent question on an adjacent page, so I would recommend covering up pages as you progress through the lab questions.

These labs do actually reset you along a correct path if you have inadvertently chosen a technology that is not appropriate for the design. Don't be disheartened if you don't score as well as you thought you would when you run through the debrief, as this is practice after all. Just aim to improve your technique with each lab so that by the final one you are eager to go and know what to expect and, more importantly, how to deal with it during your real lab exam.

Final Advice

I attended the CCDE Cisco Live Tectorial in Berlin prior to my success and booked one-on-one time with Elaine Lopes and Yuri Lukin, who were heading up the CCDE certification team at that time. The whole team was really accessible, and they were very keen to offer help and advice. This was invaluable for me—and a turning point. I learned not to be too hasty in my decisions and not to answer the questions based on the facts in front of me but to scan the documents when something wasn't clear. I was missing clues and needed to be neater in marking what was really important. My technical ability was at the correct level, however. The distracters in the questions are so well thought out that you really have to fully absorb the scenario and the requirements presented within it to be successful.

Possibly the most useful resource for me was being part of a study group that my friends Daniel Dib and Kim Pedersen started. We pretty much had the dream team in our study group. We were blessed with the presence of Russ White, the "daddy" of the CCDE exam, and I was able to ask him questions around the logic of OSPF ABR placement from one of his books, as it was puzzling me. He even gave me some brilliant last-minute advice: "read the question," he said! It proved to be simple and sound advice, which made me laugh at the time. I made sure I did read each question, at least twice. I had even filled in a table with multiple answers when I remembered the advice and read the question again and found I only needed to check one box on one column, but actually had completed two (thanks Russ!).

If you are more than an hour away from the test center, booking a hotel for the night before would be a smart move. You don't need the stress of travelling far on the same day. By taking the labs in this book and working through the debrief material, you will be in a far better position and won't have any surprises on the day.

The practical exam is very tough, but it is fair and achievable. This is what makes it so desirable. If it is your goal or ambition to become CCDE certified, you are very likely to reach it. If you are thinking, "I'll give it a shot, as I've been in the industry for 10 years and design on a daily basis," then don't be surprised if you don't get your number immediately. Just remember that if you don't pass on your first or second or even third attempt, you haven't actually failed. You will only have failed if you give up. The exam has to beat you every time, but you only have to beat it once to get your number. It has also occurred to me that if you can't explain a technology or how a solution functions or scales to a friend who isn't necessarily even technical, then you don't actually know that technology. It's a case of turning your weaknesses into your strengths. For instance, if you are a guru with IS-IS but have no real-world experience of how EIGRP may perform better in certain topologies, it's time to get the books out or speak to your study group. Be prepared for give and take from your group. Play devil's advocate to question others and offer to run a study session for your group in your area of expertise. The sum of your group's expertise will be invaluable. Even if you don't get your number, you will grow from the experience.

The exam itself is quite simply a credit to its creators. Most people don't realize the effort that goes into keeping the scenarios realistic, fresh, and protected. The team behind it is brilliant. The distracters are just so good—sometimes you see five correct answers in front of you, but only one will be appropriate to the customer and the scenario, even if not your favorite. Therefore, you just need to connect the dots and find the important requirements that, when matched with your knowledge and experience, will take you to the correct answer.

Put the books down for a few days prior to the exam. Spend time with your loved ones and be energized for the exam. Take your full break on the testing day, and pace your time. The exam status bar you will see throughout your scenarios is actually your friend, not your enemy.

You are going to need some endurance to complete four scenarios in a day. Practice with as many labs as you can as if you were taking your CCIE lab. I like to cycle, and I found I could clear my head and be energized for a long study session after a ride. I certainly couldn't run an eight-hour study session, but I could easily manage four two-hour ones.

Use the following advice as you work through the labs presented in this book and your real exam, and you should have a good chance of gaining your number. Good luck!

- Read the question.
- Connect with the scenario.
- Take time to analyze the existing environment.
- Look for missing information.
- Know what information you already have.
- Don't only base your answer on best practices.
- Do not make assumptions.
- Only make fact-based decisions.
- Work on your weaker technology areas.
- Maintain a high-level approach.
- Think as a network architect/designer, not as a CCIE.
- Focus on the "why"!

Chapter 1

CCDE Practice Lab 1: Jacobs

Jacobs

This practice lab focuses on WAN replacement/optimization in conjunction with enterprise core elements found in each CCDE lab, as per the V3.0 Blueprint. It is based on one of the three fixed core labs you will find in your practical exam.

Practice Lab Navigation

- Read, make notes, and highlight the background information for anything relevant you feel might aid a design decision.

- Answer each question before you continue to the next one.

- When you have completed a question, do not return to previous questions. You may, however, refer to any previous exhibit (email or diagram) that has been previously provided.

- Aim to complete the lab within a two-hour time frame. If you are unable to complete the lab in two hours, then make a note of where you were at the two-hour point to gauge what your score would have been and then continue on with the lab until completion. Do not move on to the review section until you are finished. This way, you will gain the maximum benefit from the practice lab experience.

Practice Lab

During this practice lab, you are the network architect for Jacobs.

Document 1: Background Information

Jacobs is a UK-based building merchant formed in 1982 that supplies the building trade with building materials. The company has over 250,000 customers—predominantly trade professionals, building companies, national contractors, and self-builders. The company began trading as an individual store in Chelsea, London, managed by the founder David Jacob. David had worked in the building trade for the previous 10 years and discovered that there were often delays associated with obtaining building materials required for specific construction stages within home building that would add significant expense to projects. David stockpiled common construction items and tools and capitalized on supplying the local trade to support their builds efficiently within the lifecycle of their projects. The business experienced strong growth due to demand and reputation, and by 1993 the company had grown to 52 stores within the inner London area. Construction demand continued to grow, and Jacobs expanded nationally within the UK in the early 2000s by purchasing a multitude of independent building merchants throughout the country (102 at current count) and by merging with Toolmate, a direct competitor brand. Integration of the independent stores was limited to a storefront change, with backend systems operating in isolation to the Jacobs network and with Toolmate stores maintaining their existing IT systems, with the exception of VoIP, which has been integrated to the Jacobs call manager and hosted within the Jacobs data center (DC), and the provision of a firewalled inter-DC link between the Toolmate and Jacobs DCs.

The majority of Jacobs' employees are based in the Jacobs, Toolmate, and independent store branches, either within the customer store or within dedicated office areas created above the store, with a small subset of IT staff located within each of the London DCs.

Jacobs prides itself on being the first in the industry to support a sustainable building initiative for multi-channel builders, with customer experience at the core of its business model. Recent initiatives have included supporting trade events, optimization of a web frontend (which has been crucial for the mobile CX experience), just-in-time delivery for projects, and tool hire. The product line has increased significantly over time to 30,000 products, and it is feared that the rationalization required to simplify operations will significantly affect the profitability of the business. Supply chain difficulties have been a significant challenge to the business post-Brexit, and Jacobs has lost some high-profile clients to its competition, which has been better positioned throughout Europe to solve supply issues.

The board of the company is keen to introduce efficiencies within the IT systems but is acutely aware that in doing so, they risk damaging a proven culture of a direct customer relationship with store management in store. Direct customer interaction within local stores is becoming more inefficient for the business, and Jacobs continues to investigate innovative processes to enhance profitability. There is a current drive to rationalize and integrate the existing networks, reduce cost, and provide simplification across the compute and network infrastructure.

Document 2: Network Background

The network has historically been separated between Jacobs entities and is served from a central Jacobs DC in the city of London and Toolmate DC in the outer London area. The network is formed of three separate WAN networks to provide DC connectivity to the remote stores. The store networks are summarized as follows:

1. **Jacobs stores (current count of 203):** Each store is dual-homed to MPLS WAN providers (Bluesky and Taco). Access to the MPLS networks is via a default route pointing to a VRRP provisioned gateway running between the CE routers with the primary MPLS network of Bluesky. Stores use VoIP for internal store-to-store communication, with a central call manager cluster hosted within the Jacobs DC and remote site survivability functionality built into the access switches with dual PSTN lines, which are only used in the event of a total WAN or VoIP failure for customers to call into the store. Each store has dual 48-port access 10/100/1Gbps switches connected in a stack to form a single logical switch, the MPLS routers are connected into separate physical switches for resiliency, and a UPS is installed with battery functionality to provide backup for critical components, with up to two hours of power in the event of a failure. The Jacobs store staff have access to all IT services within the Jacobs DC.

2. **Toolmate stores (current count of 78):** Each store is dual-homed to a single MPLS WAN provider, Lotnet. Access to the MPLS networks is via default routes with equal cost pointing to each of the CE routers for load sharing over the MPLS connections. Stores use VoIP for internal store-to-store communication, with a central call manager cluster hosted within the Jacobs DC and remote site survivability functionality built into the access switches with dual PSTN lines, which are only used in the event of a total WAN or VoIP failure for customers to call into the store. Each store has dual 48-port access 10/100/1Gbps switches connected together with an EtherChannel trunk, the MPLS routers are connected into separate physical switches for resiliency, and a UPS is installed with battery functionality to provide backup for critical components, with up to one hour of power in the event of a failure. Toolmate stores operate independently from the majority of Jacobs systems; however, access to specific systems and employee services, such as intranet and HR systems, is enabled via firewalled-controlled DCI links between the Jacobs and Toolmate DCs.

3. **Independent stores (current count of 102):** Each store is single-homed to MPLS WAN provider, Annet. Access to the MPLS networks is via the MPLS CE router, acting as the default gateway for the single VLAN provisioned on the single 48-port 10/100/1Gbps Layer 2 LAN switch in the stores. Stores use traditional telephony of varying suppliers to contact Jacobs centrally and facilitate customer communication. Each store has its own legacy IT system, which Jacobs is planning to rationalize or integrate when time and funds allow. Independent stores are provisioned without resilience, as they use their own local payment systems and telephony systems and can suffer outages to the Jacobs DC for up to six business hours without significant impact to business. Due to the way the independent store central MPLS connection is terminated in the Jacobs DC, the stores are able to access only a limited number of

shared services that are segmented from the Jacobs DC by use of a firewall. Internet access is not provisioned by Jacobs for the stores, and the WAN does not facilitate traversal of any Internet-destined traffic; some stores have therefore set up ad-hoc wireless networks with ADSL links for personal devices, and there is a strict policy in force to ensure APs are not connected to store Jacobs-managed LAN switches. Independent-store-to-independent-store communication is blocked over the MPLS network by use of a hub-and-spoke MPLS network and policy-based routing on the central DC CE router to ensure all traffic is forwarded to the DC firewall for policy.

WAN Documentation

The WAN consists of four separate MPLS provider networks, and each supplies a fully managed Layer 3 MPLS service, including CE routers, as shown in the figure and described in the list that follows.

1. **The Jacobs L3 MPLS VPN network** is provided by Bluesky and Taco for resilient Jacobs store connections into the Jacobs DC. The connections from each provider into the Jacobs DC are via 10Gbps metro Ethernet connections to each provider with

line rate capacity available. The Bluesky network operates as a primary MPLS link and the Taco network as a standby MPLS link due to costing arrangements with the providers. Jacobs stores access the MPLS networks using default static routing pointing to the VRRP gateway with the primary MPLS network of Bluesky. VRRP tracking is used, which decrements priority in the event of uplink failure for stores, so the Taco CE router is only used in the event of a Bluesky uplink circuit failure. Within the CE router configuration, each Jacobs store uses the same BGP AS of 64555 for configuration ease, and AS override is used on each provider. Store prefixes are statically redistributed into BGP by the local CE routers. iBGP is used between providers on the store site to allow connectivity between providers during failure conditions. The central DC Jacobs site uses a BGP AS of 64556 and iBGP between provider CE routers, with mutual redistribution of BGP from the MPLS network to LAN-based OSPF with metrics to ensure the Bluesky MPLS network is used as a primary connection. The Taco MPLS connection is used only in the event of a failure of Bluesky MPLS network connectivity within the DC or within one of the stores. The Layer 3 MPLS network is a full mesh configuration with store-to-store communication enabled by default, which provides optimal routing for VoIP telephony requirements. The MPLS networks are implicitly open without firewalls within Jacobs stores or DC. Each Jacobs store connects to each service provider using a 10Mbps circuit with full line rate available when required and basic QoS enabled to prioritize VoIP traffic over and above application traffic in a four-class QoS policy.

2. **The Toolmate L3 MPLS VPN network** is provided by Lotnet. Stores are dual-homed into the Toolmate MPLS network for access to the central DC and for store-to-store connectivity. The CE router connections into the DC are via 10Gbps metro Ethernet connections to each CE with a CIR of 6Gbps available on each circuit. The CE routers load-share connections for egress and ingress traffic into and out of the DC by use of BGP metric manipulation. The central DC Toolmate site uses a BGP AS of 64600 and iBGP between provider CE routers, with mutual redistribution of BGP from the MPLS network to LAN-based BGP with equal-cost routing configured to facilitate load sharing over both CE router links. The Layer 3 MPLS network is a full mesh configuration with store-to-store communication enabled by default, which provides optimal routing for VoIP telephony requirements. The MPLS network is also implicitly open without firewalls within the Toolmate stores or DC. Each Toolmate store connects to the service provider using dual 10Mbps circuits with a 5Mbps CIR and QoS enabled to prioritize VoIP traffic over and above application traffic in a six-class QoS policy. Stores use dual equal-cost static routes pointing to each MPLS CE router. Store prefixes are statically redistributed into BGP by the local CE routers.

3. **The independent store L3 MPLS VPN network** is provided by Annet. Stores are single-homed to the Layer 3 MPLS hub and spoke network. Independent stores connect to the service provider using a 10Mbps Ethernet circuit with full line rate available with no QoS. Stores use the CE router as a default gateway for the single local LAN VLAN, and store prefixes are statically redistributed into BGP by the local CE router. The CE router connection into the Jacobs DC is via a single 10Gbps metro Ethernet connection, with a CIR of 5Gbps available on the circuit. The central DC

Jacobs site uses a BGP AS of 64700 with redistribution of BGP from the MPLS network to the LAN and a summary route containing Jacobs DC reachable prefixes configured within the MPLS network to steer all DC-destined traffic toward the central DC and a shared services segment protected via a firewall. Internet-destined traffic is not serviced over the Annet MPLS network due to no available default route being present. Store-to-store communication is blocked over the hub-and-spoke network in conjunction with policy-based routing forwarding all traffic received at the DC toward the local firewall for policy decision.

Jacobs DC Network

The Jacobs DC is composed of a collapsed core architecture with 10Gbps core switches and full Layer 3 access layer running OSPF in Area 0. The WAN core is assigned Area 1 and is used as a connectivity zone for communication to the WAN and Internet. The WAN core is composed of dual 48-port 10/100/1Gbps switches with 6x 10Gbps uplinks configured in a stack forming a single logical switch. An outer and inner DMZ is formed of a firewall sandwich with dual vendor firewalls in two separate Layer 2 networks formed from dual 48-port 10/100/1Gbps Layer 2 stacked switches with 6x 10Gbps uplinks. The DMZ inner switches and firewalls host multiple load-balanced DMZ segments for publicly reachable web services for Jacobs' online retail and tool hire presence. The DMZ outer switches host the Internet CE connectivity and VPN services for B2B connections, which provide the online payment systems.

Firewalls (deployed in routed mode) are configured in a local cluster (active/active) with an LACP EtherChannel between them and the stacked switches on either side of the firewalls. A physical state and synch cable is used between firewalls for state and failover for the firewalls, which are located in the same physical network rack.

All internal applications are hosted from within the DC on Layer 3 access model 1Gbps/10Gbps switches with varying port counts, which advertise local switch prefixes using OSPF. Current port utilization is 1460 (65% of total capacity). The main business application is a typical three-tier service called "Jaystore," which synchronizes product availability with a web frontend from a database within the DC location for online and store purchases. The application was created over 10 years ago by developers within a LAN environment and, as such, does not function well when latency exceeds 20ms between the client and headend infrastructure for internal Jacobs users within the stores. Due to this issue, the network team included the TCP application in a mission-critical QoS class over the WAN for mitigation, which functions well.

Internet connectivity is provided by a single ISP (Britnet) from dual 1Gbps links in an active/standby arrangement running iBGP between ISP CE managed routers. Jacobs' external firewalls point to a VRRP address on the ISP CE routers, which receive identical partial routing via BGP from central Britnet ISP routers. Provider-assigned public IP addressing is used for external hosting using a Britnet registered /24 prefix, which is further subnetted to provide DMZ segmentation for public-facing Jacobs' services and NAT ranges for employee Internet access via a central proxy server within the DMZ.

DCI

A dual 1Gbps Layer 3 DCI link is provisioned between the Jacobs and Toolmate DCs using OSPF peering between the firewalls within Jacobs to Toolmate edge routers within the Toolmate DC. Prefixes from each DC network are advertised over the DCI, allowing machine-to-machine communication to enable Toolmate stores and online systems to broker sales for Jacobs' products and services (which is seen as crucial to the Jacobs business model) as well as access for Toolmate staff to Jacobs' intranet and HR systems and VoIP connectivity for Toolmate telephony systems to a Jacobs call manager by firewall policy. OSPF to EIGRP mutual redistribution is configured on the Toolmate DCI routers. System access to the Jacobs DC over the DCI links requires firewall changes on the Jacobs DC firewalls, which terminate the inter-DCI links. Changes require approval from Jacobs and Toolmate change management systems, which is proving to be inefficient and incurs delay for approval and manual implementation out of hours, unless an emergency change procedure is invoked to provide in-hours short notice changes. The firewalls are approaching end of life and are close to capacity in terms of CPU utilization. The following figure shows the Jacobs DC network.

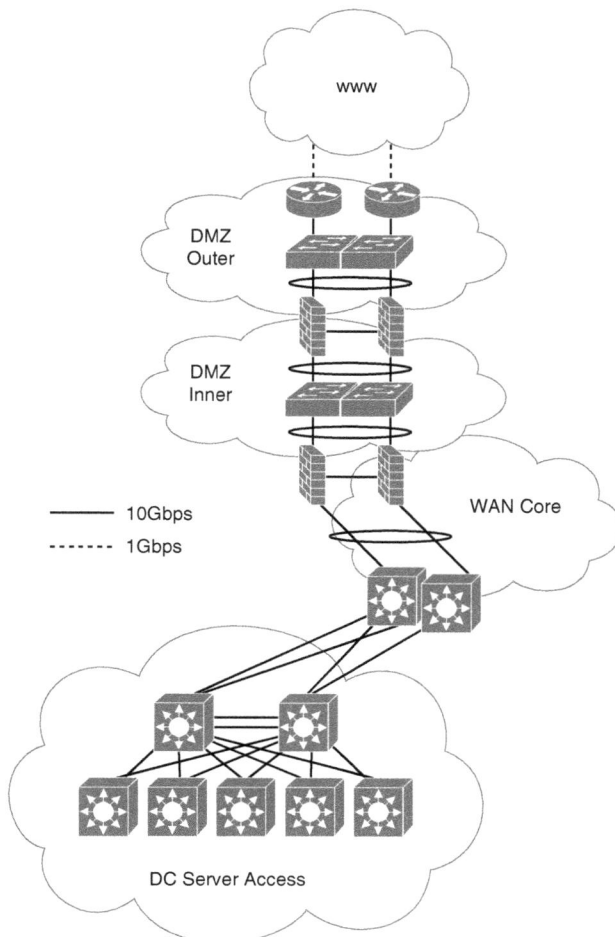

Toolmate DC Network

The Toolmate DC is composed of a collapsed core architecture with dual 48x 1/10Gbps switches configured in a stack, forming a single logical switch and full Layer 3 access layer running EIGRP over dual 10Gbps ECMP uplinks. Access switches are chassis-based modular 10/100/1Gbps switches with dual supervisors and dual PSUs, with a total current port count of 1280 (78% utilization).

A DMZ is formed of a firewall sandwich with dual vendor firewalls (deployed in routed mode) in a single Layer 2 network formed from dual 48-port 10/100/1Gbps Layer 2 switches with 6x 10Gbps uplinks connected to each other using a 2x 10Gbps Etherchannel trunk. The DMZ hosts a single non-load-balanced DMZ segment for publicly reachable web services for Toolmate's online store presence and tool hire. The red zone outer switches host the Internet CE connectivity and VPN services for B2B connections, which provide online payment systems. Firewalls are configured in an active/standby arrangement with a physical proprietary cable between firewalls for synchronization, state, and failover.

Internet connectivity is provided by a single ISP (JAnet) from dual 1Gbps links in an active/standby arrangement running iBGP between ISP CE managed routers. Toolmate's external firewalls point to a VRRP address on the ISP CE routers, which receive identical default routes (0/0) via BGP from central JAnet ISP routers. Legacy provider-independent public IP addressing migrated from a previous ISP is used for external hosting using a /25 prefix, which is subnetted to provide DMZ segmentation for public-facing Toolmate services and NAT ranges for employee Internet access via the external firewall. A default route is advertised throughout the DC and WAN for external traffic to be routed via the external firewall in the absence of a proxy server for Internet traffic. The following figure illustrates the Toolmate DC network.

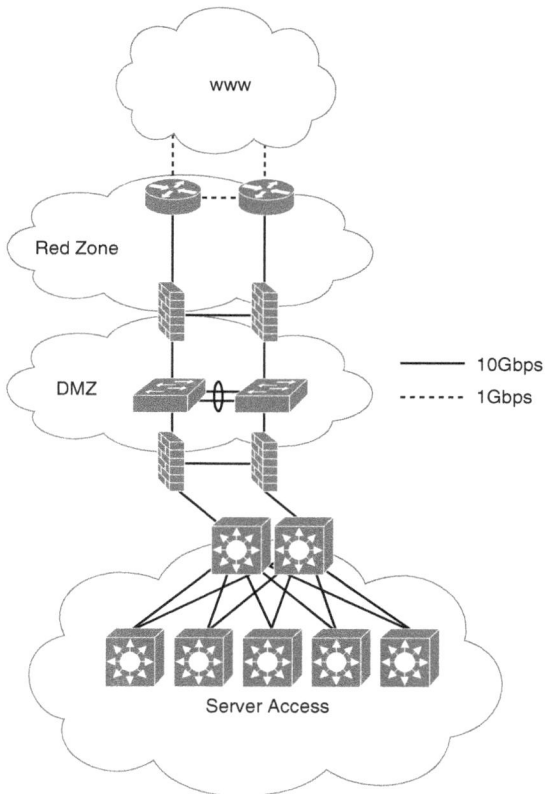

Document 3: Utilization Statistics

The figures that follow provide the WAN and Internet utilization statistics.

Jacobs Bluesky DC MPLS CE Utilization

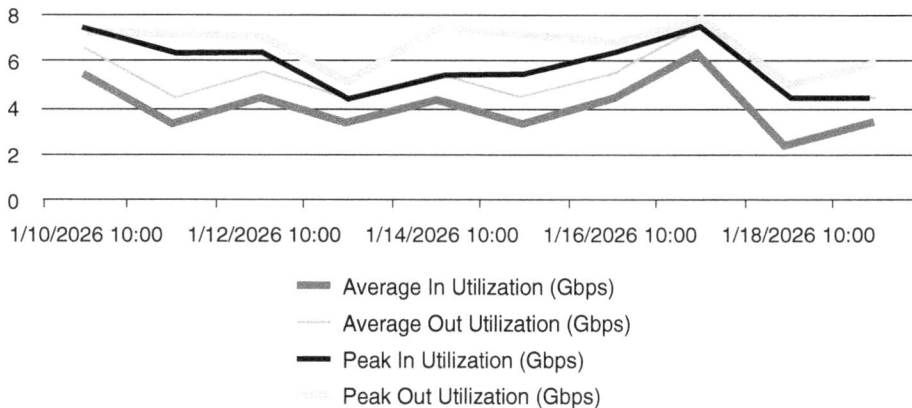

Jacobs TACO DC MPLS CE Utilization

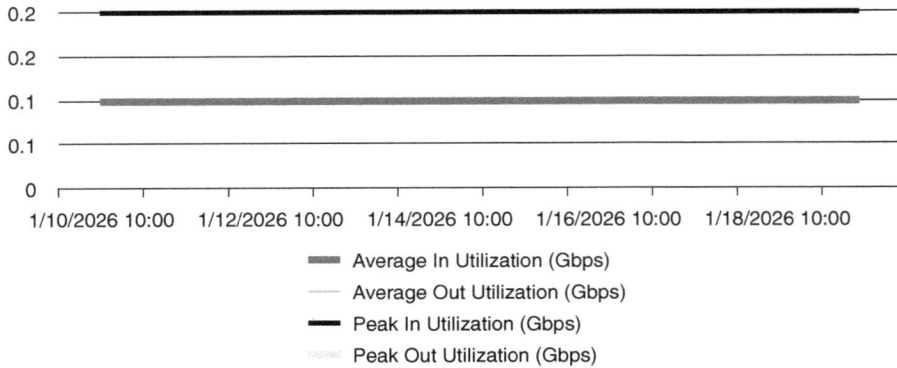

Average In Utilization (Gbps)
Average Out Utilization (Gbps)
Peak In Utilization (Gbps)
Peak Out Utilization (Gbps)

Jacobs Annet DC MPLS CE Utilization

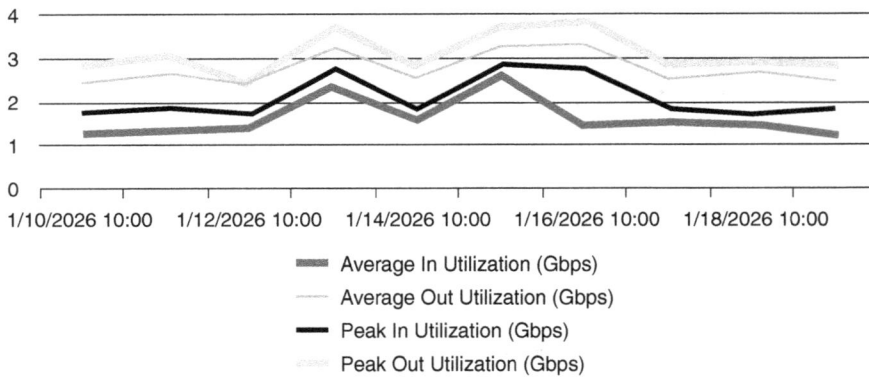

Average In Utilization (Gbps)
Average Out Utilization (Gbps)
Peak In Utilization (Gbps)
Peak Out Utilization (Gbps)

Jacobs ISP CE1

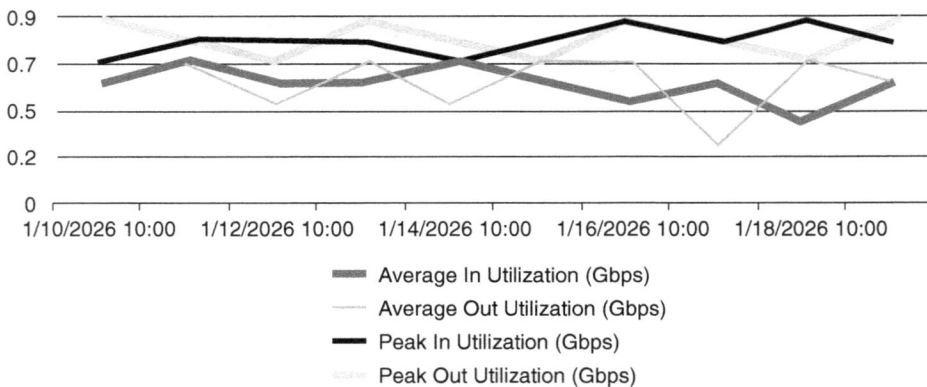

Average In Utilization (Gbps)
Average Out Utilization (Gbps)
Peak In Utilization (Gbps)
Peak Out Utilization (Gbps)

Toolmate ISP CE1

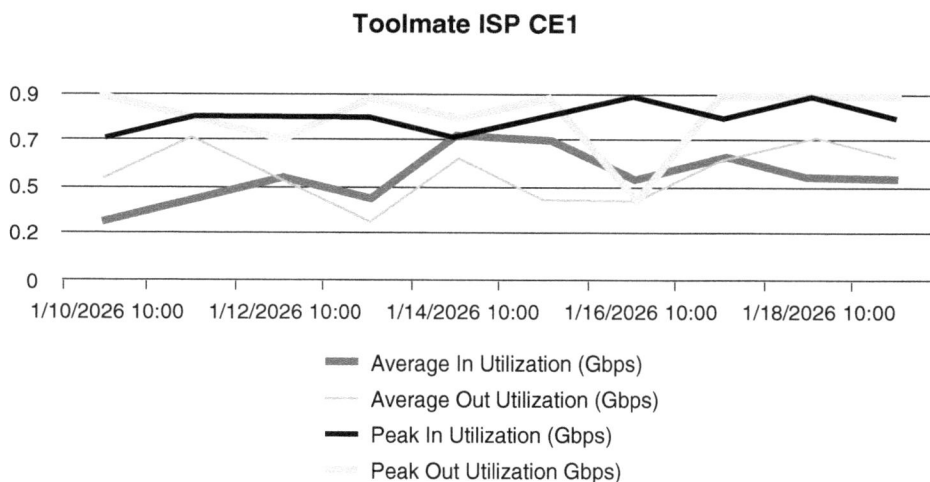

Average In Utilization (Gbps)
Average Out Utilization (Gbps)
Peak In Utilization (Gbps)
Peak Out Utilization Gbps)

Document 4: Additional Notes

There has been a recent pilot for Office 365 SaaS within the public cloud via a cloud provider (Cloudcom) reachable over the DC Internet connection for various Jacobs stores participating in a trial. Early indications are that the service has suffered intermittent delays and that user experience was not positive.

Due to a historical issue with a virtualized infrastructure device with RCA analysis citing vendor code interoperability failure that resulted in a high profile outage, Jacobs Security policy (which covers all zones of the network and store entities) now dictates that functionality of infrastructure devices should be limited to a single defined function and that separate functionality must be provisioned through separate physical infrastructure devices.

Lab Questions

Question 1

Which are the main issues facing Jacobs currently? (Choose two.)

a. Business continuity

b. An excessive number of network providers

c. Multiple single points of failure for independent stores

d. Lack of VoIP system access for independent stores

e. No integration of Toolmate and independent store IT systems

Question 2

Which of the following changes to the network could improve the scalability of the overall networks and reduce management overhead for the network teams? (Choose one.)

a. Expansion of the shared services zone for independent stores to include Toolmate services within the Jacobs DC with streamlined change control

b. Rationalization of all MPLS networks to a single provider

c. Creation of a new DR DC

d. Migration of MPLS links to SD-WAN solution

Email #1

From: James Medina

To: CCDE Candidate

Subject: MPLS Contract Renewal

Hi.

Our contract with the MPLS provider for the individual stores (Annet) is up for renewal. Turns out they have uplifted their prices by 28% for continuity of service due to a requirement to upgrade their network. We're not impressed, as it means we are effectively paying for the upgrade if we want to keep things simple and stay with them. Annet has stated they can maintain previous pricing if we migrated to a more cost-effective VPLS service using all the same equipment as is currently onsite in the stores (all the CE edge routers), as this will mean there is then no need to refresh the CE equipment. They can perform the change in a single evening for all stores at the same time, as they can script it so downtime should be minimal, and, as mentioned, the price will be the same as now, which I guess is a bonus. How does this sound? Is there an alternative technical solution you can think of to provide connectivity into the network? We only need a single connection for independent stores into the Jacobs DC, as they have their own internal system and just need a link into us for pricing changes and tool hire ordering, which they can always do by phone if there is a WAN outage. We'd rather minimize changes either in the store and centrally within the DC, but it's challenging to justify a 28% uplift without any gain or saving any pain. I made contact with Bluesky and Taco (the WAN providers for the Jacobs store MPLS networks), and they are both keen to win this business if we decide not to renew with Annet. We have a couple of months before the contract renews, so there's a limited amount of time to respond.

Rgds,

James Medina
Network Manager
Jacobs

Question 3

What is the optimal approach to the suggested MPLS changes for independent stores? (Choose one.)

a. Migrate the independent stores into one of the Jacobs MPLS network providers (Bluesky or Taco).

b. Provide an SD-WAN solution using Internet circuits at independent store locations to reach the Jacobs DC.

c. Use 4G LTE/5G transport.

d. Migrate to the VPLS service with the same MPLS provider.

e. Plan to pay the uplift to maintain continuity while researching alternative solutions in parallel.

Question 4

Jacobs believes migrating the independent stores to the Jacobs dedicated Bluesky MPLS network would be a good option to avoid an immediate uplift in pricing, which would drive future integration and provide cost leverage with its primary MPLS provider. If this direction is taken, which of the following would be the optimal option to provide connectivity into the Jacobs DC for the independent stores from the Bluesky MPLS network? (Choose one.)

a. Provision a new, separate L3 MPLS VPN within the existing Jacobs Bluesky MPLS network that breaks out into separate VRFs in the DC provisioned on the existing MPLS CE and circuit into the Jacobs DC.

b. Terminate the independent stores into the existing Jacobs Bluesky MPLS VPN and provide access to Jacobs' DC resources for the independent stores via an ACL on the headend MPLS CE.

c. Provide a new Bluesky MPLS headend CE router connecting, back to back, to the existing Bluesky headend MPLS CE router in the Jacobs DC for a new separate hub-and-spoke MPLS VPN containing the independent stores.

d. Provision a new, separate L3 MPLS VPN for independent stores within the Bluesky MPLS WAN on a new central tail circuit into the DC that breaks out into separate VRFs in the existing DC CE router.

Email #2

From: James Medina

To: CCDE Candidate

Subject: Network Integration

Hi.

I've been discussing the MPLS network issue with the CTO, and this has prompted a bigger question around finally providing integration. We both don't believe we should continue as is, and it's time to bring some innovation into the business and reduce our capex and some of the complexities of running multiple providers. The CTO believes we should be running an Internet-only VPN WAN and completely remove the overhead of MPLS running our own managed overlay networks on the Internet circuits. He stated we could reduce our Internet circuits to a single circuit in each DC (Jacobs and Toolmate) on the back of this so that the DCs can back each other up in the event of a failure and each store can have dual Internet circuits, so no single points of failure. I'm not convinced we should do this in one fell swoop and believe we are better off running a traditional hybrid SD-WAN type of network with a mix of connectivity. I've been reading up on the subject and it seems we could have the best of both worlds if we followed this path. I need your help to decide how we should progress. I've also looked into Internet-only circuits, and in some of the remote parts of the UK, the providers we contacted have latency calculators that are showing approximately 100ms latency from stores to the London DCs, so I figure we are still OK for VoIP for their ADSL circuits. The CTO has secured a budget to provide the integration/consolidation, but we need to work out the best approach for the business.

Rgds,

James Medina
Network Manager
Jacobs

Question 5

If Jacobs were to follow the CTO's instructions for a self-managed Internet-only VPN WAN solution based on the supplied information, which of the following solutions would you recommend to Jacobs to consolidate connectivity for all of the stores into the Jacobs and Toolmate DCs? (Choose one.)

a. GETVPN solution with a facility for stores to terminate VPNs in either DC should one DC Internet connection fail

b. Phase 3 DMVPN multi-VRF (Jacobs VRF, Toolmate VRF, independent store VRF) solution with a facility for stores to terminate VPNs in either DC should one DC Internet connection fail.

c. Phase 3 DMVPN single VRF solution with a facility for stores to terminate VPNs in either DC should one DC Internet connection fail.

d. Phase 1 DMVPN multi-VRF (Jacobs VRF, Toolmate VRF, independent store VRF) solution with a facility for stores to terminate VPNs in either DC should one DC Internet connection fail.

e. Hub-and-spoke IPsec VPN (Jacobs VPN, Toolmate VPN, independent store VPN), GRE tunnels with IGP, with a facility for stores to terminate VPNs in either DC should one DC Internet connection fail.

f. Hub-and-spoke IPsec VPN (Jacobs VPN, Toolmate VPN, independent store VPN), static routing with a facility for stores to terminate VPNs in either DC should one DC Internet connection fail.

Email #3

From: James Medina

To: CCDE Candidate

Subject: Hybrid WAN/SD-WAN

Hi.

We're looking into industry trends, and we're aware that there is a movement from network topology toward an application services topology. Network changes are taking too long for simple items such as bandwidth and QoS changes, so we're thinking we should definitely be moving toward some kind of hybrid WAN or SD-WAN solution. Can you have a look into this and let us know your thoughts? We could, as previously discussed, use the Internet as transport for stores in conjunction with MPLS or just use Internet only, as we have central Internet connections in the Jacobs and Toolmate DCs. From what I can gather, we would have the option to steer our traffic over specific links on an application basis. This would be fundamental to us, and we'd need the ability to be able to do this effectively in real time without raising changes for new profiles or applications as we bring them online with our providers.

Rgds,

James Medina
Network Manager
Jacobs

Question 6

If Jacobs did move to an SD-WAN type of solution with a combination of MPLS and Internet circuits per store for Jacobs and Toolmate stores and Internet-only circuits for independent stores, what would be a major benefit? (Choose one.)

a. Business continuity could be facilitated natively.

b. Cost savings of approximately 90% on Internet circuits versus MPLS circuits.

c. MPLS providers could be reduced to a single provider.

d. Security improvements.

Email #4

From: James Medina

To: CCDE Candidate

Subject: SD-WAN Thoughts

Hi.

I've been discussing the possibility of running SD-WAN with our ISPs over the existing central Jacobs and Toolmate Internet access. As you know, we have dual ISP links in each DC that are running in an active/standby arrangement. Both ISPs will reduce costs quite considerably if we decommission our standby Internet circuit in each DC and then reduce our current 1Gbps rate over the remaining 1Gbps Internet circuit in each DC (they can effectively provide a CIR in steps of 100Mbps over the access circuits). My thoughts are we can remove one ISP link at each DC and then provide resilience for each DC from the other DC for Internet SD-WAN-sourced traffic from stores. Also, as each store would require an Internet access circuit locally, we can use this for Direct Internet Access (DIA) from the store and not require anywhere near as much Internet bandwidth because we should no longer need to break out centrally to the Internet for store users. This is what I'm thinking:

1. Broadband ADSL type Internet access provisioned in each store site (independent, Jacobs, and Toolmate), sized accordingly.

2. All stores use DIA for Internet access rather than breaking out via the central DCs.

3. Annet MPLS network decommissioned for independent stores. These stores could then use SD-WAN Internet to access the Jacobs DC.

4. Taconet MPLS network decommissioned for Jacobs stores. These stores could then use an Internet SD-WAN solution and existing Bluesky MPLS network to access the Jacobs and Toolmate DCs (Jacobs stores could access their DC via Toolmate Internet connection if there is an MPLS and Internet failure within the Jacobs DC by traversing the DCI from Toolmate).

5. Lotnet second circuit MPLS network decommissioned for Toolmate stores. These stores could then use an SD-WAN solution for Internet access and existing first Lotnet MPLS network to access the Toolmate and Jacobs DCs (Toolmate stores could access their DC via the Jacobs DC Internet connection if there is an MPLS and Internet failure within the Toolmate DC by traversing the DCI from Jacobs).

Rgds,

James Medina
Network Manager
Jacobs

Question 7

If Jacobs moved to an SD-WAN solution for all store access, as detailed in the fourth email, could it, with confidence, make a design decision to remove the second ISP circuits at each DC and reduce speeds on the individual Internet circuits in the DCs by having stores use Direct Internet Access with a view reducing existing central Internet utilization and saving central ISP costs? (Choose one.)

a. Yes

b. No

Question 8

If Jacobs were to move to an SD-WAN solution, as detailed in the fourth email, with each Jacobs and Toolmate store using one MPLS link and one Internet circuit, or a single Internet circuit in independent stores for WAN connectivity, which of the following areas should take priority from a security perspective? (Choose one.)

a. Direct Internet Access from stores

b. Encryption ciphers of Internet access circuits

c. PKI infrastructure

d. DDoS protection for DCs

Email #5

From: James Medina

To: CCDE Candidate

Subject: Provider-managed SD-WAN Service

Hi.

I've been in touch with the Bluesky MPLS provider to discuss our strategy, and they offer a fully managed SD-WAN service and even a co-managed SD-WAN service. It's something we hadn't considered, as I had assumed we'd just self-manage if we went down the SD-WAN route, and I guess MPLS companies are keen to retain as much business as possible if it ultimately means loss of MPLS circuits. I need your help to ascertain the management direction we should take.

Rgds,

James Medina
Network Manager
Jacobs

Question 9

Jacobs is now considering raising an RFP (Request for Proposal) to their existing MPLS providers to bid for a fully managed SD-WAN solution that the company can use for consolidated store access to the DCs. Complete the following table to aid its decision-making process for a fully managed service versus a DIY in-house self-managed SD-WAN solution by the network team. Insert a check in the Solution Type option that provides the most benefit to Jacobs (would be most optimal) for each Function topic.

Function	Solution Type	
	Fully Managed	Self-Managed
Application-aware routing policies and QoS		
Speed of deployment		
Flexibility		
Ease of integrations		
Geographical coverage		
Control over network and data		
Skills and staffing		
Infrastructure and circuit procurement		
Underlay and overlay monitoring		

Question 10

Which of the following SD-WAN solution types would be most suitable for Jacobs? (Choose one.)

a. Fully managed MPLS service provider solution

b. Jacobs self-managed solution

Question 11

As Jacobs fully investigates SD-WAN with a view of provisioning a self-managed solution, it requires additional information on SD-WAN functions and associated "planes" to gain a better understanding of SD-WAN functionality. Check the boxes for the corresponding SD-WAN plane per function in the following table to assist in the company's understanding.

Function	Plane			
	Orchestration	Management	Control	Data
First point of authentication				
Fabric discovery				
Distribution of management and control plane controller location				
Programmatic interfaces (NETCONF/REST)				
Secure data plane establishment with edge routers				
Distributes data plane and application-aware policy to edge routers				
Centralized provisioning				
Establishment of secure control plane with control plane controllers				
Software upgrades				
Export of performance statistics				
Application-aware routing policy				

Email #6

From: James Medina

To: CCDE Candidate

Subject: SD-WAN Connectivity Technologies

Hi.

I've had the team research what technologies we can use for our connectivity to stores for SD-WAN. We have all of the following technologies available to us (varying bandwidths to suit and varying prices) for all of our store locations. Have a think about which may be better suited to our solution, as our infrastructure will natively support all of them!

4G/LTE

5G

Internet access circuits/ADSL/SDSL

MPLS circuits

Rgds,

James Medina
Network Manager
Jacobs

Question 12

Which SD-WAN underlay technology would you recommend for the store locations? (Choose two.)

  a. 4G/LTE

  b. 5G

  c. Internet access circuits/ADSL/SDSL

  d. MPLS circuits (primary site access)

  e. MPLS circuits (secondary site access)

Question 13

If Jacobs went ahead with an SD-WAN solution, which of the following items would the company need to address prior to using Internet connectivity as one path for stores to access the central resources in the Jacobs and Toolmate DCs? (Choose one.)

a. Upgrade the performance of Internet-facing firewalls in each DC.

b. Allow SD-WAN flows through Internet-facing firewalls at the DCs.

c. Upgrade Internet access circuits to 10Gbps in the DCs.

d. Decide if static routing or a dynamic protocol should be used for routing over SD-WAN Internet-based tunnels.

Email #7

From: James Medina

To: CCDE Candidate

Subject: 5G is the place to B.

Hi.

Thanks for the feedback. It has occurred to me that the Internet ADSL/SDSL circuits we've been looking at may exceed the latency requirement we have for the Jaystore app of 20ms. 5G technology definitely gets around this so I guess we will go with 5G as a secondary circuit and keep a single MPLS circuit where we have dual MPLS links now. Anywhere with a single MPLS circuit can be replaced with 5G, and we can make significant savings on our WAN opex. I did speak to the app developers for Jaystore, and they are quoting me 6 months to rewrite the application communications module based on their existing agile work load—this would be way too long for us, and it would also be expense and difficult to justify based on the amount of effort they are quoting.

I've found some competitively priced SD-WAN store-sized edge routers we can connect to 5G Internet services via an optional 5G card. For PCI compliance, they have their own full security stack, which includes VRFs, L7 firewall, IPS/IDS, protection, and URL filtering, with EIGRP and BGP LAN–side and OMP WAN–side routing. They come with dual copper Ethernet connections for access or trunking connectivity, which we can use to connect into our store network switches.

Rgds,

James Medina
Network Manager
Jacobs

Question 14

As Jacobs is intending to use SD-WAN edge routers with 5G Internet connections at stores providing Internet access to create the SD-WAN network, should the company also provide firewalls at each store location for protecting the SD-WAN edge routers and store LAN connected to the Internet? (Choose one.)

a. Yes. Firewalls should be deployed physically in front of the SD-WAN router with the Internet/5G connection.

b. Yes. Firewalls should be deployed physically behind the SD-WAN edge routers with the Internet/5G connections.

c. No. Firewalls are not required in the store due to the native firewall and security features that the SD-WAN edge routers provide.

d. No. Firewalls are not required due to SD-WAN routers only being configured to accept IPsec connections from central DC routers and all Internet traffic being forwarded to the central DC locations.

Email #8

From: James Medina

To: CCDE Candidate

Subject: Security Exception

Hi.

The security policy that dictates that functionality of infrastructure devices should be limited to a single defined function and separate functionality must be provisioned through separate physical infrastructure devices is going to add significant cost to this project. I'm going to force an exception through security with the CTO's authority so we can use SD-WAN edge routers' native security functionality and negate the requirement for store firewalls. Let's progress with the design on the assumption the exception will be approved.

In terms of underlay, as mentioned previously, I'd like to keep one MPLS circuit where we have dual MPLS circuits, and we can replace the second MPLS circuit with Internet access. Where we only have one MPLS circuit currently for independent stores, we can replace this with an Internet circuit.

I'm going to look at upgrading the Jacobs ISP link to a resilient 10Gbps solution. I'm wondering if we can remove the Toolmate ISP link if we can do this.

If you can start designing the overall SD-WAN solution, that would be great.

Rgds,

James Medina
Network Manager
Jacobs

Question 15

If Jacobs proceeds with the SD-WAN design detailed within the following figure, can the company decommission the existing central Internet access at the Toolmate DC and use a 10Gbps resilient Jacobs DC Internet connection as a secondary SD-WAN termination path for Toolmate stores in the event of an MPLS failure in the Lotnet network? (Choose one.)

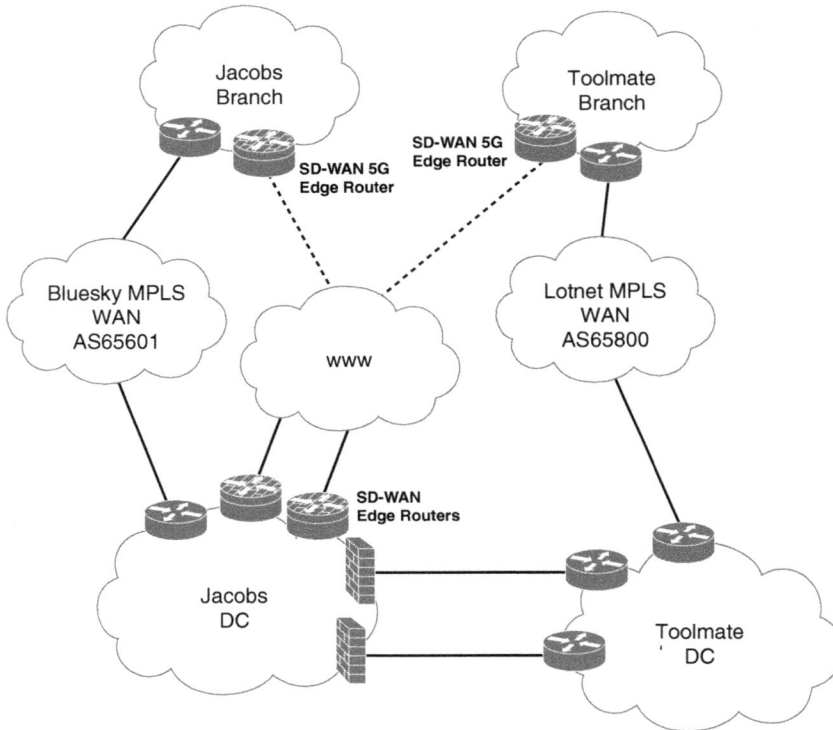

a. Yes (if the DCI firewall is configured to permit access).

b. No.

Question 16

Jacobs has decided to upgrade ISP connectivity in each DC to dual 10Gbps active/stand-by connections. Complete the design provided in the following figure for the headend SD-WAN edge router(s) placement in the Jacobs DC when the dual headend MPLS connections will be reduced to one (the Toolmate DC will be identical but with a different MPLS provider). Add as many SD-WAN edge routers (which have 4x 10Gbps interfaces) and associated Ethernet connections (all connections are 10Gbps and all existing infrastructure supports 10Gbps and has a minimum of 2x 10Gbps additional port capacity per device) as required to implement a fully resilient SD-WAN headend. You may also remove existing Ethernet connections if required.

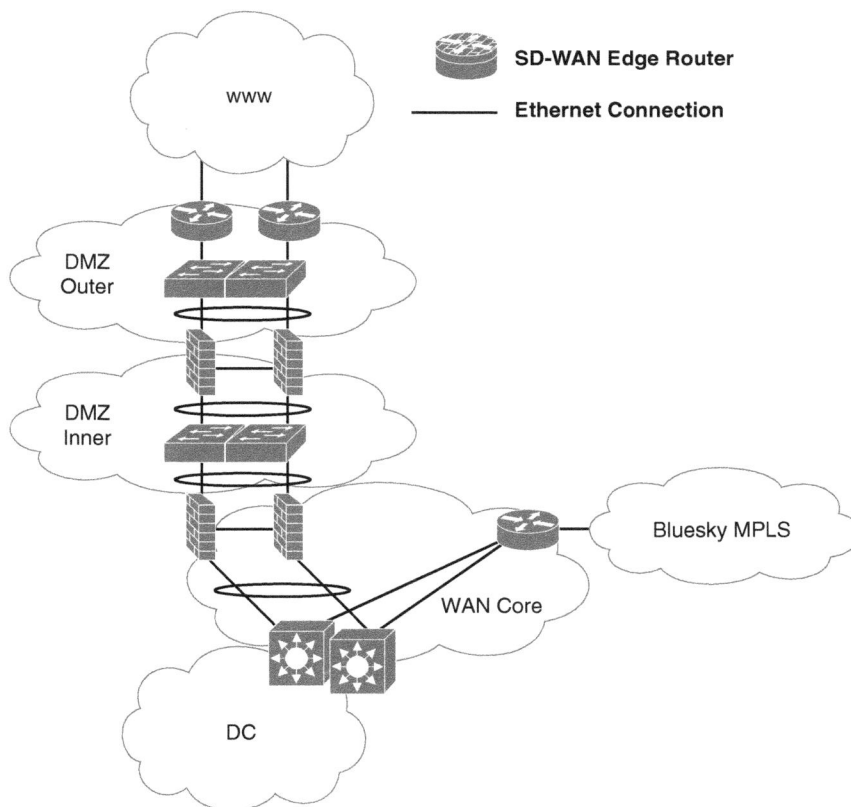

Note   The Toolmate DC would be similar, but with a different single MPLS provider. However, this question focuses only on the Jacobs DC element.

Question 17

Which of the following SD-WAN designs would you recommend for a Jacobs store.
(Choose one.)

a.

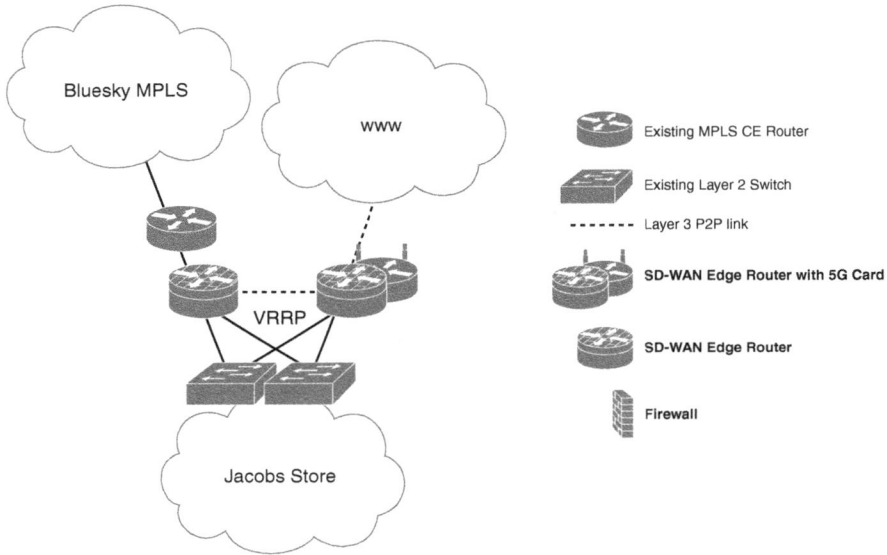

b.

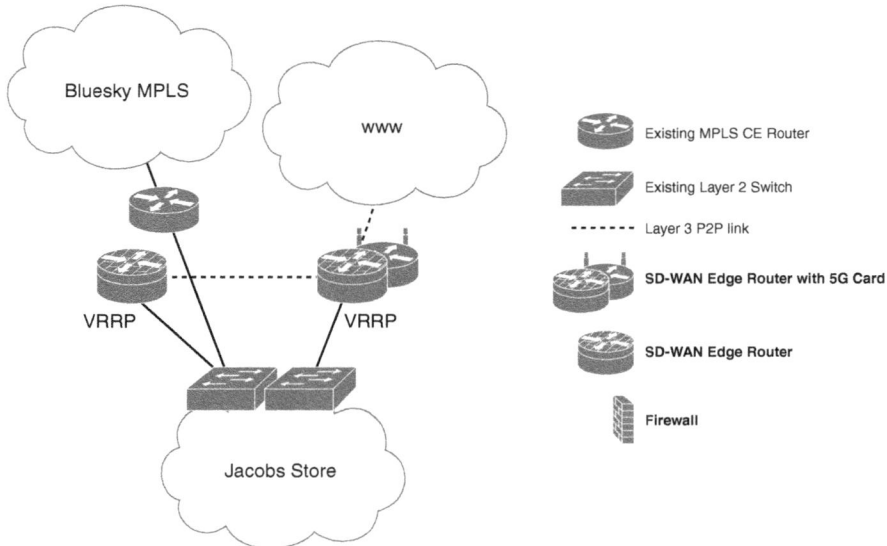

c.

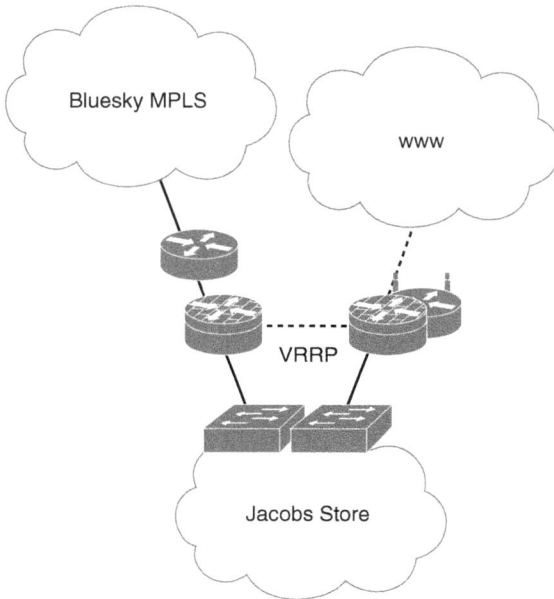
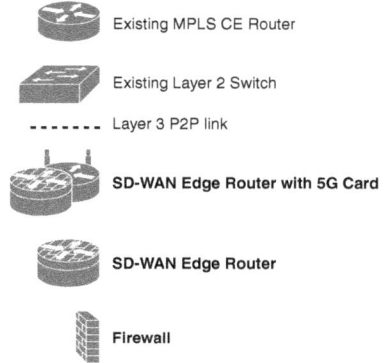

d.

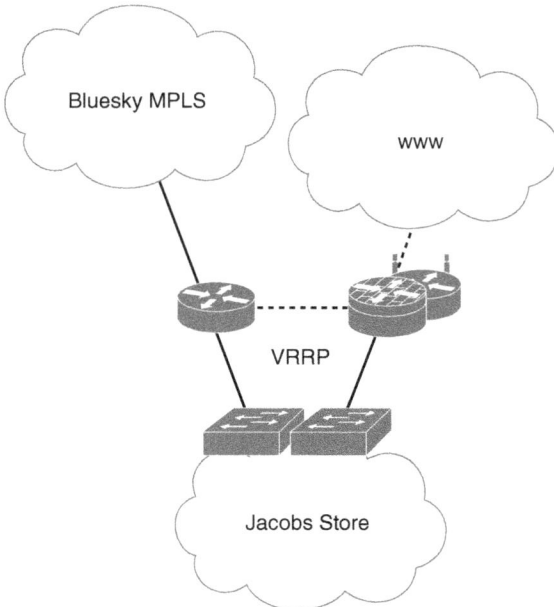
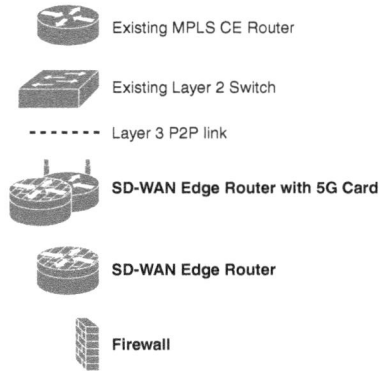

Email #9

From: James Medina

To: CCDE Candidate

Subject: SD-WAN Routing Loop Concern

Hi.

I'm a little wary of routing loops when we're setting up the SD-WAN network with its inbuilt routing protocol of OMP and whatever protocol we use our side on the DC LAN. I could use a breakdown on how you believe we can work around any potential loop with various protocols. The scenario I'm thinking of is when we have a store prefix coming in of, say, "A," as per the diagram, and this advertisement is received on the Internet SD-WAN edge router and MPLS SD-WAN edge router in one of our DCs. The edge routers will need to be running a routing protocol back to the DC LAN, so I want to make sure the SD-WAN edge routers don't end up forwarding traffic for prefix "A" toward each other via the local DC LAN, rather than direct over the SD-WAN overlay network to the store.

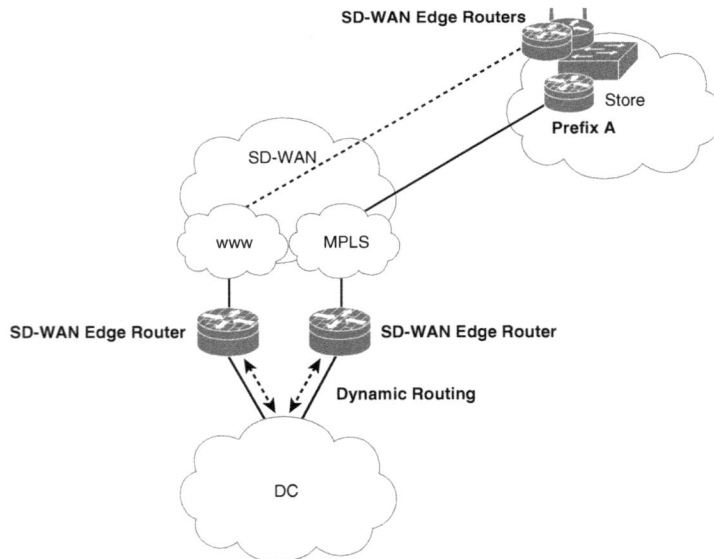

Rgds,

James Medina
Network Manager
Jacobs

Question 18

Complete the following table to assist Jacobs in understanding which loop mitigation techniques could be used in conjunction with associated dynamic routing protocol configured between SD-WAN edge routers to the DC LAN. Insert an "X" under Mitigation Technique per routing protocol, where appropriate.

Routing Protocol	Mitigation Technique			
	Route TAGs	Site of Origin	Down Bit	SD-WAN Down Bit
EIGRP				
OSPF				
BGP				
OMP				

Email #10

From: James Medina

To: CCDE Candidate

Subject: SD-WAN Routing Loop Concern

Hi.

Thanks for the loop info. It kind of makes sense.

Just a heads up: I want each store (independent, Jacobs, and Toolmate) to have an Internet SD-WAN path into each DC (Jacobs and Toolmate). My rationale is if a Jacobs store has an Internet path into the Toolmate DC as well as the Jacobs DC, the convergence in the event of an issue in the Jacobs DC on the SD-WAN side would be much quicker if the routing was already in place (and the same for a Toolmate store via the Jacobs DC). I'm still a little concerned around routing in this scenario (loops, optimum paths, etc.). Can you have a think?

Rgds,

James Medina
Network Manager
Jacobs

Question 19

Jacobs requires each store to have an SD-WAN path to each DC to aid convergence in the event of a failure condition. The company has selected eBGP to be used between the DC LAN networks in the Jacobs and Toolmate DCs and locally attached SD-WAN edge routers for the SD-WAN network to advertise DC prefixes and SD-WAN store networks. iBGP will also be used between Jacobs and Toolmate DC LAN networks over the existing DCI to provide a backup path for a Jacobs SD-WAN-enabled store via the Toolmate DC, and vice versa. How should the BGP AS number (ASN) associated to the edge routers be configured within each DC? (Choose one.)

a. The BGP ASN associated to the SD-WAN edge routers should be the same in each of the DCs.

b. The BGP ASN associated to the SD-WAN edge routers should be different in each of the DCs.

Email #11

From: James Medina

To: CCDE Candidate

Subject: Plane Speaking

Hi.

Thanks for the design of the SD-WAN edge routers in the stores and central DCs. We obviously need some controllers to enable the SD-WAN functionality on top of that infrastructure element, so we need to work out where these will be placed for reachability by the SD-WAN edge routers. The information I have back from the vendor we have selected is as follows. We will need redundant controllers in each of the following planes:

Management plane: This will be provided by a product called iManage. This is their single pane of glass that we will use for provisioning, monitoring, managing, and troubleshooting, if required.

Orchestration plane: This will be provided by a product called iOrch. It deals with authentication and authorization of all the infrastructure.

Control plane: This will be provided by a product called iCon. It provides all the data and routing plane policies to the edge routers, including application-aware routing policies, if required.

All controllers can be appliances in the DC or virtual instances in the cloud; both options use a proprietary active/standby resilience method that requires Layer 2 between controllers (physical or logical VLAN for appliances and just a VLAN for the cloud instances) and provide a single frontend IPv4 address regardless of the use of physical appliances or a cloud-based service. The vendor has offered to provide the service of all three controllers within their public cloud offering hosted in France, with resilient service in the USA, and they deal with all resiliency, backups, DR, and required certificates between controllers and SD-WAN edge routers that communicate with the controllers. The fully managed cloud offering just requires Internet access from edge routers (direct for stores or central for the DC) and works out to be the same price as the purchase of the appliances for one complete set of resilient controllers if we host ourselves over a five-year contract, which is our normal refresh period for infrastructure.

Rgds,

James Medina
Network Manager
Jacobs

Question 20

Where is the optimal hosting location for the iManage, iOrch, and iCon controllers for Jacobs? (Choose one.)

a. Within the Jacobs DC in the WAN Core area as locally clustered appliances for each controller function

b. Within the Toolmate DC as locally clustered appliances for each controller function

c. Within both Jacobs and Toolmate DCs for full resilience as remote clustered appliances (active unit in Jacobs and standby unit in Toolmate) for each controller function

d. Within both Jacobs and Toolmate DCs for full resilience as local clustered appliances (replicated service in each DC)

e. Within the vendor's private cloud for each controller function

Email #12

From: James Medina

To: CCDE Candidate

Subject: Cloud and Migration Thoughts!

Hi.

I believe it's optimal if we deploy the SD-WAN controllers in the cloud. They are natively resilient, and we won't have to deal with plumbing them in and worrying about making the deployment resilient between the Jacobs and Toolmate DCs. An additional benefit is they deal with all the required certificates between devices that can be problematic for our team and can preconfigure the SD-WAN edge routers we will purchase through them, so they will dynamically connect to the cloud controllers, meaning zero touch for our team to onboard. So thanks to your input. We will have the following future architecture.

I need your help with planning the migration to SD-WAN, which I've had drawn up below based on your input. Please have a think about the best way to bring the service online!

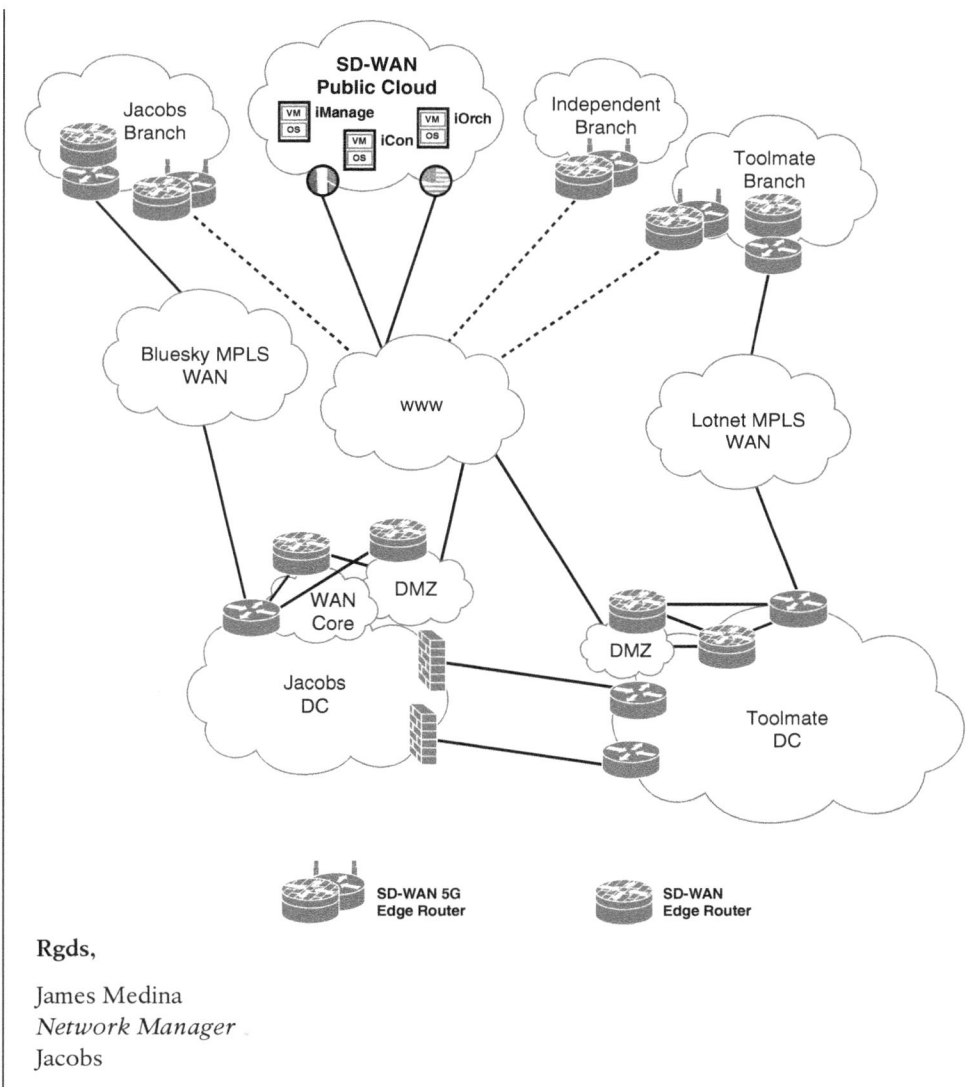

SD-WAN Public Cloud — iManage, iOrch, iCon

Jacobs Branch

Independent Branch

Toolmate Branch

Bluesky MPLS WAN

WWW

Lotnet MPLS WAN

WAN Core

DMZ

Jacobs DC

DMZ

Toolmate DC

SD-WAN 5G Edge Router

SD-WAN Edge Router

Rgds,

James Medina
Network Manager
Jacobs

Question 21

In order to board the new SD-WAN solution and migrate traffic over it for Jacobs, Toolmate, and independent stores' connectivity, arrange the following migration activities in the required sequence. The business has declared it wants to minimize any associated downtime and ensure the service is functioning correctly prior to migrating any Jacobs or Toolmate store to the SD-WAN network.

a. Connect SD-WAN edge routers to DC networks and configure eBGP between SD-WAN edge routers and the DC LAN to advertise DC LAN networks to SD-WAN. Configure DCI firewalls to allow an SD-WAN store resilience routing path between DCs and inter-DC iBGP peering.

b. Configure SD-WAN control-plane tunnels for Internet paths.

c. Configure DC firewalls for SD-WAN control plane flows to cloud service and SD-WAN edge router to SD-WAN network data plane flows and enable cloud controller service with configuration templates for all connectivity.

d. Migrate independent stores' data plane to SD-WAN by repointing local LAN gateway to the SD-WAN edge router and modify BGP metrics in DC locations.

e. Order 5G Internet connections for stores. Store SD-WAN edge routers and SD-WAN edge routers for DC locations.

f. Configure iBGP between Jacobs and Toolmate DCs to advertise SD-WAN store prefixes for a backup routing path and redistribute SD-WAN OMP to BGP and BGP to SD-WAN OMP.

g. Implement the second SD-WAN edge router on dual MPLS store sites behind the MPLS circuit / CE router being retained. Configure SD-WAN tunnels for MPLS paths.

h. Connect the independent store SD-WAN edge router with a 5G card to the local LAN, and for stores with dual MPLS routers, connect the first SD-WAN edge router with a 5G card to the LAN (low VRRP priority set with existing MPLS routers).

i. Shut down the dual MPLS store (Jacobs/Toolmate) MPLS link that will no longer be required.

j. Decommission the secondary MPLS circuits for Jacobs/Toolmate and the single MPLS circuit within independent stores.

k. Redirect Jacobs/Toolmate store traffic to Internet SD-WAN path on the current dual MPLS sites (adjust VRRP on store sites and modify BGP metrics in DC locations).

l. Shut down independent store MPLS links.

Email #13

From: James Medina

To: CCDE Candidate

Subject: Jaystore Application

Hi.

Thanks for the migration assistance. Not one store noticed any downtime! I've been asking around the stores and initial feedback is very positive, considering we are now actually using the Internet paths as well as MPLS for all our WAN traffic. I have had a couple of comments in reference to the Jaystore application being less responsive and some clipping on voice calls, though. As you know, we had QoS on the MPLS links with four classes. I think in the pressure of delivering the connectivity, we may have missed the QoS element on the 5G links. I'm going to need your assistance to make sure we improve the quality.

Rgds,

James Medina
Network Manager
Jacobs

Question 22

How can Jacobs rectify the quality issues reported post-migration? (Choose one.)

a. Duplicate the existing MPLS QoS setting into the 5G SD-WAN connections.

b. Enable TCP optimization and session persistence on the 5G SD-WAN connections.

c. Duplicate the existing MPLS QoS setting into the 5G SD-WAN connections, with the exception of store DIA traffic, which should be moved into a Scavenger queue.

d. Create an application-aware routing policy.

Question 23

Jacobs is considering Cloud onRamp for SaaS now that it has an operational SD-WAN network. What would be a benefit if the company takes this approach? (Choose one.)

a. The solution should result in a cost reduction.

b. Maintaining access through the DC to SaaS services provides an additional level of security control.

c. The solution would typically use the MPLS links as oppose to Internet circuits to access the SaaS and thus receive optimal quality.

d. The solution would have the capability to choose the path with optimal quality to reach the Office 365 cloud location (direct Internet access or via the central DC over 5G or MPLS links).

Email #14

From: James Medina

To: CCDE Candidate

Subject: Jimmy's

Hi.

I appreciate the assistance with the application routing policy and onRamp advice. I've just been thrown a curveball that I need your help with before your assignment ends. The CEO is a big fan of the fast food chain Jimmy's. As well as being well-acquainted with the menu, he is good friends with the CEO, and they fly together at his local gliding club. Between the pair of them, they have struck a deal that is going to see a small branch/store of Jimmy's in each of our Jacobs stores. The idea is the tradesmen come in early to stock up on building materials and they will undoubtedly pick up coffee, donuts, and a classic English breakfast (definitely not smashed avocado on sourdough) while their orders are being picked and loaded. Each CEO believes in the reciprocal trade that the arrangement will bring and are willing to share the setup costs. I've been told to provide a single copper Ethernet connection from our store network to them so they can reach their Jimmy's DC for their system. They just need Internet access to reach their DC and have a low-bandwidth requirement for their tills. We need to come up with a solution that keeps our internal security team happy. Help!

Rgds,

James Medina
Network Manager
Jacobs

Question 24

In order to provide the Jimmy's connectivity through a Jacobs store, which of the following options would be most suitable for communication? (Choose one.)

a. Termination of the Jimmy's Ethernet connection onto the Jacobs store switch with a B2B Internet VPN between Jacobs and Jimmy's central DC firewalls to permit secure access centrally between entities.

b. Termination of the Jimmy's Ethernet connection onto the Jacobs store switch into a new isolated VLAN, with VRF Lite configured between the store switch and Internet SD-WAN edge router to provide Internet connectivity to the VLAN.

c. Termination of the Jimmy's Ethernet connection onto the Jacobs store switch with ACL protection on the Jacobs access switch, providing access only to the Jacobs proxy server for central Internet access to a Jimmy's remote DC Internet VPN.

d. Provisioning of a new Jimmy's firewall for termination onto the Jacobs store switch for firewalled protection to only allow Jimmy's to connect to the Internet-facing SD-WAN edge router within the Jacobs store for an Internet VPN connection to the remote Jimmy's DC.

Practice Lab 1 Debrief

The lab debrief section analyzes each question, showing you what was required and how to achieve the desired results. You should use this section to produce an overall score for Practice Lab 1.

Question 1

Which are the main issues facing Jacobs currently? (Choose two.)

Requirements/constraints from supplied documentation:

A dual 1Gbps Layer 3 DCI link is provisioned between the Jacobs and Toolmate DCs using OSPF peering between the firewalls within Jacobs to Toolmate edge routers within the Toolmate DC. Prefixes from each DC network are advertised over the DCI, allowing machine-to-machine communication to enable Toolmate stores and online systems to broker sales for Jacobs products and services (which is seen as crucial to the Jacobs business model), access for Toolmate staff to Jacobs intranet and HR systems, and VoIP connectivity for Toolmate telephony systems to a Jacobs call manager by firewall policy.

Independent stores are provisioned without resilience, as they use their own local payment systems and telephony systems and can suffer outages to the Jacobs DC for up to six business hours without significant impact to business. Due to the way the independent store central MPLS connection is terminated in the Jacobs DC, the stores are only able to access a limited number of shared services, which are segmented from the Jacobs DC by use of a firewall.

Changes require approval from Jacobs and Toolmate change management systems, which is proving to be inefficient and incurs delay for approval and manual implementation out of hours unless an emergency change procedure is invoked to provide in-hours short-notice changes. The firewalls are approaching end of life and are close to capacity in terms of CPU utilization.

There is a current drive to rationalize and integrate the existing networks, reduce cost, and provide simplification across the compute and network infrastructure.

a. Business continuity

This is correct. There is no DR or standby facility for any part of the network; if the single Jacobs DC fails or becomes isolated, the company's IT would cease to function. You are informed that access from the Toolmate DC to the Jacobs DC is seen as crucial. Should the Toolmate DC or independent shared services zone fail within the Jacobs DC, just these areas/zones would be affected. However, if the DCIs, DCI firewalls, or entire Jacobs DC suffer a brownout, the Toolmate division would be just as much affected as central Jacobs. Jacobs overall would definitely benefit from some form of DR or resilience between zones/entities to provide business continuity.

b. Excessive number of network providers

This is incorrect. While this could be an issue in terms of management and complexity, there is no evidence to suggest it is a significant technical or business issue currently.

c. Multiple single points of failure for independent stores

This is incorrect. While there are multiple single points of failure for connectivity into the Jacobs DC and services, this is not a serious issue, as you are informed that independent stores can function without access for a period of time due to their own independent systems and telephony.

d. Lack of VoIP system access for independent stores

This is incorrect. While Jacobs and Toolmate stores use a central Jacobs VoIP system, there is no stated requirement for independent stores to use VoIP at this point in time.

e. No integration of Toolmate and independent store IT systems

This is correct. Systems and networks are not fully integrated. It would be beneficial to integrate the systems and rationalize WAN access to provide resilience between DCs and remove the administrative burden of the firewall change policy and end-of-life DCI firewalls for Toolmate access to Jacobs services, for example.

If you have answered this question correctly, you have scored one point.

Question 2

Which of the following changes to the network could improve the scalability of the overall networks and reduce management overhead for the network teams? (Choose one.)

Requirements/constraints from supplied documentation:

Changes require approval from Jacobs and Toolmate change management systems, which is proving to be inefficient and incurs delay for approval and manual implementation out of hours unless an emergency change procedure is invoked to provide in-hours short-notice changes. The firewalls are approaching end of life and are close to capacity in terms of CPU utilization.

a. Expansion of the shared services zone for independent stores to include Toolmate services within the Jacobs DC with streamlined change control

This is correct. Jacobs is clearly lacking integration between entities currently. It has a limited shared services zone for independent store resources and an almost tactical approach to provisioning access to specific services from Toolmate over the DCI and firewalls to the Jacobs DC. You are informed that the current change process is inefficient and the firewalls are approaching end of life and are running at capacity. Expansion of the shared services zone would typically reduce the need for emergency out-of-hours changes to provision access, and streamlining the change control inefficiencies would certainly reduce management overhead.

b. Rationalization of all MPLS networks to a single provider

This is a suboptimal answer. Rationalization would help overall management, but there is no information to suggest this would improve scalability. There is no evidence to suggest that there is an issue with the use of multiple providers, and using a single provider would actually introduce fate sharing, resulting with a single point of failure within the WAN.

c. Creation of a new DR DC

This is a suboptimal answer. It would definitely improve resilience, but it wouldn't necessarily improve scale, and management overhead would definitely increase with an additional site and resulting DR policy.

d. Migration of MPLS links to SD-WAN solution

This is a suboptimal answer. At this point in time, there is no evidence to suggest this would improve scale. It may reduce costs, but in terms of the sheer number of remote stores and separate entities currently, the complexity and management would definitely increase in the short term.

If you have answered this question correctly, you have scored one point.

Email #1

From: James Medina

To: CCDE Candidate

Subject: MPLS Contract Renewal

Hi.

Our contract with the MPLS provider for the individual stores (Annet) is up for renewal. Turns out they have uplifted their prices by 28% for continuity of service due to a requirement to upgrade their network. We're not impressed, as it means we are effectively paying for the upgrade if we want to keep things simple and stay with them. Annet has stated they can maintain previous pricing if we migrated to a more cost-effective VPLS service using all the same equipment as is currently onsite in the stores (all the CE edge routers), as this will mean there is then no need to refresh the CE equipment. They can perform the change in a single evening for all stores at the same time, as they can script it so downtime should be minimal, and, as mentioned, the price will be the same as now, which I guess is a bonus. How does this sound? Is there an alternative technical solution you can think of to provide connectivity into the network? We only need a single connection for independent stores into the Jacobs DC, as they have their own internal system and just need a link into us for pricing changes and tool hire ordering, which they can always do by phone if there is a WAN outage. We'd rather minimize changes either in the store and centrally within the DC, but it's challenging to justify a 28% uplift without any gain or saving any pain. I made contact with Bluesky and Taco (the WAN providers for the Jacobs store MPLS networks), and they are both keen to win this business if we decide not to renew with Annet. We have a couple of months before the contract renews, so there's a limited amount of time to respond.

Rgds,

James Medina
Network Manager
Jacobs

Question 3

What is the optimal approach to the suggested MPLS changes for independent stores? (Choose one.)

Requirements/constraints from supplied documentation:

Independent stores are provisioned without resilience, as they use their own local payment systems and telephony systems and can suffer outages to the Jacobs DC for up to six business hours without significant impact to business.

We only need a single connection for independent stores into the Jacobs DC, as they have their own internal system and just need a link into us for pricing changes and tool hire ordering, which they can always do by phone if there is a WAN outage. We'd rather minimize changes either in the store and centrally within the DC, but it's challenging to justify a 28% uplift without any gain or saving any pain. I made contact with Bluesky and Taco WAN providers for the Jacobs store MPLS networks, and they are both keen to win this business from Annet if we decide not to renew with Annet.

Independent-store-to-independent-store communication is blocked over the MPLS network by use of a hub-and-spoke MPLS network and policy-based routing on the central DC CE router to ensure all traffic is forwarded to the DC firewall for policy. The following figures show the utilization statistics.

Jacobs Bluesky DC MPLS CE Utilization

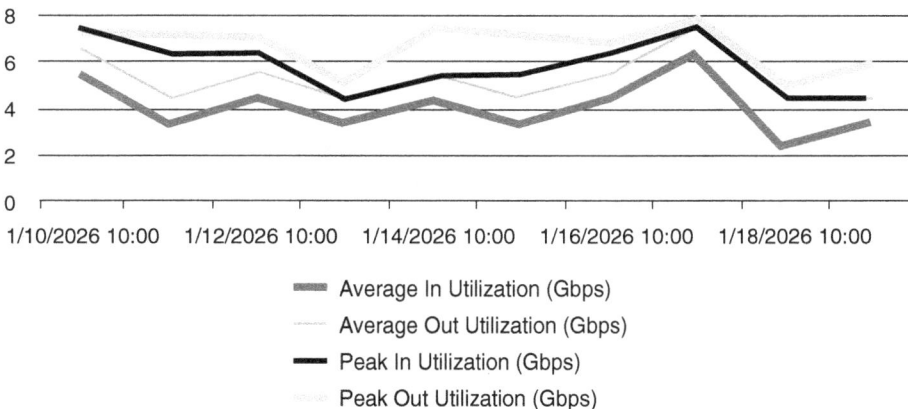

Average In Utilization (Gbps)
Average Out Utilization (Gbps)
Peak In Utilization (Gbps)
Peak Out Utilization (Gbps)

Jacobs Annet DC MPLS CE Utilization

Legend:
- Average In Utilization (Gbps)
- Average Out Utilization (Gbps)
- Peak In Utilization (Gbps)
- Peak Out Utilization (Gbps)

Jacobs ISP CE1

Legend:
- Average In Utilization (Gbps)
- Average Out Utilization (Gbps)
- Peak In Utilization (Gbps)
- Peak Out Utilization (Gbps)

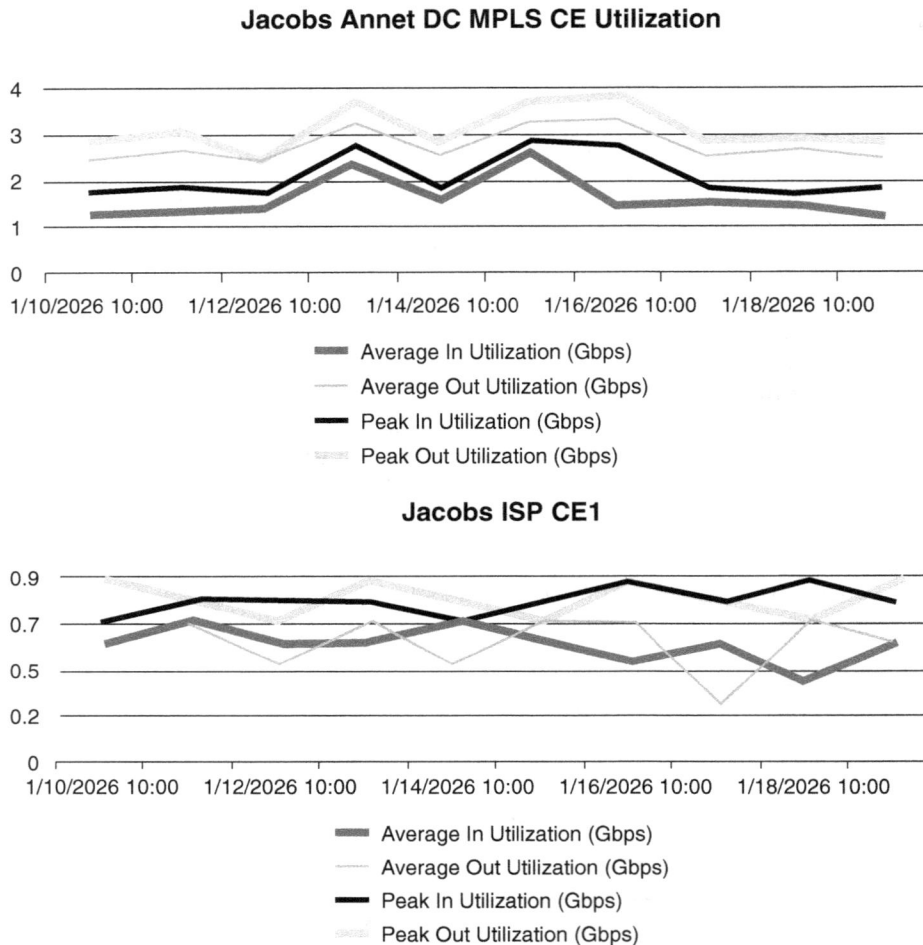

a. Migrate the independent stores into one of the Jacobs MPLS network providers (Bluesky or Taco).

This is incorrect. This could be a reasonable option, but it would require new MPLS tail circuits for independent stores to the new WAN provider (Bluesky or Taco) and additional service costs from the selected Jacobs WAN provider. You should be able to determine from utilization statistics that the combined traffic flow of independent stores and Jacobs MPLS stores' MPLS traffic would actually exceed the 10Gbps MPLS circuit provisioned within the central Jacobs DC. A new MPLS tail circuit would be required within the DC to accommodate combined traffic requirements. The solution would typically require an additional VPN within the existing MPLS network and separation of the new and existing VPN, as it connects into the

Jacobs DC WAN core. You don't have the information to state that this would be more cost effective; as such, you would be making assumptions based on costs and data, so technically this could be a good option. However, realistically, there are too many unknowns in terms of cost, capacity, and delivery timings for this to be a valid option. The customer has stated they want to minimize change, and this solution would be a major project with each of the independent stores requiring migration of service to the new MPLS network and disruption within the Jacobs DC to terminate the required new connectivity as well as incorporating the existing policy-based routing complexity setup for the independent stores, so in reality this answer can fairly simply be ruled out.

b. Provide an SD-WAN solution using Internet circuits at independent store locations to reach the Jacobs DC.

This is a suboptimal answer. This could be a good option, as in general costs would be favorable circuit-wise if Internet connectivity was provided, and it would likely be provisioned fairly quickly, but it would be a major project to deploy SD-WAN technology to the total number of stores and within the central DC. Also, the customer does not want to make significant changes. These reasons aside, you should be able to tell from the utilization statistics that the DC Internet connection at Jacobs is running close to saturation, and this solution would clearly require additional capacity on this central link to terminate the SD-WAN Internet-based connections from the stores, thus rendering this option unfeasible at this point in time.

c. Use 4G LTE/5G transport.

This is incorrect. 4G LTE or 5G in itself as a transport mechanism wouldn't connect the independent stores to the Jacobs DC. This technology would need to be combined with an SD-WAN-type solution to tie it together.

d. Migrate to the VPLS service with the same MPLS provider.

This is a suboptimal answer. This would create significant change, which would by default actually break the connectivity. Each independent store uses the CE MPLS router as the default gateway for its connected VLAN. In order for the migration to be successful, there would need to be some dynamic or static routing configured between all locations to reach store networks and the Jacobs DC, as the routing would no longer be provided by the MPLS network. Imagine all of the stores effectively connecting to each other on the same VLAN in the center of the WAN. This wouldn't scale with dynamic routing adjacencies, so static routes would need to be configured at a minimum from the store to reach the DC within the VPLS connection. There is also an issue, as you have been informed, that store-to-store communication is currently being blocked by policy-based routing at the central DC. This would be more complex to manage in a VPLS solution. Technically, it would be achievable, but it is disruptive, and it isn't the most elegant of solutions. Also, it requires a fair amount of change, which the customer is reluctant to perform. If you did select this option, give yourself half a point. The question has been designed to ensure you are able to fully evaluate the options and associated implications.

e. Plan to pay the uplift to maintain continuity while researching alternative solutions in parallel.

This is the optimum answer based on the information you have available up to this point. Clearly, no changes would be required, which saves the pain the customer has referenced. Also, some time would be available to research alternatives, as opposed to diving headfirst into some unknown costs/challenges of SD-WAN or new MPLS connectivity. Sometimes maintaining the status quo is an acceptable option.

If you have answered this question correctly, you have scored one point.

Question 4

Jacobs believes migrating the independent stores to the Jacobs' dedicated Bluesky MPLS network would be a good option to avoid an immediate uplift in pricing, which would drive future integration and provide cost leverage with its primary MPLS provider. If this direction is taken, which of the following would be the optimal option to provide connectivity into the Jacobs DC for the independent stores from the Bluesky MPLS network? (Choose one.)

Requirements/constraints from supplied documentation:

Independent-store-to-independent-store communication is blocked over the MPLS network by use of a hub-and-spoke MPLS network and policy-based routing on the central DC CE router to ensure all traffic is forwarded to the DC firewall for policy. The following figures show utilization of Jacobs' Bluesky DC MPLS CE and Jacobs' Annet DC MPLS CE links, respectively.

Jacobs Bluesky DC MPLS CE Utilization

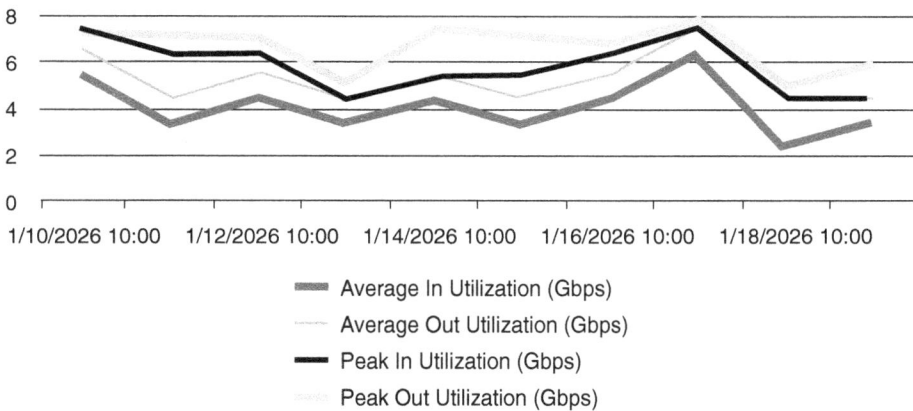

Jacobs Annet DC MPLS CE Utilization

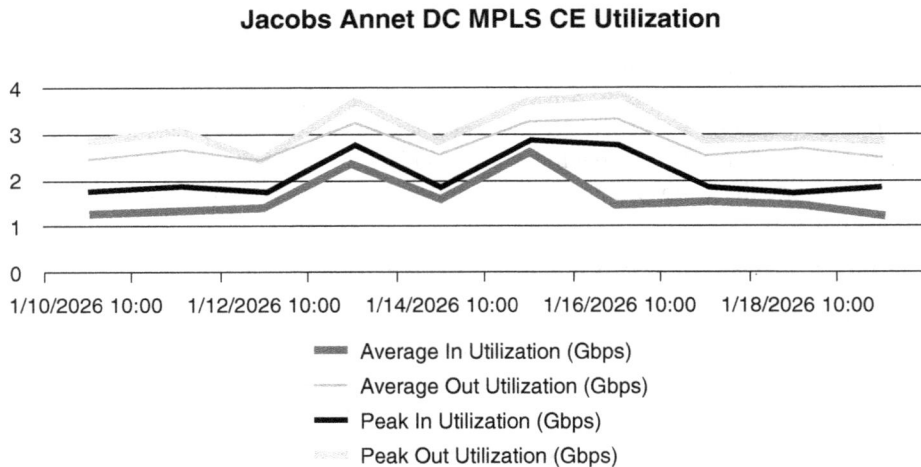

— Average In Utilization (Gbps)
— Average Out Utilization (Gbps)
— Peak In Utilization (Gbps)
— Peak Out Utilization (Gbps)

a. Provision a new, separate L3 MPLS VPN within the existing Jacobs Bluesky MPLS network that breaks out into separate VRFs in the DC provisioned on the existing MPLS CE and circuit into the Jacobs DC.

This is incorrect. Some form of separation would, however, be required between the two networks as a matter of principle. The separate VPN would be a good option, but the overall solution isn't possible due to DC capacity issues on the existing Bluesky CE circuit. By checking the existing capacity statistics on the Bluesky MPLS DC connectivity, you should notice that the link is close to capacity. Should a new VPN be created for the independent stores, there would be contention issues on the central DC Bluesky MPLS link into Jacobs.

b. Terminate the independent stores into the existing Jacobs Bluesky MPLS VPN and provide access to Jacobs' DC resources for the independent stores via an ACL on the headend MPLS CE.

This is incorrect. By default, this would allow independent stores Layer 3 access to the Jacobs stores on the MPLS network, which is fully meshed. Also, a stateless ACL wouldn't be the correct security feature to use on the headend CE, even if the MPLS network was set up in a hub-and-spoke configuration over MPLS for the independent stores. The current solution forces all traffic received at the headend into the Jacobs firewall for policy, but this solution does not reflect this. As detailed in the explanation for Answer A, there is also no capacity available for this solution.

c. Provide a new Bluesky MPLS headend CE router connecting, back to back, to the existing Bluesky headend MPLS CE router in the Jacobs DC for a new, separate hub-and-spoke MPLS VPN containing the independent stores.

This is incorrect. This solution would typically also require a new circuit into the MPLS provider to function, but there is no detail of a new circuit within the option, and the existing capacity of the existing solution would not allow the scale required to also provide connectivity for the independent stores.

d. Provision a new, separate L3 MPLS VPN for independent stores within the Bluesky MPLS WAN on a new central tail circuit into the DC that breaks out into separate VRF in the existing DC CE router.

This is the optimum answer. There isn't sufficient capacity on the existing Bluesky central DC circuit to provide connectivity for the independent stores, and clearly separation would be required between the two networks so that the independent networks couldn't just join the Jacobs store MPLS VPN. The additional VPN could be terminated within the DC on a separate VRF on the CE router or VLAN within the Jacobs DC to provide separation and connectivity to the existing firewall used for the independent stores' policy. The question is really ensuring you are analyzing all of the data you have available, in that the independent stores are currently using more combined bandwidth centrally than is available on the existing Bluesky tail circuit to the DC paired with the separation required for independent stores.

If you have answered this question correctly, you have scored one point.

Email #2

From: James Medina

To: CCDE Candidate

Subject: Network Integration

Hi.

I've been discussing the MPLS network issue with the CTO, and this has prompted a bigger question around finally providing integration. We both don't believe we should continue as is, and it's time to bring some innovation into the business and reduce our capex and some of the complexities of running multiple providers. The CTO believes we should be running an Internet-only VPN WAN and completely remove the overhead of MPLS running our own managed overlay networks on the Internet circuits. He stated we could reduce our Internet circuits to a single circuit in each DC (Jacobs and Toolmate) on the back of this so that the DCs can back each other up in the event of a failure and each store can have dual Internet circuits, so no single points of failure. I'm not convinced we should do this in one fell swoop and believe we are better off running a traditional hybrid SD-WAN type of network with a mix of connectivity. I've been reading up on the subject and it seems we could have the best of both worlds if we followed this path. I need your help to decide how we should progress. I've also looked into Internet-only circuits, and in some of the remote parts of the UK, the providers we contacted have latency calculators that are showing approximately 100ms latency from stores to the London DCs, so I figure we are still OK for VoIP for their ADSL circuits. The CTO has secured a budget to provide the integration/consolidation, but we need to work out the best approach for the business.

Rgds,

James Medina
Network Manager
Jacobs

Question 5

If Jacobs were to follow the CTO's instructions for a self-managed Internet-only VPN WAN solution based on the supplied information, which of the following solutions would you recommend to Jacobs to consolidate connectivity for all of the stores into the Jacobs and Toolmate DCs? (Choose one.)

Requirements/constraints from supplied documentation:

The CTO believes we should be running an Internet-only VPN WAN and completely remove the overhead of MPLS running our own managed overlay networks on the Internet circuits. He stated we could reduce our Internet circuits to a single circuit in each DC (Jacobs and Toolmate) on the back of this so that the DCs can back each other up in the event of a failure and each store can have dual Internet circuits, so no single points of failure.

I've also looked into Internet-only circuits, and in some of the remote parts of the UK, the providers we contacted have latency calculators that are showing approximately 100ms latency from stores to the London DCs, so I figure we are still OK for VoIP for their ADSL circuits.

a. GETVPN solution with a facility for stores to terminate VPNs in either DC should one DC Internet connection fail

This is incorrect. GETVPN would be suitable for an MPLS-only WAN with private IP addressing, but the feature is not compatible with the Internet circuits due to an incompatibility with NAT. GETVPN maintains address preservation between inner and outer IP headers, and this is not feasible with the NAT required over the Internet—an easy one to rule out.

b. Phase 3 DMVPN multi-VRF (Jacobs VRF, Toolmate VRF, independent store VRF) solution with a facility for stores to terminate VPNs in either DC should one DC Internet connection fail

This is the optimal answer from the available options at this point in time. A DMVPN network would function well over the Internet with a minimum of three VRFs required, based on the existing DC setup for Jacobs, Toolmate, and independent stores. As there would only be a single Internet circuit within each of the Jacobs and Toolmate DCs, the Jacobs stores would need a secure way to access their home DC if their associated Internet circuit failed within the Jacobs DC, and vice versa for Toolmate branches. The DCI link would need to be configured for connectivity for the stores in the event of an Internet failure within one of the DCs (post-termination on the DC with functioning Internet access). Existing VoIP calls between stores in each network would continue to function with the stipulated 100ms latency, as these would utilize spoke-to-spoke tunnels over DMVPN Phase 3. If the calls had to route via the hub in the DC, the latency would increase to 200ms, which would border on being unacceptable for VoIP quality, with the industry standard latency maximum recognized as being 150ms.

   c. Phase 3 DMVPN single-VRF solution with a facility for stores to terminate VPNs in either DC should one DC Internet connection fail

   This is incorrect. A single VRF solution wouldn't provide any separation or segmentation between the separate entities natively and would be highly complex to administer. This solution would require a hub-and-spoke deployment denying spoke-to-spoke communication, with all traffic routed to central firewall for policy decisions. VoIP quality between stores would also be unacceptable with the latency into and out of the DC for store-to-store communications.

   d. Phase 1 DMVPN multi-VRF (Jacobs VRF, Toolmate VRF, independent store VRF) solution with a facility for stores to terminate VPNs in either DC should one DC Internet connection fail

   This is incorrect. A multi-VRF DMVPN solution would function well, as detailed in Answer A, but DMVPN Phase 1 means no dynamic spoke-to-spoke tunnels. Also, communication via the DMVPN hub would be required, which then doubles the latency of VoIP calls to an unacceptable level.

   e. Hub-and-spoke IPsec VPN (Jacobs VPN, Toolmate VPN, independent store VPN), GRE tunnels with IGP, with a facility for stores to terminate VPNs in either DC should one DC Internet connection fail

   This is a suboptimal answer. The solution would function, but there are negative aspects associated with it. Primarily, VoIP quality would be degraded, as store-to-store calls would need to traverse the DC location and incur additional latency. Secondly, significant management overhead is involved in the configuration and management of the IPsec peers due to the sheer number of stores, and the headend routers would also have to be specified appropriately to accommodate the number of dynamic routing neighbors and to process the IPsec traffic. Scalability would be questionable with this solution.

   f. Hub-and-spoke IPsec VPN (Jacobs VPN, Toolmate VPN, independent store VPN), static routing with a facility for stores to terminate VPNs in either DC should one DC Internet connection fail

   This is a suboptimal answer for the reasons detailed in the explanation for Answer D. Scalability would be improved, however, due to not having to maintain dynamic routing adjacencies over the IPsec connections and because of simplification due to static routing.

If you have answered this question correctly, you have scored one point.

Email #3

From: James Medina

To: CCDE Candidate

Subject: Hybrid WAN/SD-WAN

Hi.

We're looking into industry trends, and we're aware that there is a movement from network topology toward an application services topology. Network changes are taking too long for simple items such as bandwidth and QoS changes, so we're thinking we should definitely be moving toward some kind of hybrid WAN or SD-WAN solution. Can you have a look into this and let us know your thoughts? We could, as previously discussed, use the Internet as transport for stores in conjunction with MPLS or just use Internet only, as we have central Internet connections in the Jacobs and Toolmate DCs. From what I can gather, we would have the option to steer our traffic over specific links on an application basis. This would be fundamental to us, and we'd need the ability to be able to do this effectively in real time without raising changes for new profiles or applications as we bring them online with our providers.

Rgds,

James Medina
Network Manager
Jacobs

Question 6

If Jacobs did move to an SD-WAN type of solution with a combination of MPLS and Internet circuits per store for Jacobs and Toolmate stores and Internet-only circuits for independent stores, what would be a major benefit? (Choose one.)

Requirements/constraints from supplied documentation: N/A

a. Business continuity could be facilitated natively.

This is correct. A forthright statement, and one you would have to evaluate carefully prior to committing to, the question is designed to ensure you consider the required design and the effect it will have on the existing network. Each DC has central Internet connections but does not have each MPLS provider's networks present; as such, if the Toolmate DC suffered a catastrophic failure, there would be no feasible access from a Toolmate store to required services within the Jacobs DC. The Internet links could be used in this failure scenario to natively provide a backup to the Jacobs DC for the Toolmate branches or Jacobs stores, access to the Jacobs DC via Toolmate, and the ability to traverse the DCI if the Jacobs MPLS provider(s) fail.

b. Cost savings of approximately 90% on Internet circuits versus MPLS circuits.

This is incorrect. You would be making an assumption here, unless these figures have been provided within an email or background information. You shouldn't make assumptions in the CCDE lab; if you feel you have to, you have missed some vital information and will need to go back over the documentation you have available to you to make an informed decision.

c. MPLS providers could be reduced to a single provider.

This is incorrect. There are currently three MPLS providers serving each area of the network. The MPLS provider serving the independent stores (Annet) would no longer be required, as the stores would use Internet circuits. You would be making an assumption that Jacobs and Toolmate stores use the same provider, as this would entail one entity migrating its MPLS connections to the other provider, which would require significant effort.

d. Security improvements.

This is incorrect. The security challenges would increase when migrating from private to public circuits.

If you have answered this question correctly, you have scored one point.

Email #4

From: James Medina

To: CCDE Candidate

Subject: SD-WAN Thoughts

Hi.

I've been discussing the possibility of running SD-WAN with our ISPs over the existing central Jacobs and Toolmate Internet access. As you know, we have dual ISP links in each DC that are running in an active/standby arrangement. Both ISPs will reduce costs quite considerably if we decommission our standby Internet circuit in each DC and then reduce our current 1Gbps rate over the remaining 1Gbps Internet circuit in each DC (they can effectively provide a CIR in steps of 100Mbps over the access circuits). My thoughts are we can remove one ISP link at each DC and then provide resilience for each DC from the other DC for Internet SD-WAN-sourced traffic from stores. Also, as each store would require an Internet access circuit locally, we can use this for Direct Internet Access (DIA) from the store and not require anywhere near as much Internet bandwidth because we should no longer need to break out centrally to the Internet for store users. This is what I'm thinking:

1. Broadband ADSL type Internet access provisioned in each store site (independent, Jacobs, and Toolmate), sized accordingly.

2. All stores use DIA for Internet access rather than breaking out via the central DCs.

3. Annet MPLS network decommissioned for independent stores. These stores could then use SD-WAN Internet to access the Jacobs DC.

4. Taconet MPLS network decommissioned for Jacobs stores. These stores could then use an Internet SD-WAN solution and existing Bluesky MPLS network to access the Jacobs and Toolmate DCs (Jacobs stores could access their DC via Toolmate Internet connection if there is an MPLS and Internet failure within the Jacobs DC by traversing the DCI from Toolmate).

5. Lotnet second circuit MPLS network decommissioned for Toolmate stores. These stores could then use an SD-WAN solution for Internet access and existing first Lotnet MPLS network to access the Toolmate and Jacobs DCs (Toolmate stores could access their DC via the Jacobs DC Internet connection if there is an MPLS and Internet failure within the Toolmate DC by traversing the DCI from Jacobs).

Rgds,

James Medina
Network Manager
Jacobs

Question 7

If Jacobs moves to an SD-WAN solution for all store access, as detailed in the fourth email, could it, with confidence, make a design decision to remove the second ISP circuits at each DC and reduce speeds on the individual Internet circuits in the DCs by having stores use Direct Internet Access with a view toward reducing existing central Internet utilization and saving central ISP costs? (Choose one.)

Requirements/constraints from supplied documentation:

1. Broadband ADSL type Internet access provisioned in each store site (independent, Jacobs, and Toolmate), sized accordingly.

2. All stores use DIA for Internet access rather than breaking out via the central DCs.

3. Annet MPLS network decommissioned for independent stores. These stores could then use SD-WAN Internet to access the Jacobs DC.

4. Taconet MPLS network decommissioned for Jacobs stores. These stores could then use an Internet SD-WAN solution and existing Bluesky MPLS network to access the Jacobs and Toolmate DCs (Jacobs stores could access their DC via Toolmate Internet connection if there is an MPLS and Internet failure within the Jacobs DC by traversing the DCI from Toolmate).

5. Lotnet second circuit MPLS network decommissioned for Toolmate stores. These stores could then use an SD-WAN solution for Internet access and existing first Lotnet MPLS network to access the Toolmate and Jacobs DCs (Toolmate stores could access their DC via the Jacobs DC Internet connection if there is an MPLS and Internet failure within the Toolmate DC by traversing the DCI from Jacobs).

The following figures illustrate Jacobs and Toolmate ISP utilization statistics.

Jacobs ISP CE1

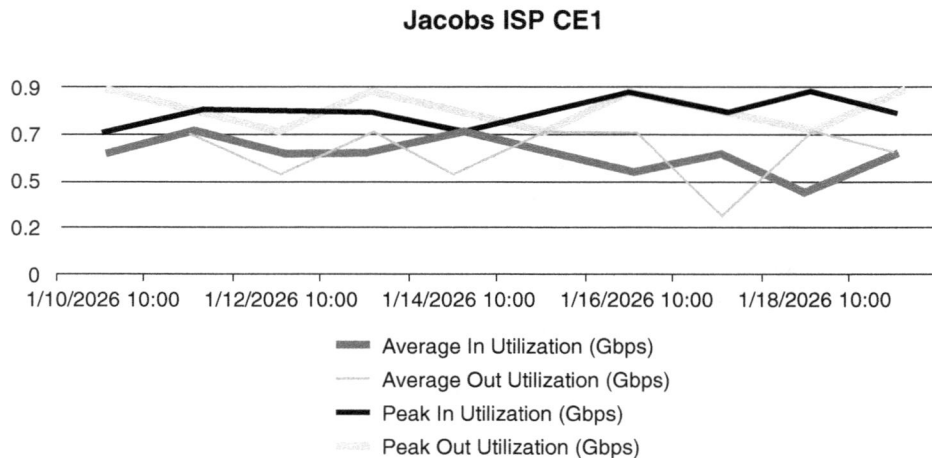

- Average In Utilization (Gbps)
- Average Out Utilization (Gbps)
- Peak In Utilization (Gbps)
- Peak Out Utilization (Gbps)

Toolmate ISP CE1

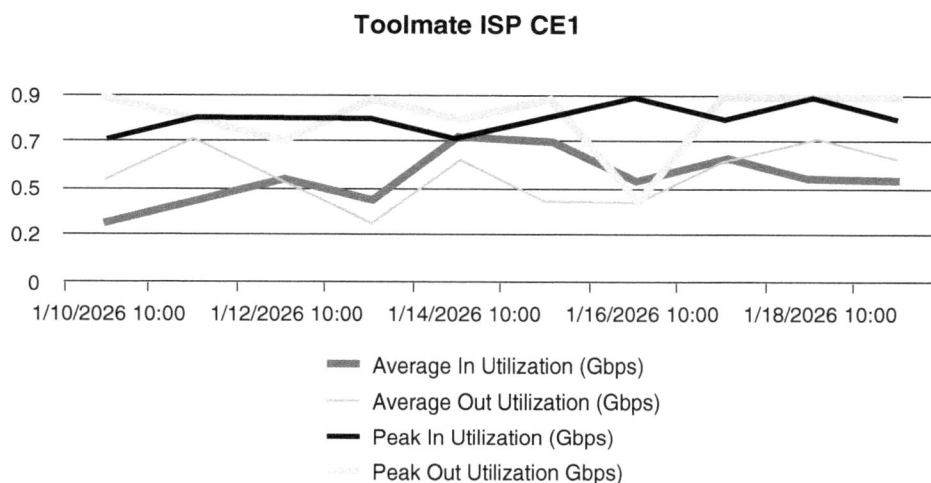

Legend:
- ▬▬ Average In Utilization (Gbps)
- ┄┄ Average Out Utilization (Gbps)
- ▬▬ Peak In Utilization (Gbps)
- ┄┄ Peak Out Utilization Gbps)

a. Yes

This is incorrect. As Internet-destined traffic will be breaking out locally at the stores using DIA, it might seem that central Internet access traffic over DC links will be reduced, but of course the stores will be using the local Internet links to access the DCs for the SD-WAN-based VPN. Even though Jacobs might be able to remove a second standby ISP circuit at each site now that cross-site resilience has been introduced, it wouldn't be able to reduce the capacity of circuits and would most likely need to up-speed these connections so they could accommodate traffic in MPLS failure conditions when the SD-WAN network only has the ISP circuits available for use.

b. No

This is correct. As per the explanation for Answer A, the SD-WAN network would actually be using more bandwidth over Internet circuits. This is a relatively straight-forward question designed to ensure you are following the scenario and evaluating the data you have available. Occasionally, you can get a question that is answerable in seconds, and the subsequent question could take 20 minutes!

If you have answered this question correctly, you have scored one point.

Question 8

If Jacobs were to move to an SD-WAN solution as detailed in the fourth email, with each Jacobs and Toolmate store using one MPLS link and one Internet circuit, or a single Internet circuit in independent stores for WAN connectivity, which of the following areas should take priority from a security perspective? (Choose one.)

Requirements/constraints from supplied documentation:

Provider-assigned public IP addressing is used for external hosting using a Britnet registered /24 prefix, which is further subnetted to provide DMZ segmentation for public-facing Jacobs services and NAT ranges for employee Internet access via a central proxy server within the DMZ.

a. Direct Internet Access from stores

This is the optimal answer. You are informed that Jacobs stores currently use a proxy server for Internet access, where policy would typically be applied for users accessing the Internet. If the stores accessed the Internet directly from local circuits, policy would need to be defined and applied locally within the store; otherwise, Jacobs would be introducing significant risk to its IT environment.

b. Encryption ciphers of Internet access circuits

This is a suboptimal answer. Encryption ciphers would in reality be an implementation item; the Internet connections would of course require encryption, but the exact details are not "key" at this point in time from a security perspective.

c. PKI infrastructure

This is a suboptimal answer. The PKI infrastructure is effectively an implementation item. CA authority, digital certificates, and such will of course be required, but the exact details are not "key" at this point in time from a security perspective.

d. DDoS protection for DCs

This is incorrect. The DC Internet connections are not new. Jacobs and Toolmate DCs already have an online presence for online retailing; as such, any requirements for DDoS protection wouldn't necessarily change as part of this new solution.

If you have answered this question correctly, you have scored one point.

Email #5

From: James Medina

To: CCDE Candidate

Subject: Provider-managed SD-WAN Service

Hi.

I've been in touch with the Bluesky MPLS provider to discuss our strategy, and they offer a fully managed SD-WAN service and even a co-managed SD-WAN service. It's something we hadn't considered, as I had assumed we'd just self-manage if we went down the SD-WAN route, and I guess MPLS companies are keen to retain as much business as possible if it ultimately means loss of MPLS circuits. I need your help to ascertain the management direction we should take.

Rgds,

James Medina
Network Manager
Jacobs

Question 9

Jacobs is now considering raising an RFP (Request for Proposal) to their existing MPLS providers to bid for a fully managed SD-WAN solution that the company can use for consolidated store access to the DCs. Complete the following table to aid its decision-making process for a fully managed service versus a DIY in-house self-managed SD-WAN solution by the network team. Insert a check in the Solution Type option that provides the most benefit to Jacobs (would be most optimal) for each Function topic.

Function	Solution Type	
	Fully Managed	**Self-Managed**
Application-aware routing policies and QoS		x
Speed of deployment	x	
Flexibility		x
Ease of integrations		x
Geographical coverage	x	
Control over network and data		x
Skills and staffing	x	
Infrastructure and circuit procurement	x	
Underlay and overlay monitoring	x	

- **Application-aware routing policies and QoS:** SD-WAN offers attractive options for traffic engineering over available underlay links to provide optimum routing toward specific applications based on set criteria. In order to create the policies required and to provide maximum flexibility, Jacobs itself would be in a better position to administer this element with its application knowledge and ability to create and modify policies without delay and process in comparison to the service provider.

- **Speed of deployment:** Deploying an SD-WAN solution is a significant project when the remote store count is high. The service provider would be in a much better position to deal with circuit ordering and implementation of service in comparison to an enterprise.

- **Flexibility:** Flexibility is an open term, but you would undoubtedly achieve more flexibility in a self-managed solution versus a service provider, which would have a contracted service with SLAs, a fixed number of changes per month, and a notice period for changes, for example.

- **Ease of integrations:** In terms of integrating the solution, Jacobs would be in a better position than a service provider in terms of understanding its own IT environment and the ability to integrate systems and facilitate migration.

- **Geographical coverage:** A service provider would typically have enhanced geographical coverage in comparison to an enterprise. Jacobs would have a store presence, for example, in a specific location, but would it also be able to deploy IT skills in the event of an issue in that area as easily as a service provider?

- **Control over network and data:** A self-managed solution would undoubtedly have enhanced control over the network and underlying data in comparison to a remote service provider.

- **Skills and staffing:** This one is debatable, but in general a service provider is going to have a larger pool of staff with a higher skill level than an enterprise. It is the service provider's primary business function.

- **Infrastructure and circuit procurement:** Economies of scale would dictate that the service provider be able to provide efficiencies in cost and delivery for commodities such as infrastructure and circuit procurement.

- **Underlay and overlay monitoring:** A service provider would typically have the correct toolset and skilled employees to provide an enhanced monitoring solution in comparison to an enterprise, especially when a significant number of the circuits would be their own MPLS circuits.

If you have answered this question, correctly, you have scored two points. Partial scoring would be available within the CCDE lab. I'll let you do the math on this one. If you have one or two check marks in the wrong section, you can determine your own score!

Question 10

Which of the following SD-WAN solution types would be most suitable for Jacobs? (Choose one.)

Requirements/constraints from supplied documentation:

From what I can gather, we would have the option to steer our traffic over specific links on an application basis. This would be fundamental to us, and we'd need the ability to be able to do this effectively in real time without raising changes for new profiles or applications as we bring them online with our providers.

Network changes are taking too long for simple items such as bandwidth changes. We're thinking we should definitely be moving toward some kind of hybrid WAN solution.

a. Fully managed MPLS service provider solution

This is a suboptimal answer. The fully managed solution does appear to offer more benefits than the self-managed solution, but per the requirements, Jacobs does require the flexibility that a self-managed solution brings for application-aware routing and QoS, whereas a service provider is likely to require some level of change and delay.

b. Jacobs self-managed solution

This is correct. The self-managed solution suits Jacobs' requirement to bring new applications online and provide application-aware policies without requiring a service provider to be involved and thus incur delay. You are also informed that, historically, even simple changes have been taking too long. Cost aside, it might be beneficial for a service provider to fully manage an SD-WAN solution, especially if the skills are not available in house, and economies of scale are useful for circuit ordering, delivery times, and the ability to provide a monitoring solution without the requirement for new tooling within the enterprise.

If you have answered this question correctly, you have scored one point.

Question 11

As Jacobs fully investigates SD-WAN with a view of provisioning a self-managed solution, it requires additional information on SD-WAN functions and associated "planes" to gain a better understanding of SD-WAN functionality. Check the boxes for the corresponding SD-WAN plane per function in the following table to assist in the company's understanding.

Function	Plane			
	Orchestration	Management	Control	Data
First point of authentication	x			
Fabric discovery			x	
Distribution of management and control plane controller location	x			
Programmatic interfaces (NETCONF/REST)		x		
Secure data plane establishment with edge routers				x
Distributes data plane and application-aware policy to edge routers			x	
Centralized provisioning		x		
Software upgrades		x		
Export of performance statistics				x
Application-aware routing policy				x

- **Orchestration plane:** The orchestration plane typically authenticates and authorizes all of the SD-WAN infrastructure devices.

- **Management plane:** The management plane deals with provisioning, onboarding, and monitoring and would deal with the overall management and troubleshooting of the SD-WAN solution.

- **Control plane:** The control plane manages all policies (data plane and routing) for the SD-WAN edge routers in the environment.

- **The data plane:** The data plane is the path the traffic flows over the SD-WAN overlay network in order to reach the required destination.

If you have answered this question correctly, you have scored two points. As per previous questions, partial scoring is available. There are effectively 11 straightforward questions incorporated into this single overall question. You can't expect to be awarded too many points for general knowledge items, though, and these question types should be seen as a simple way to earn 1 or 2 quick points and then move on to more complex questions where you will need thinking time in order to apply knowledge.

Email #6

From: James Medina

To: CCDE Candidate

Subject: SD-WAN Connectivity Technologies

Hi.

I've had the team research what technologies we can use for our connectivity to stores for SD-WAN. We have all of the following technologies available to us (varying bandwidths to suit and varying prices) for all of our store locations. Have a think about which may be better suited to our solution, as our infrastructure will natively support all of them!

4G/LTE

5G

Internet access circuits/ADSL/SDSL

MPLS circuits

Rgds,

James Medina
Network Manager
Jacobs

Question 12

Which SD-WAN underlay technology would you recommend for the store locations? (Choose two.)

Requirements/constraints from supplied documentation:

Jaystore syncs product availability from a database within the DC location for online purchases and store purchases. The application was developed over 10 years ago and by developers within a LAN environment. As such, it does not function well when latency exceeds 20ms between the client and headend infrastructure. Due to this issue, the network team included the TCP application into a mission-critical QoS class over the WAN for mitigation.

1. Broadband ADSL type Internet access provisioned in each store site (independent, Jacobs, and Toolmate), sized accordingly.

2. All stores use DIA for Internet access rather than breaking out via the central DCs.

3. Annet MPLS network decommissioned for independent stores. These stores could then use SD-WAN Internet to access the Jacobs DC.

4. Taconet MPLS network decommissioned for Jacobs stores. These stores could then use an Internet SD-WAN solution and existing Bluesky MPLS network to access the Jacobs and Toolmate DCs (Jacobs stores could access their DC via Toolmate Internet connection if there is an MPLS and Internet failure within the Jacobs DC by traversing the DCI from Toolmate).

5. Lotnet second circuit MPLS network decommissioned for Toolmate stores. These stores could then use an SD-WAN solution for Internet access and existing first Lotnet MPLS network to access the Toolmate and Jacobs DCs (Toolmate stores could access their DC via the Jacobs DC Internet connection if there is an MPLS and Internet failure within the Toolmate DC by traversing the DCI from Jacobs).

a. 4G/LTE

This is incorrect. You were told from previous information that an Internet circuit will be required; however, if 5G is available, there would need to be a convincing reason why you would consider 4G/LTE instead of 5G. Also, this technology is likely to provide a latency of over 50ms, which exceeds the 20ms requirement for the Jaystore application.

b. 5G

This is correct. You were told from previous information that an Internet circuit will be required, and 5G is optimal (in comparison to Answers A and C). It's well known that this technology is likely to provide a low latency of approximately 10ms, which would mitigate the known Jaystore application latency requirement.

c. Internet access circuits/ADSL/SDSL

This is a suboptimal answer. You were told from previous information that an Internet circuit will be required; however, in comparison to 5G (Answer B), ADSL/SDSL would be less favorable. Making a choice between the two at this level without having cost or speed requirements factored into the question is difficult, but you should have determined that 5G can offer everything that ADSL/SDSL circuits can offer in terms of speed, along with the lower latency characteristics, which suit the Jaystore application latency requirement. ADSL/SDSL latency characteristics, on the other hand, would be variable.

d. MPLS circuits (primary site access)

This is correct. The MPLS circuits are functioning already. You would typically maintain one circuit as part of the SD-WAN deployment, as the customer has previously mentioned within emails.

e. MPLS circuits (secondary site access)

This is incorrect. The whole vision/intent of the SD-WAN solution was to move away from dual MPLS circuits. A primary MPLS circuit is appropriate, but a secondary MPLS circuit would defeat the objective of the project and offer no advantages.

If you answered this question correctly, you have scored one point. If you selected Answer C instead of B in conjunction with D, then award yourself half a point. If you have been following the scenario, the fourth email details the vision for the circuits. You really just needed to determine which Internet access method is most suitable based on the Jaystore requirement.

Question 13

If Jacobs went ahead with an SD-WAN solution, which of the following items would the company need to address prior to using Internet connectivity as one path for stores to access the central resources in the Jacobs and Toolmate DCs? (Choose one.)

Requirements/constraints from supplied documentation:

The following figures illustrate the Jacobs and Toolmate ISP utilization statistics.

Jacobs ISP CE1

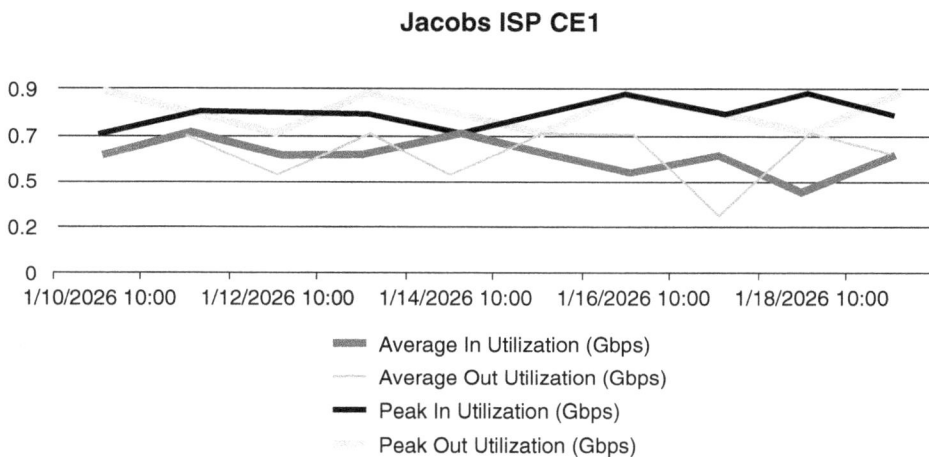

Legend:
- Average In Utilization (Gbps)
- Average Out Utilization (Gbps)
- Peak In Utilization (Gbps)
- Peak Out Utilization (Gbps)

Toolmate ISP CE1

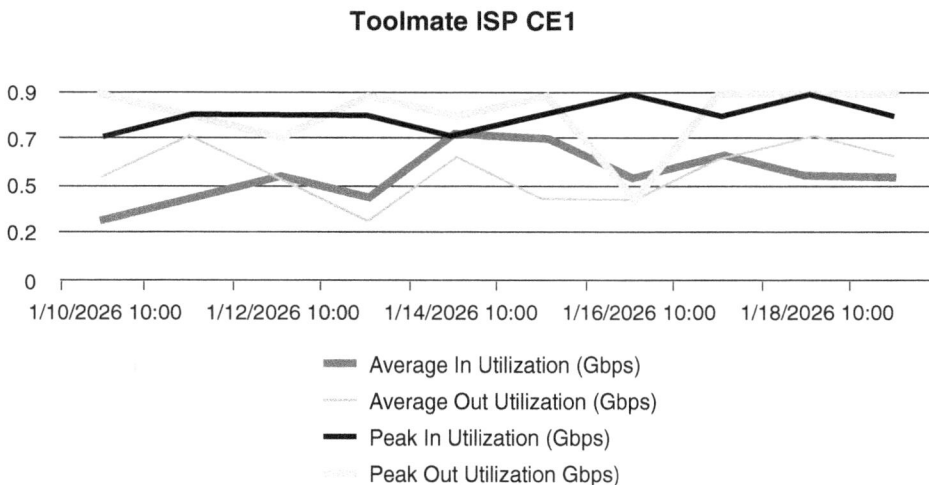

Legend:
- Average In Utilization (Gbps)
- Average Out Utilization (Gbps)
- Peak In Utilization (Gbps)
- Peak Out Utilization Gbps)

a. Upgrade the performance of Internet-facing firewalls in each DC.

This is a suboptimal answer, as there is no evidence to suggest the Internet firewalls would require a performance or even throughput upgrade. External firewalls in an SD-WAN solution would typically pass VPN traffic onto SD-WAN edge routers, as opposed to terminating the SD-WAN VPN traffic, where additional performance might be required to perform this functionality.

b. Allow SD-WAN flows through Internet-facing firewalls at the DCs.

This is incorrect. Flows would require enabling, but this would be an implementation task at the time of deployment. The question is really trying to see if you are looking at this from a design perspective and something that could make or break the deployment, as opposed to an implementation task.

c. Upgrade Internet access circuits to 10Gbps in the DCs.

This is correct. Current ISP usage at the Jacobs and Toolmate DCs is close to the maximum available 1Gbps. The existing circuits could not accommodate additional traffic migrated from legacy MPLS connections.

d. Decide if static routing or a dynamic protocol should be used for routing over the SD-WAN Internet-based tunnels.

This is incorrect. A routing protocol would be required (typically OMP), but this would be an implementation task at the time of deployment. The question is really trying to see if you are looking at this from a design perspective, as per the explanation in Answer B.

If you answered this question correctly, you have scored one point.

Email #7

From: James Medina

To: CCDE Candidate

Subject: 5G is the place to B.

Hi.

Thanks for the feedback. It has occurred to me that the Internet ADSL/SDSL circuits we've been looking at may exceed the latency requirement we have for the Jaystore app of 20ms. 5G technology definitely gets around this so I guess we will go with 5G as a secondary circuit and keep a single MPLS circuit where we have dual MPLS links now. Anywhere with a single MPLS circuit can be replaced with 5G, and we can make significant savings on our WAN opex. I did speak to the app developers for Jaystore, and they are quoting me 6 months to rewrite the application communications module based on their existing agile work load—this would be way too long for us, and it would also be expense and difficult to justify based on the amount of effort they are quoting.

I've found some competitively priced SD-WAN store-sized edge routers we can connect to 5G Internet services via an optional 5G card. For PCI compliance, they have their own full security stack, which includes VRFs, L7 firewall, IPS/IDS, protection, and URL filtering, with EIGRP and BGP LAN–side and OMP WAN–side routing. They come with dual copper Ethernet connections for access or trunking connectivity, which we can use to connect into our store network switches.

Rgds,

James Medina
Network Manager
Jacobs

Question 14

As Jacobs is intending to use SD-WAN edge routers with 5G Internet connections at stores providing Internet access to create the SD-WAN network, should the company also provide firewalls at each store location for protecting the SD-WAN edge routers and store LAN connected to the Internet? (Choose one.)

Requirements / constraints from supplied documentation:

I've found some competitively priced SD-WAN store-sized edge routers we can connect to 5G Internet services via an optional 5G card. For PCI compliance, they have their own full security stack, which includes VRFs, L7 firewall, IPS/IDS, protection, and URL filtering, with EIGRP and BGP LAN–side and OMP WAN–side routing. They come with dual copper Ethernet connections for access or trunking connectivity, which we can use to connect into our store network switches.

Due to a historical issue with a virtualized infrastructure device with RCA analysis citing vendor code interoperability failure that resulted in a high-profile outage, Jacobs security policy (which covers all zones of the network and store entities) now dictates that functionality of infrastructure devices should be limited to a single defined function and that separate functionality must be provisioned through separate physical infrastructure devices.

Also, as each store will have an Internet access circuit locally, we can use this for DIA from the store and not require anywhere near as much Internet bandwidth, as we should no longer need to break out centrally to the Internet. This is what I'm thinking:

All stores use DIA for Internet access rather than breaking out via the DCs.

a. Yes. Firewalls should be deployed physically in front of the SD-WAN router with the Internet/5G connection.

This is incorrect. Even though you are informed the SD-WAN edge routers have their own security stack, including firewalling, the Jacobs security policy dictates that infrastructure devices must be limited to single functionality. Combining edge routing/5G connectivity with firewall functionality would breach this policy, and firewalls are therefore required; however, there isn't a connection point for a firewall in front of a wireless 5G connection. Logically, the firewall could be placed in front of the edge router, but not physically.

b. Yes. Firewalls should be deployed physically behind the SD-WAN edge routers with the Internet/5G connections.

This is correct. Even though you are informed the SD-WAN edge routers have their own security stack, including firewalling, the Jacobs security policy dictates that infrastructure devices must be limited to single functionality. Combining edge routing/5G connectivity with firewall functionality would breach this policy, and firewalls are therefore required. You can only physically connect the firewall behind the SD-WAN edge router in the 5G use case, so the firewall would be placed between the store LAN and edge router, providing the security functionality.

c. No. Firewalls are not required in the store due to the native firewall and security features that the SD-WAN edge routers provide.

This is incorrect. Even though you are informed the edge routers have their own security stack, including firewalling, the Jacobs security policy dictates that infrastructure devices must be limited to single functionality. Combining edge routing/5G connectivity with firewall functionality would breach this policy.

d. No. Firewalls are not required due to SD-WAN routers only being configured to accept IPsec connections from central DC routers and all Internet traffic being forwarded to the central DC locations.

This is incorrect, as per the explanation for Answer C, and Jacobs has indicated that it does require DIA for store access to the Internet.

As a side note, a firewall positioned in front of an SD-WAN edge router effectively only has visibility of encrypted packets for the SD-WAN control and data planes. Firewalls placed behind SD-WAN edge routers would have visibility of traffic ingressing and egressing the local LAN.

If you have answered this question correctly, you have scored one point.

Email #8

From: James Medina

To: CCDE Candidate

Subject: Security Exception

Hi.

The security policy that dictates that functionality of infrastructure devices should be limited to a single defined function and separate functionality must be provisioned through separate physical infrastructure devices is going to add significant cost to this project. I'm going to force an exception through security with the CTO's authority so we can use SD-WAN edge routers' native security functionality and negate the requirement for store firewalls. Let's progress with the design on the assumption the exception will be approved.

In terms of underlay, as mentioned previously, I'd like to keep one MPLS circuit where we have dual MPLS circuits, and we can replace the second MPLS circuit with Internet access. Where we only have one MPLS circuit currently for independent stores, we can replace this with an Internet circuit.

I'm going to look at upgrading the Jacobs ISP link to a resilient 10Gbps solution. I'm wondering if we can remove the Toolmate ISP link if we can do this.

If you can start designing the overall SD-WAN solution, that would be great.

Rgds,

James Medina
Network Manager
Jacobs

Question 15

If Jacobs proceeds with the SD-WAN design detailed within the following figure, can the company decommission the existing central Internet access at the Toolmate DC and use a 10Gbps resilient Jacobs DC Internet connection as a secondary SD-WAN termination path for Toolmate stores in the event of an MPLS failure in the Lotnet network? (Choose one.)

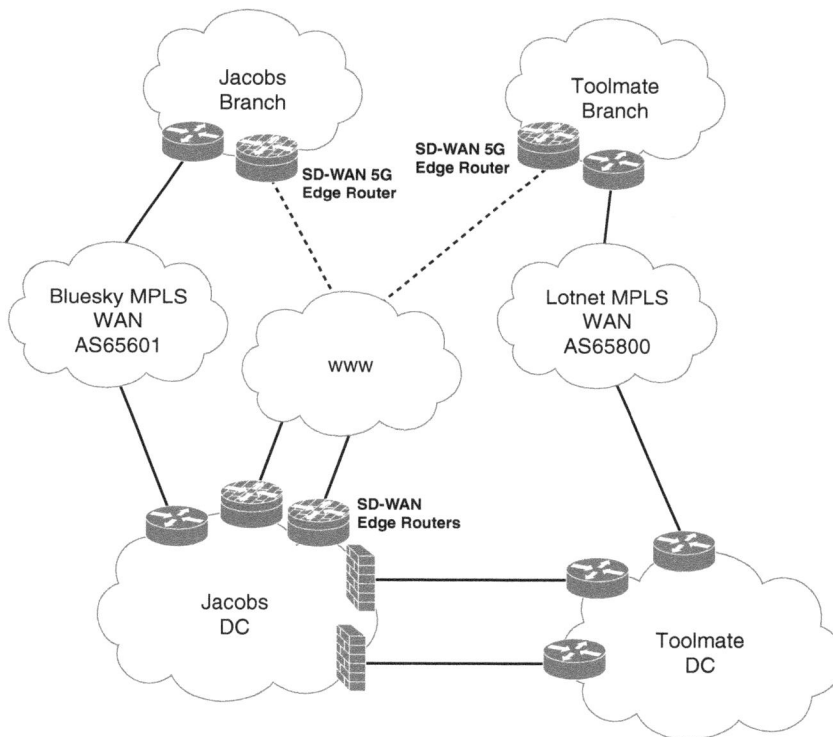

Requirements/constraints from supplied documentation:

In terms of underlay, I'd like to keep one MPLS circuit where we have dual MPLS circuits, and we can replace the second MPLS circuit with Internet access. Where we have only one MPLS circuit currently for independent stores, we can replace this with an Internet circuit.

The DMZ hosts a single non-load-balanced DMZ segment for publicly reachable web services for the Toolmate online presence. The red zone outer switches host the Internet CE connectivity and VPN services for B2B connections, which provide the online payment systems.

I'm going to look at upgrading the Jacobs ISP link to a resilient 10Gbps solution. I'm wondering if we can remove the Toolmate ISP link if we can do this.

   a. Yes (if the DCI firewall is configured to permit access).

   This is incorrect. While it is true that the Jacobs DC Internet path could actually provide termination of SD-WAN access from Toolmate stores and onward over the DCI
   links back to the Toolmate DC, the central Internet access from the Toolmate DC is
   still required for public-facing Toolmate services.

   b. No.

   This is correct. The central Internet access from the Toolmate DC is still required for
   public-facing Toolmate services.

This question is designed to make you evaluate information on hand before you provide
your answer. It's quite simple in reality, but you need to follow the story without getting too engrossed in the SD-WAN side and overlooking the day-to-day operation of the
existing network. By analyzing the information you have available to you and pairing this
with your technical knowledge and experience, you will ultimately gain your CCDE number. If you answered this question correctly, you have scored one point.

Question 16

Jacobs has decided to upgrade ISP connectivity in each DC to dual 10Gbps active/standby connections. Complete the design illustrated in the following figure for the head-end SD-WAN edge router(s) placement in the Jacobs DC when the dual headend MPLS connections will be reduced to one (the Toolmate DC will be identical, with a different MPLS provider). Add as many SD-WAN edge routers (which have 4x 10Gbps interfaces) and associated Ethernet connections (all connections are 10Gbps and all existing infra-structure supports 10Gbps and has a minimum of 2x 10Gbps additional port capacity per device) as required to implement a fully resilient SD-WAN headend. You may also remove existing Ethernet connections, if required.

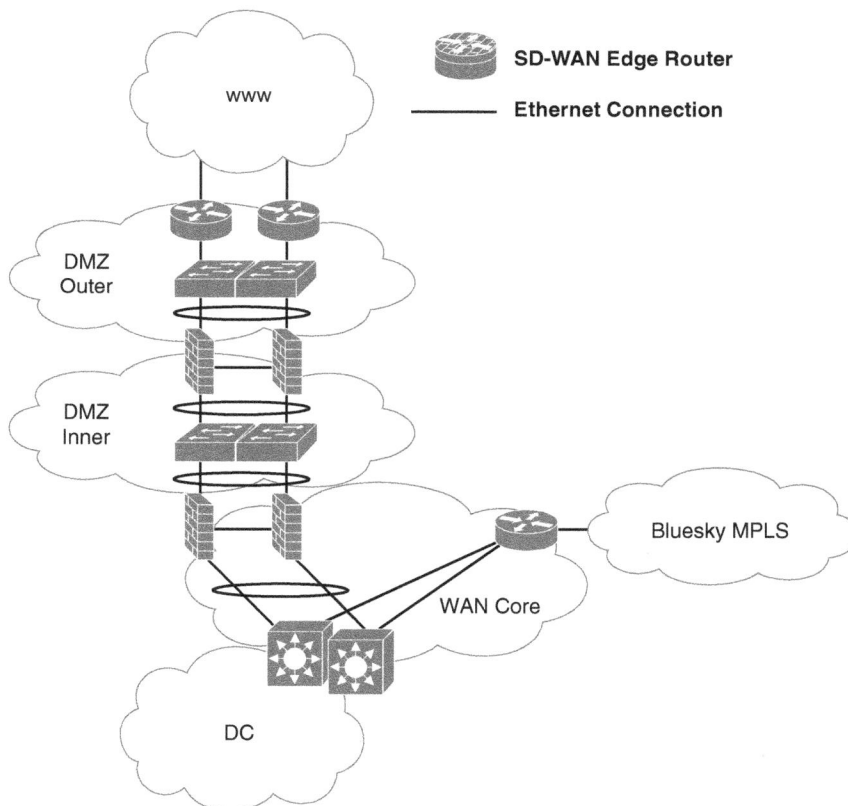

For your information, the Toolmate DC would be similar, with a different single MPLS provider, but this question focuses purely on the Jacobs DC element.

Requirements/constraints from supplied documentation:

Complete the design for the SD-WAN edge router(s) placement in the Jacobs DC when the dual headend MPLS connections will be reduced to one. Add as many SD-WAN edge routers (which have 4x 10Gbps interfaces) and associated Ethernet connections (all connections are 10Gbps, and all existing infrastructure supports 10Gbps and has a minimum of 2x 10Gbps additional port capacity per device) as required to implement a fully resilient SD-WAN headend. You may also remove existing Ethernet connections, if required.

Jacobs has decided to upgrade ISP connectivity in each DC to dual 10Gbps active/standby connections.

The following figure details the optimal design—a fully resilient SD-WAN headend requires two edge routers. One interface of each router requires Internet access and, as such, should be connected within the inner DMZ.

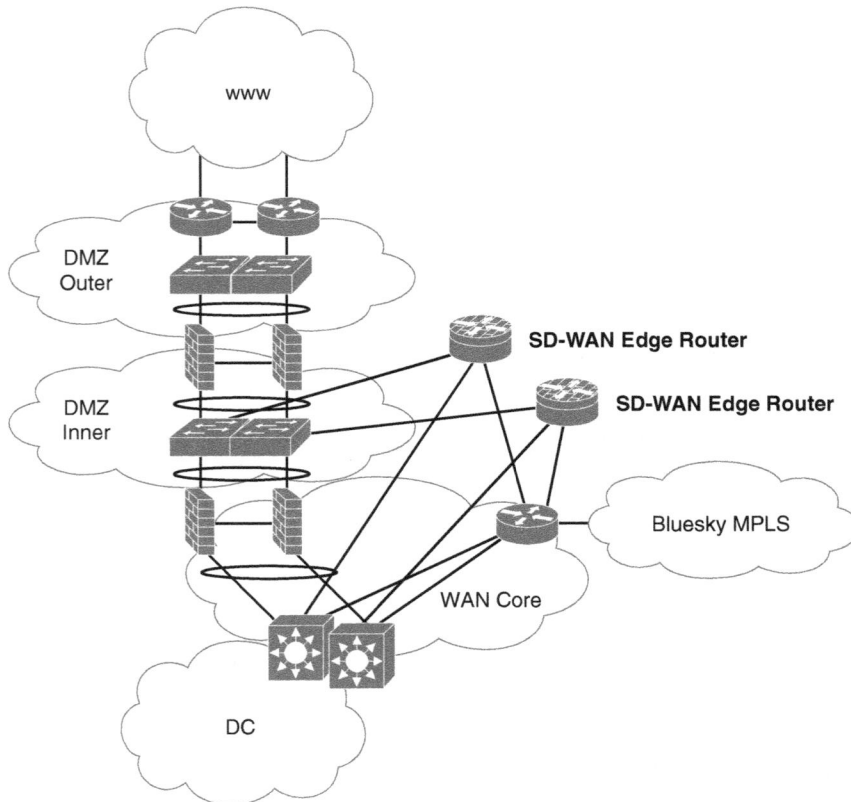

This approach provides additional security, allowing only the required ports needed for SD-WAN functionality and ensuring the SD-WAN edge routers are not directly accessible on the Internet and subject to attack, as they would be if located within the outer DMZ. An additional interface from each edge router requires terminating directly on the MPLS headend router and a further interface connected to the DC (via the WAN core in this example). This topology facilitates traffic flow from the DC directly to the SD-WAN edge routers, which then make a routing decision to forward traffic directly over the connected MPLS or Internet route with no single points of failure. Variations to this topology include not having a connection from the SD-WAN edge routers directly to the MPLS router (you were informed a minimum of two physical ports are available on each infra-structure device). This topology would function, but it is suboptimal in that traffic that traverses the MPLS network from the SD-WAN edge routers would need to "ping-pong" over the DC to the edge router interface to reach the MPLS network. Another variation is connecting the MPLS router directly to the SD-WAN edge routers and removing the DC-to-MPLS router links. This provides an optimal traffic flow from DC to edge routers to MPLS for MPLS-destined traffic, but it does not facilitate a smooth migration when some stores are not on the SD-WAN network, and traffic should flow directly from the MPLS network to the DC and not via the in-path edge router. A final variation worth considering that would also score full points is if you dual-homed the SD-WAN edge routers' DC side versus single-homed, as shown in the correct design to the LAN core. There are sufficient interfaces available on each side based on information supplied within the question, but it doesn't really provide a huge gain, as the maximum throughput of the MPLS link and ISP link would be 10Gbps, but it does mitigate a dual failure scenario (you have been asked to ensure the design is fully resilient and not that it should cater for multiple failures).

If you answered this question correctly, you have scored three points.

Question 17

Which of the following SD-WAN designs would you recommend for a Jacobs store? (Choose one.)

In terms of underlay, I'd like to keep one MPLS circuit where we have dual MPLS circuits, and we can replace the second MPLS circuit with Internet access. Where we have only one MPLS circuit currently for independent stores, we can replace this with an Internet circuit.

The security policy that dictates that functionality of infrastructure devices should be limited to a single defined function and separate functionality must be provisioned through separate physical infrastructure devices is going to add significant cost to this project. I'm going to request an exception through security so we can use edge routers' native security functionality and negate the requirement for store firewalls. Let's progress with the design on the assumption the exception will be approved.

I've found some competitively priced SD-WAN store-sized edge routers we can connect to 5G Internet services via an optional 5G card. For PCI compliance, they have their own full security stack, which includes VRFs, L7 firewall, IPS/IDS, protection, and URL filtering with EIGRP and BGP LAN–side and OMP WAN–side routing. They come with dual copper Ethernet connections for access or trunking connectivity, which we can use to connect into our store network switches.

Jacobs stores access the MPLS networks using default static routing pointing to the VRRP gateway with the primary MPLS network of Bluesky.

a.

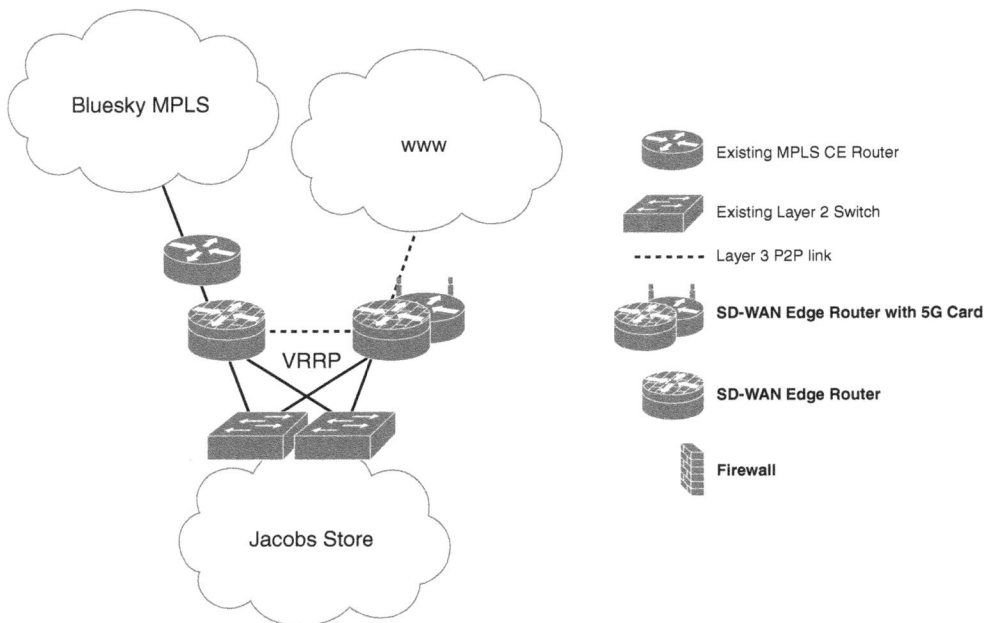

This is incorrect. Dual SD-WAN edge routers connected to each of the Layer 2 switches in the store provide resilience. SD-WAN edge routers connect to a common VLAN linking them to the LAN, and VRRP is used from the LAN to the SD-WAN edge routers with a Layer 3 point-to-point link between edge routers, which can be used to route between SD-WAN routers for specific failure conditions and application routing policies. The solution, however, wouldn't function because the switch to SD-WAN edge router connections would need to be EtherChannels to operate correctly in this scenario. (The switch side is acceptable to leave without channeling and have STP block links. The SD-WAN edge router side, however, would not function because a physical interface could not be assigned to the same IP subnet or VLAN without channeling enabled—the diagram would have shown the links joined as an EtherChannel if channeling was part of the design.) Be wary of making a simple error if you were drawn to this option. Be sure to take the time to evaluate options for sound, networking practices.

b.

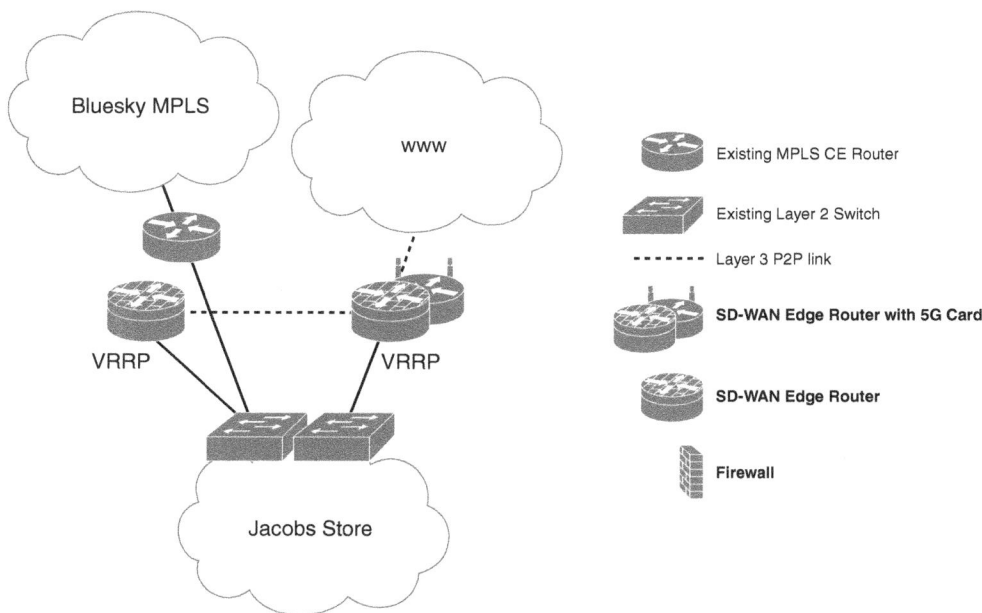

This is a suboptimal answer. Dual SD-WAN edge routers connected to each of the Layer 2 switches in the store provide resilience. SD-WAN edge routers connect to a common VLAN linking them to the LAN, and VRRP is used from the LAN to the SD-WAN edge routers with a Layer 3 point-to-point link between edge routers, which can be used to route between SD-WAN routers for specific failure conditions and application routing policies. The solution would provide a relatively straightforward migration path, but there is no real benefit for the SD-WAN edge routers not to connect directly to the transport media because traffic would need to trombone/ping-pong through the SD-WAN edge routers from the store LAN on the same physical interfaces that connect the SD-WAN edge routers to the LAN (traffic flow from the store would be LAN to SD-WAN edge router to LAN to MPLS CE router, for example).

c.

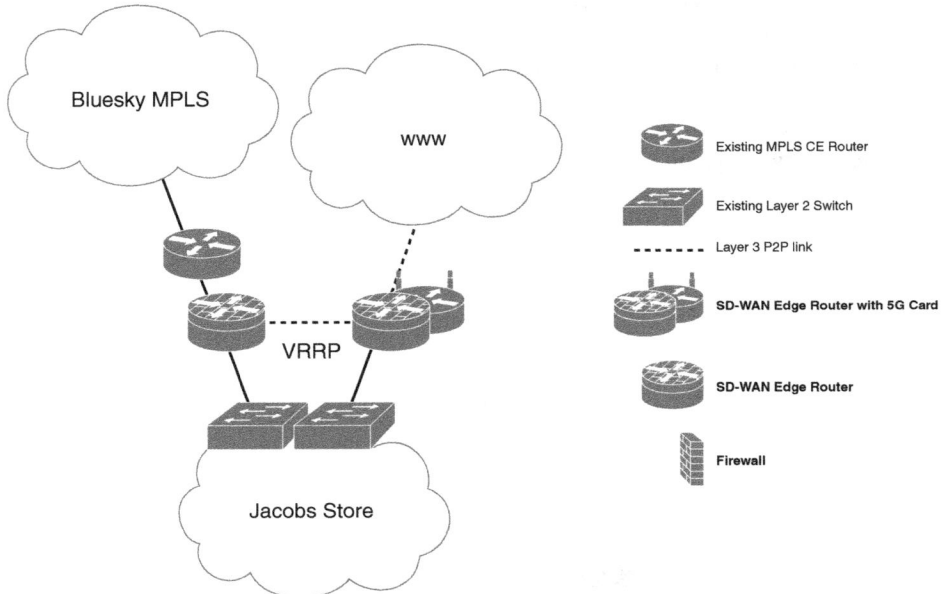

This is the optimal solution. Dual SD-WAN edge routers connected to each of the Layer 2 switches in the store provide resilience. Each SD-WAN edge router connects to a single transport media. VRRP is used from the store to direct traffic to SD-WAN edge routers over a common VLAN connecting the SD-WAN edge routers to the LAN with a Layer 3 point-to-point link between SD-WAN edge routers, which can be used to route between SD-WAN routers for specific failure conditions and application routing policies. Traffic naturally flows from the LAN through the SD-WAN edge routers for optimal traffic forwarding.

d.

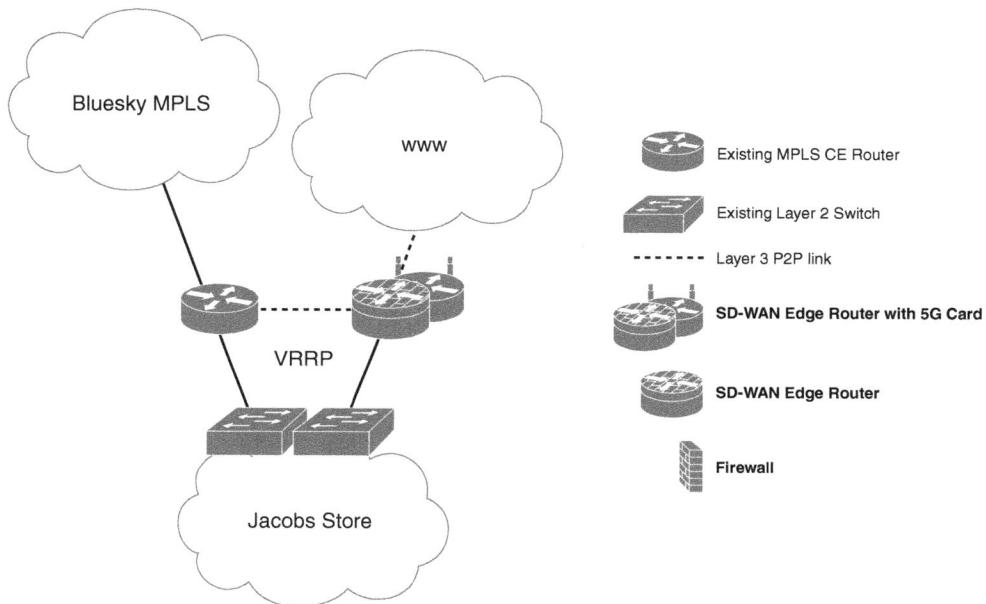

This is incorrect. A single SD-WAN edge router connects to one of the Layer 2 switches in the store, creating a single point of failure. The SD-WAN edge router connects to a single transport media, and VRRP is used from the store to direct traffic to the SD-WAN edge or MPLS CE router over a common VLAN with a Layer 3 point-to-point link between the SD-WAN edge router and MPLS CE router, which can be used to route for specific failure conditions. The solution would function correctly, but there is a single point of failure with a single SD-WAN edge router in the store location.

If you answered this question correctly, you have scored one point. If you selected Answer B, award yourself half a point.

Email #9

From: James Medina

To: CCDE Candidate

Subject: SD-WAN Routing Loop Concern

Hi.

I'm a little wary of routing loops when we're setting up the SD-WAN network with its inbuilt routing protocol of OMP and whatever protocol we use our side on the DC LAN. I could use a breakdown on how you believe we can work around any potential loop with various protocols. The scenario I'm thinking of is when we have a store prefix coming in of, say, "A," as per the diagram, and this advertisement is received on the Internet SD-WAN edge router and MPLS SD-WAN edge router in one of our DCs. The edge routers will need to be running a routing protocol back to the DC LAN, so I want to make sure the SD-WAN edge routers don't end up forwarding traffic for prefix "A" toward each other via the local DC LAN, rather than direct over the SD-WAN overlay network to the store.

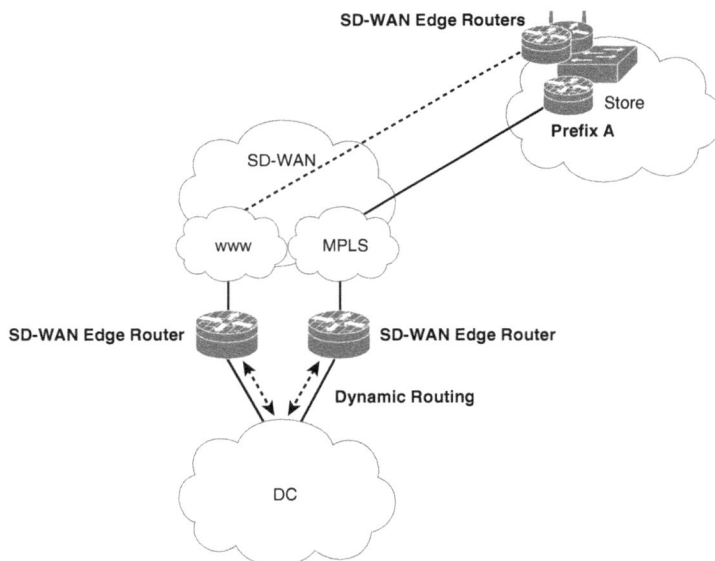

Rgds,

James Medina
Network Manager
Jacobs

Question 18

Complete the following table to assist Jacobs in understanding which loop mitigation techniques could be used in conjunction with the associated dynamic routing protocol configured between SD-WAN edge routers to the DC LAN. Insert an "X" under Mitigation Technique per routing protocol, where appropriate.

Requirements/constraints from supplied documentation: None. General routing/ SD-WAN routing knowledge.

Routing Protocol	Mitigation Technique			
	Route TAGs	Site of Origin	Down Bit	SD-WAN Down Bit
EIGRP				X
OSPF			X	
BGP		X		
OMP				

- **EIGRP** provides loop mitigation by using an SD-WAN down bit. Redistribution of OMP to EIGRP invokes setting the External Protocol field to OMP-Agent. The OMP-Agent setting is used on a neighboring router to set the SD-WAN down bit, which ultimately increases the AD value of the prefix to 252. This AD value is higher than the default OMP AD value of 251 and hence the prefix learned via the SD-WAN overlay is preferred over the prefix advertisement from the EIGRP neighbor.

- **OSPF** uses the classic down bit for loop mitigation, as described in RFC 4577. When the OMP prefix is redistributed in OSPF, the down bit is set within the Options field of an LSA Type 3. When this Type 3 LSA is propagated from the first edge router to the second edge router via the DC LAN, the second edge router will reject the Type 3 LSA and a loop cannot form.

- **BGP** uses Site of Origin (SoO) in conjunction with the SD-WAN site ID. An extended community is required within the network to transport the attribute within the BGP network. SD-WAN edge routers within the DC requires configuration of the same SD-WAN site ID for the SoO. When an edge router receives a prefix with the same SoO as configured locally, it drops the route advertisement and hence a loop cannot form.

- **OMP** is used within the overlay SD-WAN network and would not be used for SD-WAN edge routers to communicate with the DC LAN; as such, you would not select any of the mitigation techniques for OMP.

  Route TAGs are not used as a loop-prevention mechanism, as currently OMP does not support route TAGs for redistribution.

Award yourself a half point per correct answer.

Email #10

From: James Medina

To: CCDE Candidate

Subject: SD-WAN Routing Loop Concern

Hi.

Thanks for the loop info. It kind of makes sense.

Just a heads up: I want each store (independent, Jacobs, and Toolmate) to have an Internet SD-WAN path into each DC (Jacobs and Toolmate). My rationale is if a Jacobs store has an Internet path into the Toolmate DC as well as the Jacobs DC, the convergence in the event of an issue in the Jacobs DC on the SD-WAN side would be much quicker if the routing was already in place (and the same for a Toolmate store via the Jacobs DC). I'm still a little concerned around routing in this scenario (loops, optimum paths, etc.). Can you have a think?

Rgds,

James Medina
Network Manager
Jacobs

Question 19

Jacobs requires each store to have an SD-WAN path to each DC to aid convergence in the event of a failure condition. The company has selected eBGP to be used between the DC LAN networks in the Jacobs and Toolmate DCs and locally attached SD-WAN edge routers for the SD-WAN network to advertise DC prefixes and SD-WAN store networks. iBGP will also be used between Jacobs and Toolmate DC LAN networks over the existing DCI to provide a backup path for a Jacobs SD-WAN-enabled store via the Toolmate DC, and vice versa. How should the BGP AS number (ASN) associated to the edge routers be configured within each DC? (Choose one.)

Requirements/constraints from supplied documentation:

Jacobs has selected eBGP to be used between the DC LAN networks in the Jacobs and Toolmate DCs and locally attached SD-WAN edge routers for the SD-WAN network to advertise DC prefixes and SD-WAN store networks. iBGP will also be used between the Jacobs and Toolmate DC LAN networks over the existing DCI to provide a backup path for a Jacobs SD-WAN-enabled store via the Toolmate DC, and vice versa.

a. The BGP ASN associated to the SD-WAN edge routers should be the same in each of the DCs.

This is correct. A routing loop could be present due to a DCI link between DCs with iBGP routing configured over the DCI. A prefix received from a store would be received in each DC and advertised between DCs over the DCI. Use of the same ASN will ensure that learning of identical prefixes on SD-WAN edge routers is avoided due to the AS-PATH attribute blocking prefixes with identical AS sources by the remote DC toward the LAN and across the DCI.

b. The BGP ASN associated to the SD-WAN edge routers should be different in each of the DCs.

This is incorrect. A routing loop could be present due to a DCI link between DCs with iBGP routing configured over the DCI. If the ASNs are different, BGP's own loop-avoidance mechanism of the same ASN being dropped wouldn't be engaged, and DCs may use the DCI link to forward traffic to a remote store rather than directly via the local SD-WAN edge routers under normal (non-failure) operation.

If you have answered this question correctly, you have scored one point.

Email #11

From: James Medina

To: CCDE Candidate

Subject: Plane Speaking

Hi.

Thanks for the design of the SD-WAN edge routers in the stores and central DCs. We obviously need some controllers to enable the SD-WAN functionality on top of that infrastructure element, so we need to work out where these will be placed for reachability by the SD-WAN edge routers. The information I have back from the vendor we have selected is as follows. We will need redundant controllers in each of the following planes:

Management plane: This will be provided by a product called iManage. This is their single pane of glass that we will use for provisioning, monitoring, managing, and troubleshooting, if required.

Orchestration plane: This will be provided by a product called iOrch. It deals with authentication and authorization of all the infrastructure.

Control plane: This will be provided by a product called iCon. It provides all the data and routing plane policies to the edge routers, including application-aware routing policies, if required.

All controllers can be appliances in the DC or virtual instances in the cloud; both options use a proprietary active/standby resilience method that requires Layer 2 between controllers (physical or logical VLAN for appliances and just a VLAN for the cloud instances) and provide a single frontend IPv4 address regardless of the use of physical appliances or a cloud-based service. The vendor has offered to provide the service of all three controllers within their public cloud offering hosted in France, with resilient service in the USA, and they deal with all resiliency, backups, DR, and required certificates between controllers and SD-WAN edge routers that communicate with the controllers. The fully managed cloud offering just requires Internet access from edge routers (direct for stores or central for the DC) and works out to be the same price as the purchase of the appliances for one complete set of resilient controllers if we host ourselves over a five-year contract, which is our normal refresh period for infrastructure.

Rgds,

James Medina
Network Manager
Jacobs

Question 20

Where is the optimal hosting location for the iManage, iOrch, and iCon controllers for Jacobs? (Choose one.)

Requirements/constraints from supplied documentation:

All controllers can be appliances in the DC or virtual instances in the cloud; both options use a proprietary active/standby resilience method that requires Layer 2 between controllers (physical or logical VLAN for appliances and just a VLAN for the cloud instances) and provide a single frontend IPv4 address regardless of the use of physical appliances or a cloud-based service. The vendor has offered to provide the service of all three controllers within their public cloud offering hosted in France, with resilient service in the USA, and they deal with all resiliency, backups, DR, and required certificates between controllers and SD-WAN edge routers that communicate with the controllers. The fully managed cloud offering just requires Internet access from edge routers (direct for stores or central for the DC) and works out to be the same price as the purchase of the appliances for one complete set of resilient controllers if we host ourselves over a five-year contract, which is our normal refresh period for infrastructure.

a. Within the Jacobs DC in the WAN Core area as locally clustered appliances for each controller function

   This is incorrect. Although it appears to be a reasonable choice, if there was an issue in the Jacobs DC and some or all of the controllers were isolated or Internet access was unavailable, then the SD-WAN would not operate for new connections, changes, and troubleshooting. Existing VPNs would continue to function, however.

b. Within the Toolmate DC as locally clustered appliances for each controller function

   This is incorrect. As per the explanation for Answer A, although it appears to be a reasonable choice, if there was an issue in the Toolmate DC and some or all of the controllers were isolated or Internet access was unavailable, then the SD-WAN would not operate for new connections, changes, and troubleshooting. Existing VPNs would continue to function, however.

c. Within both Jacobs and Toolmate DCs for full resilience as remote clustered appliances (active unit in Jacobs and standby unit in Toolmate) for each controller function

   This is incorrect. This topology of split controllers would require Layer 2 propagation between the Jacobs and Toolmate DCs, which is not currently in place and would require serious rework for the network connectivity and existing Layer 3 firewalls terminating the DCI links.

d. Within both Jacobs and Toolmate DCs for full resilience as local clustered appliances (replicated service in each DC)

This is a suboptimal answer. While deploying resilient controllers per location would provide full resilience in the event of a site issue, it would cost double the price of the single set of resilient appliances and cloud offering.

e. Within the vendor's private cloud for each controller function

This is the optimal answer. You are told the public cloud offering is hosted in France and the USA, but there are no reported issues with data sovereignty for the UK company. A cloud offering is popular in SD-WAN deployments and vastly simplifies the solution while offering native resilience for the same cost as appliances in this instance. Internet reachability is crucial for the cloud offering, and this is achieved by direct access over the local store 5G Internet connections or via central Internet access within the DC locations. Cloud deployments may not be the optimal approach for a government entity, but they would suit Jacobs well.

If you have answered this question correctly, you have scored one point.

Email #12

From: James Medina

To: CCDE Candidate

Subject: Cloud and Migration Thoughts!

Hi.

I believe it's optimal if we deploy the SD-WAN controllers in the cloud. They are natively resilient, and we won't have to deal with plumbing them in and worrying about making the deployment resilient between the Jacobs and Toolmate DCs. An additional benefit is they deal with all the required certificates between devices that can be problematic for our team and can preconfigure the SD-WAN edge routers we will purchase through them, so they will dynamically connect to the cloud controllers, meaning zero touch for our team to onboard. So thanks to your input. We will have the following future architecture.

I need your help with planning the migration to SD-WAN, which I've had drawn up below based on your input. Please have a think about the best way to bring the service online!

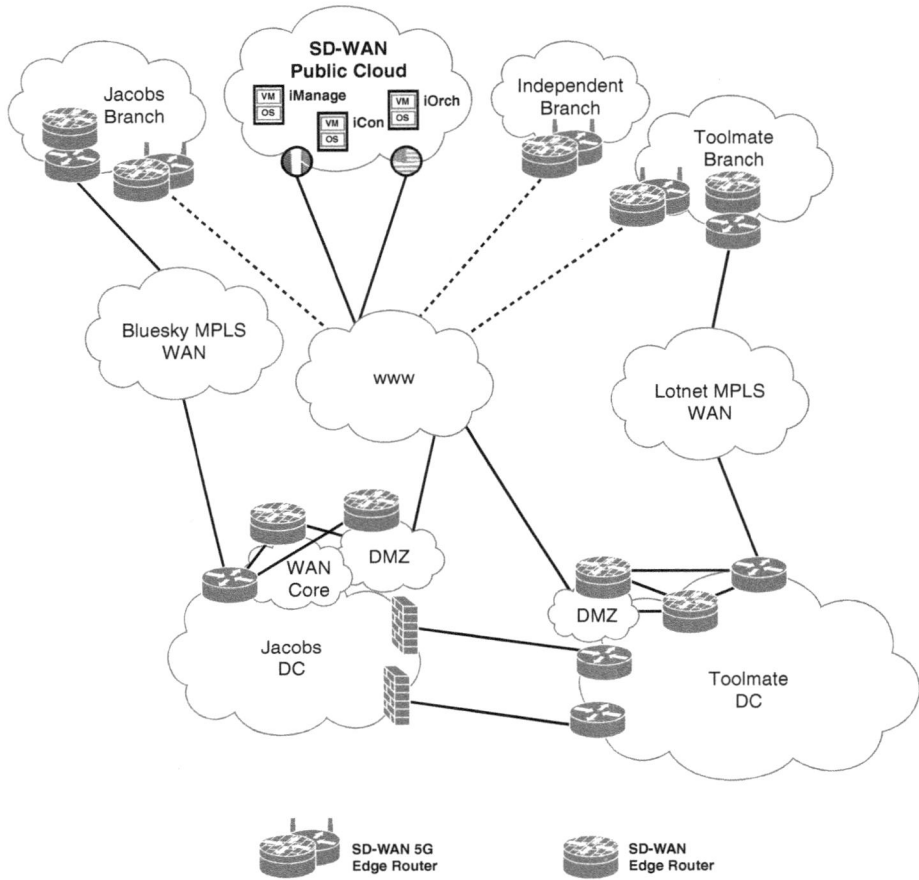

SD-WAN Public Cloud

iManage · iCon · iOrch

Jacobs Branch

Independent Branch

Toolmate Branch

Bluesky MPLS WAN

www

Lotnet MPLS WAN

WAN Core

DMZ

Jacobs DC

DMZ

Toolmate DC

SD-WAN 5G Edge Router

SD-WAN Edge Router

Rgds,

James Medina
Network Manager
Jacobs

Question 21

In order to board the new SD-WAN solution and migrate traffic over it for Jacobs, Toolmate, and independent stores' connectivity, arrange the following migration activities in the required sequence. The business has declared it wants to minimize any associated downtime and ensure the service is functioning correctly prior to migrating any Jacobs or Toolmate store to the SD-WAN network.

Requirements/constraints from supplied documentation:

The business has declared it wants to minimize any associated downtime and ensure the service is functioning correctly prior to migrating any Jacobs or Toolmate store to the SD-WAN network.

The migration steps have been simplified for the scenario and omit specific boarding and testing phases but cover the associated tasks at a high level. There are obviously numerous steps involved in an SD-WAN migration, and it can be quite daunting when you see the number of tasks laid out in front of you, but you don't actually need to be an SD-WAN expert or even have experience with the technology to sequence the steps correctly in this lab, as this is primarily a routing scenario. Any specific SD-WAN technology could be dealt with as a "black box," such as OMP for example, but it's still plain routing. The methodology of these implementation- or migration-type questions is simply "make before you break" so that you don't cause any unnecessary outage, and if any tasks will take time, such as ordering circuits or hardware, then they obviously need to be completed prior to other tasks.

a. Order 5G Internet connections for stores. Store SD-WAN edge routers and SD-WAN edge routers for DC locations.

Clearly this has to be the first step, as it can be initiated without the need for any change to the network and will take time. There would be hundreds of circuit and hardware orders for this project. Jacobs might wish it had signed up for a fully managed solution at this point in time!

b. Configure DC firewalls for SD-WAN control plane flows to cloud service and SD-WAN edge router to SD-WAN network data plane flows and enable cloud controller service with configuration templates for all connectivity.

The SD-WAN edge routers within the DC will need to communicate with the cloud controllers and are situated behind firewalls in the DMZ environment within Jacobs and Toolmate, so these flows will need to be permitted. The cloud controllers will need to be configured to set up site IDs, TLOCs, and all of the SD-WAN specifics to bring up secure tunnels between edge routers in the stores and DC locations. It makes sense to have the controllers and environment ready prior to installing any SD-WAN edge routers, so this step is preferable sequenced prior to Step C but can in reality be sequenced after it.

c. Connect SD-WAN edge routers to DC networks and configure eBGP between SD-WAN edge routers and the DC LAN to advertise DC LAN networks to SD-WAN. Configure DCI firewalls to allow an SD-WAN store resilience routing path between DCs and inter-DC iBGP peering.

Once the edge routers are physically installed within the DC, effectively in parallel to the existing infrastructure (there would be no associated downtime), they will initiate communication to the cloud controllers, so the controllers need to be accessible and configured appropriately. BGP can be enabled between the local DC LAN and SD-WAN edge routers to advertise the DC LAN prefixes (at this point in time, it would be simply sharing the DC prefixes with the SD-WAN network and there would of course be no store prefixes being discovered). The DCI firewalls between Jacobs and Toolmate require configuration to allow inter-DC peering and traffic flow between DCs should there be an issue in one DC, and SD-WAN traffic can then traverse the DCI link for resilience.

d. Configure iBGP between Jacobs and Toolmate DCs to advertise SD-WAN store prefixes for a backup routing path and redistribute SD-WAN OMP to BGP and BGP to SD-WAN OMP.

This step should be completed after Step C; otherwise, the peering would fail.

e. Connect the independent store SD-WAN edge router with a 5G card to the local LAN, and for stores with dual MPLS routers, connect the first SD-WAN edge router with a 5G card to the LAN (low VRRP priority set with existing MPLS routers).

This step should be completed after Step D and prior to Step F. This wouldn't incur any downtime, as this connection would be in parallel to existing connectivity. The Jacobs and Toolmate stores with dual MPLS routers in a VRRP configuration would have the new Internet-facing SD-WAN edge router as a third router within the VRRP group with a low priority assigned, so it wouldn't become the primary gateway and blackhole traffic.

f. Configure SD-WAN control-plane tunnels for Internet paths.

This step has to happen after Step E because tunnels would be configured and the control plane would be established, ready for the data-plane traffic when required.

g. Migrate independent stores' data plane to SD-WAN by repointing local LAN gateway to the SD-WAN edge router and modify BGP metrics in DC locations.

This step cannot happen until Step F has been completed. The brief is that the service should be proved prior to Jacobs or Toolmate stores being migrated, so the logical response to this is to migrate the independent stores first. You were previously informed that these stores can actually tolerate downtime for a short period, and they of course only had a single MPLS link previously. Migration would involve steering traffic on the store LAN to the SD-WAN edge router, which is up and running at this point in time, so downtime would be minimal.

h. Shut down independent store MPLS links.

This step cannot happen until the independent stores have been migrated onto the SD-WAN path over Internet connections in Step G. This step could be delayed toward the end of the migration, so it is acceptable at any point past Step G.

i. Redirect Jacobs/Toolmate store traffic to Internet SD-WAN path on the current dual MPLS sites (adjust VRRP on store sites and modify BGP metrics in DC locations).

This step cannot happen until the independent stores have been migrated (and tested) onto the SD-WAN network in Step G and after the SD-WAN Internet-facing edge routers have been installed in Jacobs/Toolmate stores in Step E and the control plane enabled in Step F.

j. Implement the second SD-WAN edge router on dual MPLS store sites behind the MPLS circuit / CE router being retained. Configure SD-WAN tunnels for MPLS paths.

This step cannot be completed prior to Step I; otherwise, there would be a single point of failure with a single MPLS connection available for the duration of the change (as this change requires disconnecting one MPLS CE router from the LAN and inserting the SD-WAN edge router in between). The Internet SD-WAN path implemented in Step I is functioning at this point, so there would be dual routes available to the store. This is the "make before you break" methodology.

k. Shut down the dual MPLS store (Jacobs/Toolmate) MPLS link that will no longer be required.

This step cannot be completed prior to Step J when the SD-WAN network is functioning with an Internet and MPLS path; otherwise, there would be a single point of failure.

l. Decommission the secondary MPLS circuits for Jacobs/Toolmate and the single MPLS circuit within independent stores.

This is clearly the final step in the migration path and may typically only be actioned after a suitable duration of stability on the new SD-WAN network.

If you have answered this correctly, you have scored three points—you earned them! Partial scoring is available for this question. Steps B and C could also be swapped sequence-wise for a full score.

Email #13

From: James Medina

To: CCDE Candidate

Subject: Jaystore Application

Hi.

Thanks for the migration assistance. Not one store noticed any downtime! I've been asking around the stores and initial feedback is very positive, considering we are now actually using the Internet paths as well as MPLS for all our WAN traffic. I have had a couple of comments in reference to the Jaystore application being less responsive and some clipping on voice calls, though. As you know, we had QoS on the MPLS links with four classes. I think in the pressure of delivering the connectivity, we may have missed the QoS element on the 5G links. I'm going to need your assistance to make sure we improve the quality.

Rgds,

James Medina
Network Manager
Jacobs

Question 22

How can Jacobs rectify the quality issues reported post-migration? (Choose one.)

Requirements/constraints from supplied documentation:

We are now actually using the Internet paths as well as MPLS for all of our WAN traffic. I have had a couple of comments in reference to the Jaystore application being less responsive and some clipping on voice calls, though. As you know, we had QoS on the MPLS links with four classes, and I think in the pressure of delivering the connectivity, we may have missed the QoS element on the 5G links

The main application is Jaystore, which syncs product availability from a database within the DC location for online purchases and store purchases. The application was developed over 10 years ago by developers within a LAN environment and as such does not function well when latency exceeds 20ms between the client and headend infrastructure. Due to this issue, the network team included the TCP application into a mission-critical QoS class over the WAN for mitigation.

Control plane: This will be provided by a product called iCon. It provides all data and routing plane policies to the edge routers, including application-aware routing policies, if required.

   a. Duplicate the existing MPLS QoS setting into the 5G SD-WAN connections.

      This is a suboptimal answer. Although mirroring the QoS settings could potentially help, it would only assist at times of congestion pushing data onto the actual 5G link. Clearly there would be no further QoS applied over the Internet path.

   b. Enable TCP optimization and session persistence on the 5G SD-WAN connections.

      This is incorrect. TCP optimization and session persistence can optimize latency and reduced throughput for high-latency links, but the Internet access is provisioned over 5G, which is well known for high throughput and low latency.

   c. Duplicate the existing MPLS QoS setting into the 5G SD-WAN connections, with the exception of store DIA traffic, which should be moved into a Scavenger queue.

      This is incorrect. As per the explanation for Answer A, this wouldn't guarantee that Jaystore is prioritized over the Internet path. You don't have sufficient information provided in reference to the requirement for a Scavenger queue, and the DIA traffic could include valid cloud-destined traffic, which shouldn't be associated with a Scavenger-type queue.

   d. Create an application-aware routing policy.

      This is the optimal answer. An application-aware routing policy could be created on the SD-WAN network with SLA parameters set that dynamically reroute (in real time) the Jaystore application traffic over the link that meet, set criteria, such as the stringent latency requirement in conjunction with packet loss and such. The policy could be as simple as just using the MPLS link for Jaystore and VoIP and using the 5G link for all other applications, as the application runs well over the original MPLS links.

If you have answered this question correctly, you have scored one point.

Question 23

Jacobs is considering Cloud onRamp for SaaS now that it has an operational SD-WAN network. What would be a benefit if the company takes this approach? (Choose one.)

Requirements/constraints from supplied documentation:

There has been a recent pilot for Office 365 SaaS within the public cloud via a cloud provider (Cloudcom) reachable over the DC Internet connection for various Jacobs stores participating in a trial. Early indications are that the service has suffered intermittent delays and the user experience was not positive.

a. The solution should result in a cost reduction.

This is incorrect. There are no compelling reasons to suggest costs would actually be reduced by utilizing a Cloud onRamp solution.

b. Maintaining access through the DC to SaaS services provides an additional level of security control.

This is incorrect. Although the statement may be valid, this would actually be a potential benefit of not using Cloud onRamp and accessing the cloud services via the central Internet connection within the DC for stores.

c. The solution would typically use the MPLS links as opposed to Internet circuits to access the SaaS and thus receive optimal quality.

This is incorrect. The SaaS is running in the public cloud and is therefore accessible via the Internet (you are not informed of any "direct connect" type of circuit between the cloud provider and Jacobs DC). Accessing the SaaS via MPLS would only be of potential benefit if there was a direct connect circuit to the cloud provider within the DC, and not via a store's MPLS circuit to then egress the central Internet connection.

d. The solution would have the ability to choose the path with optimal quality to reach the Office 365 cloud location (direct Internet access or via the central DC over 5G or MPLS links).

This is the optimal answer. With Cloud OnRamp for SaaS, the SD-WAN solution can measure performance of an SaaS application through all available paths available to a connected store. You were informed that an early trial to Office 365 in the public cloud suffered from a poor user experience. Typically, a score rating is assigned to available paths in the control plane, which will be dynamically adjusted and reflected in the data plane based on real-time performance attributes such as latency and packet loss. For Jacobs, the store paths to the public cloud would be direct Internet access over the 5G Internet connections or via the central DC to the public cloud via either the MPLS path or even initially over the 5G Internet connection (it sounds unlikely that the Internet path to the DC would be chosen, but there could be certain scenarios when a less reliable portion of the Internet could be avoided by selecting this path).

If you have answered this question correctly, you have scored one point. If you selected Answer A, award yourself half a point.

Email #14

From: James Medina

To: CCDE Candidate

Subject: Jimmy's

Hi.

I appreciate the assistance with the application routing policy and onRamp advice. I've just been thrown a curveball that I need your help with before your assignment ends. The CEO is a big fan of the fast food chain Jimmy's. As well as being well-acquainted with the menu, he is good friends with the CEO, and they fly together at his local gliding club. Between the pair of them, they have struck a deal that is going to see a small branch/store of Jimmy's in each of our Jacobs stores. The idea is the tradesmen come in early to stock up on building materials and they will undoubtedly pick up coffee, donuts, and a classic English breakfast (definitely not smashed avocado on sourdough) while their orders are being picked and loaded. Each CEO believes in the reciprocal trade that the arrangement will bring and are willing to share the setup costs. I've been told to provide a single copper Ethernet connection from our store network to them so they can reach their Jimmy's DC for their system. They just need Internet access to reach their DC and have a low-bandwidth requirement for their tills. We need to come up with a solution that keeps our internal security team happy. Help!

Rgds,

James Medina
Network Manager
Jacobs

Question 24

In order to provide the Jimmy's connectivity through a Jacobs store, which of the following options would be most suitable for communication? (Choose one.)

Requirements/constraints from supplied documentation:

I've found some competitively priced SD-WAN store-sized edge routers we can connect to 5G Internet services via an optional 5G card. For PCI compliance, they have their own full security stack, which includes VRFs, L7 firewall, IPS/IDS, protection, and URL filtering with EIGRP and BGP LAN–side and OMP WAN–side routing. They come with dual copper Ethernet connections for access or trunking connectivity, which we can use to connect into our store network switches.

We need to come up with a solution that keeps our internal security team happy.

a. Termination of the Jimmy's Ethernet connection onto the Jacobs store switch with a B2B Internet VPN between Jacobs and Jimmy's central DC firewalls to permit secure access centrally between entities.

This is incorrect. If you selected this option, it's definitely time to have a coffee break. The CEOs may have a good relationship, but this would mean providing the Jimmy's store connectivity through the Jacobs network, and it's guaranteed that either enterprise's security team would veto this type of connection.

b. Termination of the Jimmy's Ethernet connection onto the Jacobs store switch into a new isolated VLAN with VRF Lite configured between the store switch and Internet SD-WAN edge router to provide Internet connectivity to the VLA.

This is the optimal answer. It would require some downtime converting the access links on the store access switch for the SD-WAN edge router to a trunk and creating VRF Lite connectivity through from the new VLAN on the access switch to the Internet-facing SD-WAN edge router to provide Internet connectivity to the new VLAN via the external Internet connection on the SD-WAN edge router. The SD-WAN edge router would of course require some NAT configuration. The Jacobs store switch would need some Layer 2 hardening to ensure behavior such as VLAN hopping wouldn't be possible once VRF Lite was provisioned.

c. Termination of the Jimmy's Ethernet connection onto the Jacobs store switch with ACL protection on the Jacobs access switch, providing access only to the Jacobs proxy server for central Internet access to a Jimmy's remote DC Internet VPN.

This is incorrect. The Jacobs store is Layer 2, so an ACL would not be feasible, and you certainly wouldn't want to rely on an ACL to protect access through the Jacobs network to reach a remote VPN.

d. Provision of a new Jimmy's firewall for termination onto the Jacobs store switch for firewalled protection to only allow Jimmy's to connect to the Internet-facing SD-WAN edge router within the Jacobs store for an Internet VPN connection to the remote Jimmy's DC.

This is incorrect. A firewall sounds like a good option, but this would only provide protection for the Jimmy's network and not offer any protection for the Jacobs network. Connectivity would be possible with this approach, but the Jacobs security team would never sign off on it.

If you have answered this question correctly, you have scored one point.

Summary

Glad it's over or are you hungry for more? This was an introduction into your V3 lab for content, complexity, and volume—we can call it the warmup for this book. Although it's primarily based on SD-WAN, you can see that you don't need to be an expert in this field. As long as you have an understanding of the technology as outlined in the V3 blueprint, you should be able to rely on your routing knowledge to be successful in this lab. You were spared some of the complexity of TLOCs and colors as well as VPN0s and VPN1s, and this should allow you to treat a specific technology as a "black box" if you are not an expert in that field. If you haven't worked on an SD-WAN design previously, hopefully you have gained some further insight and can research specific areas that may need strengthening.

Accurate scoring of the lab isn't crucial, and neither is completing the lab strictly within two hours. The important factors are that you just experienced the level of complexity you will meet in the real exam and that you have benefited from the exercise of determining the correct answers based on the stipulated requirements. You should realize that being successful in the CCDE exam isn't solely about best practice or industry trends; it's about connecting with the scenario and following it as well as answering the design-related questions based on the constraints and requirements provided to you within the background information, documents, and specific questions. If you found it too hard to select the optimum answer, you likely missed a constraint or requirement and can use this lab as practice to determine which information is worth making a note of and developing a skill to analyze design requirements to aid your design decisions.

If you do want to score yourself, a maximum of 30.5 points were available in this lab. If you scored over 21 points (approximately 70%), you have a very good chance of being successful on your CCDE exam.

Chapter 2

CCDE Practice Lab 2: Squid Energy

This practice lab has a focus on large-scale IoT deployment in conjunction with enterprise core elements found in each CCDE lab, as per the V3.0 Blueprint. It is based on one of the three fixed core labs you will find in your practical exam.

Practice Lab Navigation

- Read, make notes, and highlight the background information for anything relevant you feel might aid a design decision.

- Answer each question before you continue to the next one.

- When you have completed a question, do not return to previous questions. You may, however, refer to any previous exhibit (email or diagram) that has been previously provided.

- Aim to complete the lab within a two-hour time frame. If you are unable to complete the lab in two hours, then make a note of where you were at the two-hour point to gauge what your score would have been and then continue on with the lab until completion. Do not move on to the review section until you are finished. This way, you will gain the maximum benefit from the practice lab experience.

Practice Lab

During this practice lab, you are the network architect for Squid Energy.

Document 1: Company Background Information

Squid Energy is a UK company formed in 1999 after the UK electricity markets fully opened up for competition post-denationalization of the service in the previous decade. The enterprise capitalized on comparative competition from the numerous new energy suppliers, allowing end consumers to switch to a supplier that best met their needs, which previously wasn't possible with a state monopoly.

Squid started on a small scale, with a modest cash injection from local venture capitalists, allowing the company to set up an office in central London and hire call center staff to deal with marketing campaigns and to assist consumers with the switching process. Squid knew from the offset that it could avoid business and technical complexity by not being involved in power generation and transmission and simply aimed to resell energy. It was apparent that the national power infrastructure required modernization and expansion and that large power companies would be focused on these areas, leaving opportunity for smaller companies such as Squid. Profit margins were relatively modest initially and relied on regular negotiation of wholesale power purchase agreements from the largest power providers in the market, which were then resold to consumers on separate contracts through the power providers' infrastructure. Squid found competition to be fierce within the market for its first 10 years of operation and was close to dissolution had it not been for further investment from its own board members. The board members decided prior to the cash injection, and in order to make the business viable for the future, that Squid needed to differentiate its service. Its unique selling point should be that it supplies only renewable energy, with minimal to zero carbon footprint, in order to be able to charge a premium to environmentally conscious consumers to increase profit margin from its service. The further investment and subsequent partnering with production companies that generated power though solar, hydro, or wind turbine means proved to be successful, and the customer base rapidly expanded to 300,000. However, the growth in customer base introduced issues of scale to the business. Squid began to encounter problems with service delivery, as it simply couldn't meet the customer demand. Churn became an issue when customers were unable to switch suppliers in the previously advertised time scales, and invoices were often incorrect during the switch over from the incumbent supplier, leading to negative publicity and significant management overhead for accounting. Accurate meter reading proved to be and continues to be the main problem encountered. Up until the customer base rapidly expanded, meter readings were typically estimated with field staff only rarely being required to visit customer homes to confirm readings during move events or meter replacements. The growing customer base, however, introduced significant demand for field meter readings, and Squid found that opex costs spiraled due to hiring and training of new field engineers and associated vehicle and fuel costs. Squid began investigating ways in which to reduce or eradicate the field engineer costs by use of contracting competitor engineers while in the area and researching smart meter technology.

Squid commissioned a group of industry consultants who convinced the board members to innovate from the outside-in, as if they were their own customers rather than from the inside-out, as they had traditionally been doing. The new approach identified issues that, when resolved, would create a huge impact for the business. It became apparent that avenues such as online meter reading and enhanced estimation by use of artificial intelligence or by implementation of smart meters would solve the company's problems, but it was reluctant to invest due to the significant capex required for the new technology with the required associated network infrastructure. The company was also wary of a well-publicized cyberattack on Ukraine's power network in 2015 and was adamant that it could not find itself in that position. Squid acknowledged the fact that the business would remain stagnant until it was in a position to raise the necessary capex funds and was delighted when the UK government announced that in order to reduce CO_2 emissions, it would provide funding to energy companies in order to supply smart meter technology to end consumers by 2025.

Document 2: UK Power Background Information

- **Generation:** Power generation is the physical location where and the method in which electricity is generated. Generation is typically achieved via fossil fuels, nuclear reaction, hydro-electric, and solar and wind plants. Generated power is fed into transmission lines at high voltage for optimal efficiency and minimal loss. Substations within generator plants interface between the plant and transmissions systems.

- **Transmission:** The National Grid in the UK is responsible for the transmission of power at high voltage (400kV and 275kV). Transmission of power over the UK is mainly above ground on the pylon network, with a growing number of subterranean systems. Transmission substations deliver power to distribution substations around the UK.

- **Distribution:** Power distribution fans out power from transmission networks around the UK and delivers power to the end consumer. Power is stepped down to lower voltages by transformers and delivered to the consumer at 240V A/C. Power is terminated at the consumer location to a power meter where the boundary of responsibility ends for the local power distribution company. Power delivery from the meter to the end devices is the responsibility of the consumer.

The following diagram provides high-level detail of the power system in the UK.

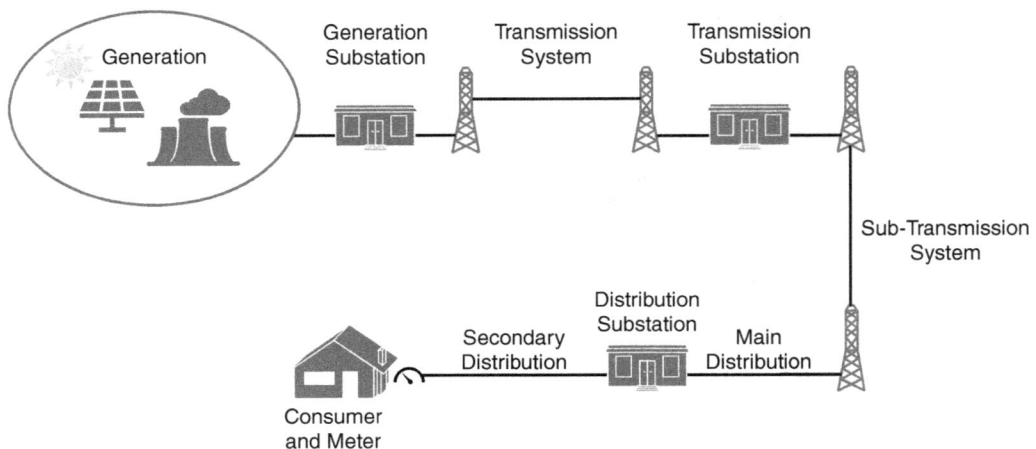

Document 3: Squid Network Background Information

Squid's network reflects the company's desire to operate with low complexity where possible. The network is formed of an on-premise infrastructure within the central London location and is supported in house by a small IT team. Two Internet-facing firewalls configured in an active/standby arrangement connect to a single ISP on 1Gbps line rate Ethernet circuits to create a business-to-business (B2B) zone within the DMZ for third-party connectivity, a DMZ for web hosting, and an internal LAN for user and server access. IPsec VPNs connect from the B2B zone to the National Grid transmission infrastructure and to various national distribution third-party companies (33 at current count) in order to process payment for the electricity used by Squid's consumers.

The DMZ zone also provides Remote Access Service for employee access to the Squid internal network and public-facing web servers for customer information and initiation to switch suppliers to Squid, which is then processed manually.

The internal Squid network is formed of a chassis-based LAN collapsed core/aggregation/access model with a current port count of 480x 1Gbps Ethernet ports for user and server connectivity on separate VLANs. A default route on the internal and DMZ networks points to the local firewall pair.

Telephony for call center staff is provided on legacy PABX systems.

There are five full-time IT employees who are responsible for firewall rule changes and web server configuration, along with other IT-related duties.

The following diagram details the network at a high level.

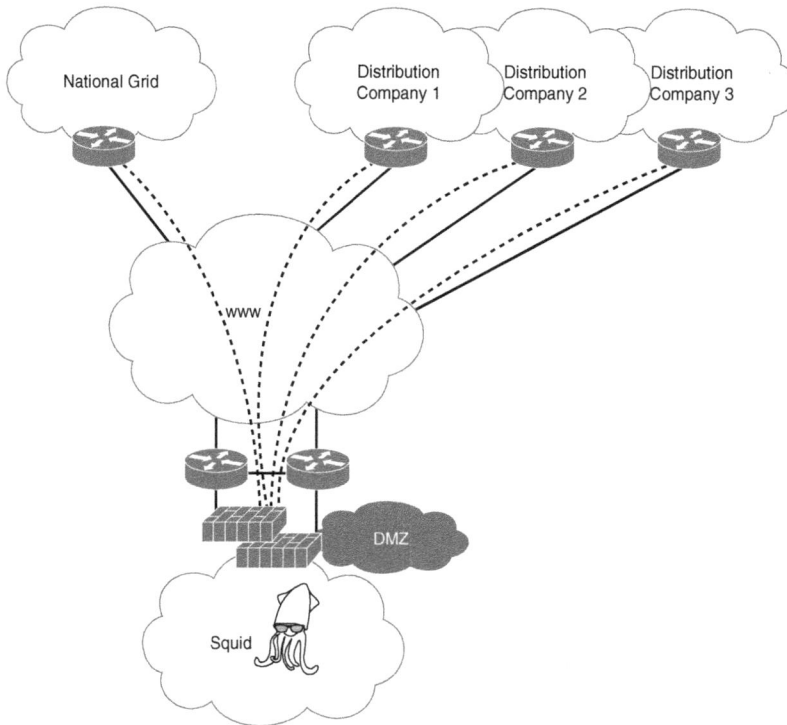

Document 4: Relevant Background Information

Squid Energy is well placed to take advantage of the government grants being offered to provide smart meter technology to end consumers. The company feels this is the opportunity it has been waiting for in order to grow the business while reducing opex costs.

The company is keen to continue its environmentally conscious brand image and also believes it should offer home electric vehicle (EV) charging points throughout the UK, with a reduced cost for Squid subscribers in comparison to competitors. It is believed that, even though an effective loss leader, it will gain market share for end subscribers even if this area of the business operates on a cost-neutral basis. However, Squid does not want to be responsible for EV charger hardware or implementation costs and therefore aims to package these costs within products for consumers.

Email #1

From: Mich Fara-Day

To: CCDE Candidate

Subject: Welcome to Squid

Hi.

Welcome aboard. We're really glad to have you join us for a six-month assignment. You came highly recommended, and we're keen to get you to work on our latest initiative. As you well know, we've been having difficulty with our meter reading and billing, and we have to cut costs to reduce overall opex yet improve the service we deliver to our customers. The government has recently introduced a generous grant to the tune of £50 per end consumer to entice a move away from legacy meters and be more aware of energy use and costs. We have conducted some research with our existing customer base and have found there is a reluctance to make the change, as it will involve cutting power briefly. The consumers are slow to realize that they can actually achieve some cost savings and reduce carbon footprints by being more aware of their energy use. In summary, we believe we can only make them switch and make the meter rollout viable if we offer a £10 credit to their account, so we really only have £40 per customer to play with.

I'll worry about the overall finance element, but you do need to keep this in mind as you don't have an open checkbook available. If you can save money where possible, then please do. You can probably guess it's not just a case of getting our field engineers to swap meters over; we need to create the infrastructure behind the meters to collate the data and use it for billing and make it available for consumers. This is where you come in. We would be the first to tell you that our own network is pretty basic, and I would imagine not fit to start hosting the service, which is going to need to scale to a couple of million meters (if our marketing team has done its homework correctly) over the next five years. We have to assume we will migrate our current base of 300K customers gradually onto the smart meter program and grow from there. We have a lot of work to do in terms of how we deliver this, but I need you to start some architectural thinking around how this would all work. I don't know if these meters will connect back to us over a private WAN or the Internet, so at this phase I want to keep my options open and make sure we can support private and public addressing if need be. I've attached a high-level specification of a smart meter we think will be suitable versus a more expensive one. The price is right at £20 a unit, and the other one has some additional features at £28 a unit. I'll let you do the math in terms of the numbers we are talking about! Both communicate to a basic display in the home to show current usage over a HAN (home area network) connection, which is built into each device and included in the unit price. We want to start the ordering process for a pilot ASAP, so please take a look at the options we have.

Feature	Meter 1: SMARTS 2.0 (£20)	Meter 2: Zenith V3 (£28)
WAN Connectivity	4/5G + Wi-Fi Mesh	2/3/4/5G + Wi-Fi Mesh
HAN Connectivity	Zigbee (dual band, additional £3 per unit), Wi-Fi, Ethernet, Bluetooth	Zigbee, dual-band Zigbee, Wi-Fi, Ethernet, Bluetooth
Electric Metering	✓	✓
Gas Metering	✓	(Additional £2 per unit software activation option)
IPsec Encryption Support	✓	✓
TLS Support	X	X
Digital Certificates	✓	✓
IP Version	4 (6 on roadmap)	4/6
DHCP Support	✓	✓
Static/Fixed IP Support	✓	✓
Call Home Installation	✓	✓
Inbuilt Firewall	X	X
NAT Compatible	X	X
Remote Supply Disconnect	✓	✓

Rgds,

Mich Fara-Day
CTO Squid Energy

Lab Questions

Question 1

Which smart meter would you recommend to Squid to supply to end consumers? (Choose one.)

a. SMARTS 2.0 meter

b. SMARTS 2.0 meter with dual-band optional upgrade

c. Zenith V3 meter

d. Zenith V3 meter with gas-metering software activation option

Question 2

Which IP version should be deployed on the smart meters? (Choose one.)

a. IPv4

b. IPv6

Email #2

From: Mich Fara-Day

To: CCDE Candidate

Subject: Zenith WAN Options

Hi.

Thanks for selecting the Zenith smart meter. Our CFO wasn't really pleased we had to go with this one, but I explained we needed IPv6 support to make this scale. We're going to have to get these meters to communicate to our central DC facility over some form of WAN from a consumer's home location, which can be quite rural. I need you to come up with a recommendation of how we should achieve this. The facts I can gather from the meter company are as follows:

Typical IP packet size: **1000 bytes (includes IPsec overhead if used)**

IP protocol: **UDP**

Maximum packet per second rate (typically seen during firmware upgrades): **100**

Latency requirement normal operation: **Sub 80ms**

Power requirements: **10 watts**

WAN charges are relatively low with the cellular 2/3/4/5G network, ranging from 2G being the lowest cost to 5G being the highest cost.

Rgds,

Mich Fara-Day
CTO Squid Energy

Question 3

Based on the information supplied to date, which WAN technology would be most suitable for the meter rollout for Squid? (Choose one.)

a. 2G

b. 3G

c. 4G

d. 5G

e. Wireless mesh

Email #3

From: Mich Fara-Day

To: CCDE Candidate

Subject: Cellular Connectivity

Hi.

Historically, we've split the UK up into five different areas for marketing and service delivery/support. I think it makes sense if we create our new smart meter service in the same manner. I've decided to run with a 4G cellular service for WAN connectivity for the meters and have spoken to numerous cellular providers. A company called Jaketel offers 4G coverage to 94% of the UK and can provide us with data-only SIMs that we can fit into the smart meters we deploy. Jaketel stated it can configure multiple access point names (APNs) for us, which is the equivalent of a data service. This can be either private without access to the Internet or other Jaketel data subscribers or public with access to the Internet and other Jaketel data subscribers. Cost-wise, the private APN is marginally more expensive than the private. Jaketel also stated that in terms of IP address we are good with IPv6—either fixed (static), DHCP-based, or an SLAAC approach. The APNs Jaketel configures can fit into our five area footprint (there will be multiple APNs per area to assist with scale), and I'm told we can install our own equipment within its APNs to backhaul each area's traffic back to a central location. If I'm honest, this didn't mean a great deal to me other than coverage. I'm happy enough with 94% coverage, and I'm sure we can even extend some coverage in rural areas with additional antennas if really required and if we have to we can use a different supplier for the more complex installs, but we don't want to be seen to turn customers down. I do need you to evaluate the other aspects of the service though.

Rgds,

Mich Fara-Day
CTO Squid Energy

Question 4

Which network APN mode should be selected for the 4G SIM network from Jaketel for the smart meter WAN network that will provide communications from the meters to a central location? (Choose one.)

a. Public APN

b. Private APN

Question 5

Which type of IPv6 address assignment would you recommend for smart meters within the Jaketel APN? (Choose one.)

a. Provider assigned (PA)

b. Provider independent (PI)

Email #4

From: Mich Fara-Day

To: CCDE Candidate

Subject: IPv6 Address Allocation/Type

Hi.

I need your help to determine what type of IPv6 addressing we use on the smart meter network and how it should be allocated. We have to be able to route to the meters directly for software updates from our central DC. All we need to do for ID is to be able to know which IPv6 address belongs to which customer at their physical address location. To do this, we can allocate an IPv6 address prior to installation time before the meter is shipped to the installers that we can allocate centrally, or I'm told we can use DHCPv6 within each APN in Jaketel. When the meter has an IPv6 address and calls home, it registers its IPv6 address with the central application with a site ID that references the customer address, so we're covered either way. We're also thinking of registering each meter on its own /64 segment to give us some segmentation between devices and scale for the future. (Yeah I know, that's a lot of scale!)

Rgds,

Mich Fara-Day
CTO Squid Energy

Question 6

Which IPv6 address type should be used for the smart meter that would provide as minimal administrative overhead as possible? (Choose one.)

a. Global Unicast Address (GUA)

b. Link Local (LLA)

Question 7

Squid has chosen to use Global Unicast Addressing (GUA) because it didn't want the meters to provision their own IPv6 addresses and needed to route to them from their DC location. Which address allocation mode should be used for the smart meter IPv6 addressing? (Choose one.)

a. Manual configuration

b. Stateless autoconfiguration

c. Stateful autoconfiguration

Question 8

If Squid has decided to use stateful autoconfiguration with DHCPv6 servers based in Jaketel APNs, how long would you recommend the lease be set for? (Choose one.)

a. One day

b. One week

c. One month

d. One year

Email #5

From: Mich Fara-Day

To: CCDE Candidate

Subject: IPv6 Address Block

Hi.

Thanks for the info on addressing. We've evaluated your responses and decided to run with PI GUAs issued by DHCPv6. If we need to run with other providers, it will provide some additional flexibility. I need to request a block of addresses from Jaketel, which I guess goes to RIPE on our behalf on the PI side, so I could use your help in requesting a large enough block. This is what we've determined so far:

1. We have five regions/areas, as you know, but we want to have the ability to scale to 256 max if we expand into Europe in the future.

2. We want to have the ability to have up to 256 APNs in each region.

3. We want to run up to 65,000 smart meters per APN.

4. We want each smart meter to have an individual /64 prefix.

5. Smart meters use a form of unnumbered IPv6 addressing from their main /64 prefix over the APN, so we don't need to worry about any prefixes for the APN/WAN. The /64 prefix will also be used for the HAN for displays and any other devices that require access to the meter or further connectivity to our systems.

Rgds,

Mich Fara-Day
CTO Squid Energy

Question 9

Which size IPv6 prefix should be requested from RIPE for Squid's smart meter roll out? (Choose one.)

   a. /24

   b. /32

   c. /40

   d. /48

   e. /60

Email #6

From: Mich Fara-Day

To: CCDE Candidate

Subject: WAN to Central Location Design

Hi.

Marketing worked out that we will need to scale to 400,000 customers per region/area, which is formed with multiple APNs. Jaketel apparently runs its own MPLS network also and has priced up a way of backhauling aggregated APN traffic onto our central location.

I did read about an Internet-based attack in the Ukraine power network some time ago, and that cannot be permitted here, so I'll need you to make it as secure as possible. Therefore, everything should be encrypted outside of our own DC. I was informed that we can use a DHCPv6 option in the offer to the smart meters that gives the meters the ability to connect to a remote IPsec peer of our choice that we configure on the DHCPv6 server. Hopefully, we can make use of this feature. If you can absorb the information below and then get started on a design, that will allow us to connect the smart meters to the cellular network and then onto a DC, which is likely going to be a co-located area where we can rent some rack space in London and where we will install the associated compute environment. I'm just not convinced our own DC is up to this. I've discussed some of the security aspects with our security leads, and they have requested we run an appliance-based IPS/IDS that can monitor the traffic flow into the co-lo before it reaches the compute environment to enhance security over and above a perimeter firewall, which will also be required in front of the connection to the meters.

As mentioned previously, Jaketel said we can connect our own infrastructure devices within each region in order to connect back to a central location. These devices will effectively have a logical connection into each APN provisioned within that region. Jaketel is going to provide a Layer 3 MPLS VPN for us to assist with backhauling WAN cellular traffic to the central location, which will be our co-lo, and we can just connect up a local 10Gbps fiber connection into our co-lo area, as a Jaketel PE is conveniently sited in the same co-lo building.

In terms of infrastructure devices at our disposal, we have 10Gbps routers with six interfaces and 10Gbps VPN routers with four interfaces. The VPN routers are capable of terminating 500,000 VPNs connections, and we have firewalls that are VPN compatible with 4x 10Gbps interfaces and can also terminate up to 500,000 VPNs. The smart meters will connect to the Jaketel APN on bootup thanks to their SIM card and a pre-configured APN on the Jaketel side. Also, as mentioned, we can preload some configuration to point to a remote VPN of our choice to make use of Jaketel's IPsec feature using DHCPv6 options. Oh, and the IPS/IDS device—due to the number of flows that can go through it, the price is eye-watering. I need you to use as few of these as possible, and they have 2x 10Gbps interfaces (an in and an out, so they work in series). All routers and firewalls can run OSPF and BGP with dual-stack IPv4 and IPv6, and we calculate the overall peak aggregate traffic load into the co-lo would not exceed 6Gbps.

Rgds,

Mich Fara-Day
CTO Squid Energy

Question 10

Design the WAN connectivity in order to provide IPv6 connectivity from the smart meters back to the co-located environment. Your design should use single infrastructure devices and connections at this point in time; resilience can be addressed at a later stage. Add the required infrastructure devices, as shown in the following diagram key, as required, and use 10Gbps Ethernet connections or IPsec tunnels. Any infrastructure device placed within the MPLS network can be assumed to have a 10Gbps direct connection to the MPLS network without the need to specifically add it within the diagram.

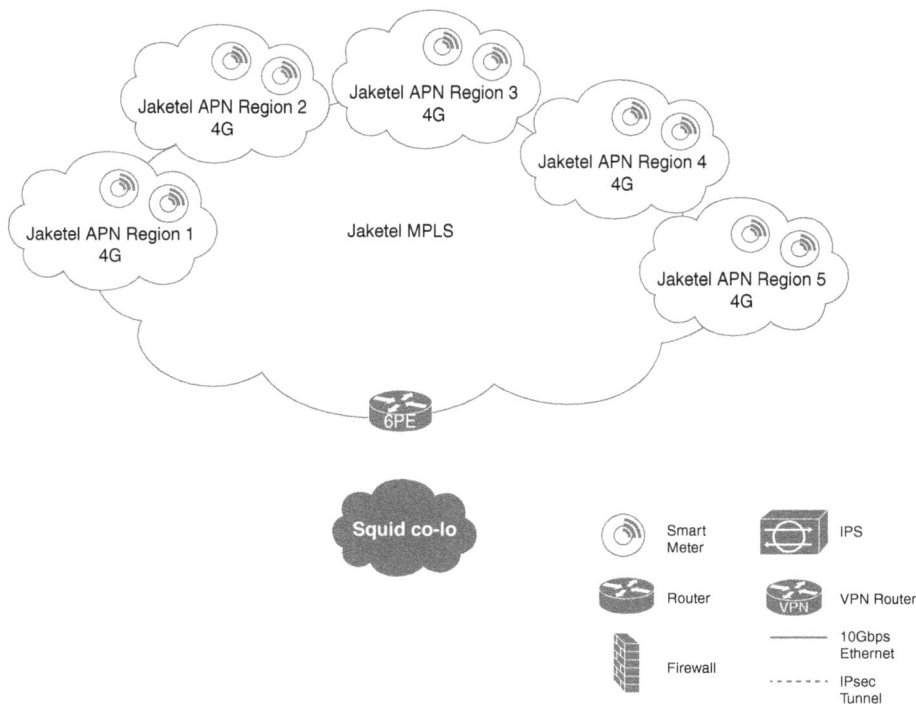

Email #7

From: Mich Fara-Day

To: CCDE Candidate

Subject: WAN to Co-lo Design

Hi.

Thanks for your help in the overall WAN design. We're going for the design outlined below. We can work out the resilience at a later date. We'll just double up on infrastructure and connectivity to ensure we have no single points of failure. The VPN routers placed within the APN regions terminate the IPsec VPN connections from the smart meters from their local APN, and then each region VPN router has L3 MPLS VPN connectivity through the central 6PE to the co-lo edge router to the central firewall. The firewall has an IPsec VPN connection to each region's VPN router, so all traffic is encrypted end-to-end and the IPS/IDS appliance is able to monitor all flows. We decided not to run the IPsec VPN tunnels direct from the meters to the firewall, as this approach didn't scale as well.

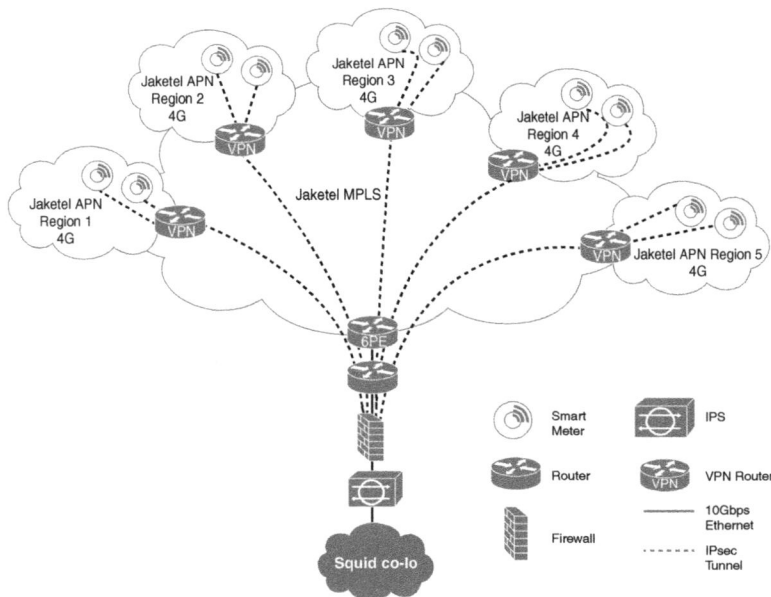

Rgds,

Mich Fara-Day
CTO Squid Energy

Question 11

As detailed in the email, Squid chose to run IPsec VPN connections from the smart meters to the region/APN edge VPN routers. How would you recommend the IPsec authentication be deployed for meters to VPN routers for maximum security and minimal administrative overhead? (Choose one.)

   a. Certificate-based with self-signed X.509 certificates on smart meters

   b. Certificate-based PKI infrastructure with a dedicated CA located within Squid's DC/co-lo

   c. Certificate-based PKI infrastructure with a shared CA located within the Internet

   d. Manual pre-shared key configuration on IPsec peers

Question 12

As detailed in the email, Squid has chosen to run IPsec VPN connections from the region/APN edge VPN routers to the co-lo firewall to aggregate and encrypt meter traffic flowing into the co-lo. How would you recommend IPsec be deployed for VPN routers to the firewall for the five IPsec tunnels with maximum security and minimal administrative overhead? (Choose one.)

a. Certificate-based PKI infrastructure with a dedicated CA located within Squid's DC

b. Manual pre-shared key configuration on IPsec peers

Question 13

Squid has decided to implement certificates with a PKI infrastructure with a root CA in order for the smart meters to be authenticated and encrypt traffic. Which is the optimal method of provisioning the required certificates onto the smart meters?

a. SCEP

b. Embedded meter self-signed certificate

c. CMP

d. EST

Email #8

From: Mich Fara-Day

To: CCDE Candidate

Subject: Dynamic Routing

Hi.

Thanks for your help with the security side, I'm going to get our security guys to fully design the PKI. It has occurred to me we don't have any routing defined for the WAN-to-co-lo design. I initially thought we'd just run static routes, but I'd rather run a dynamic routing protocol to provide additional flexibility and resilience as we scale out and add multiple routing devices to remove existing single points of failure. I was going to ask you to evaluate a bunch of protocols, but I'm going to save you the bother, as our team members only have experience with OSPF. It's going to be too much of a learning curve for them to learn a new protocol, so we'll just bump up their knowledge from V2 to V3 to accommodate the IPv6. I did ask them if we needed to bother with areas for the routing, and their eyes glazed over, so this one's on you. Can you have a think and let us know which OSPF design is going to be optimal for us? From the co-lo network we will just have a default route pointing to the co-lo edge firewall to reach the meters.

Rgds,

Mich Fara-Day
CTO Squid Energy

Question 14

Which of the following OSPF WAN designs would be most suitable for Squid to provide dynamic routing from the regions into the co-lo environment to discover IPv6 prefixes assigned to the smart meters? (Choose one.)

a.

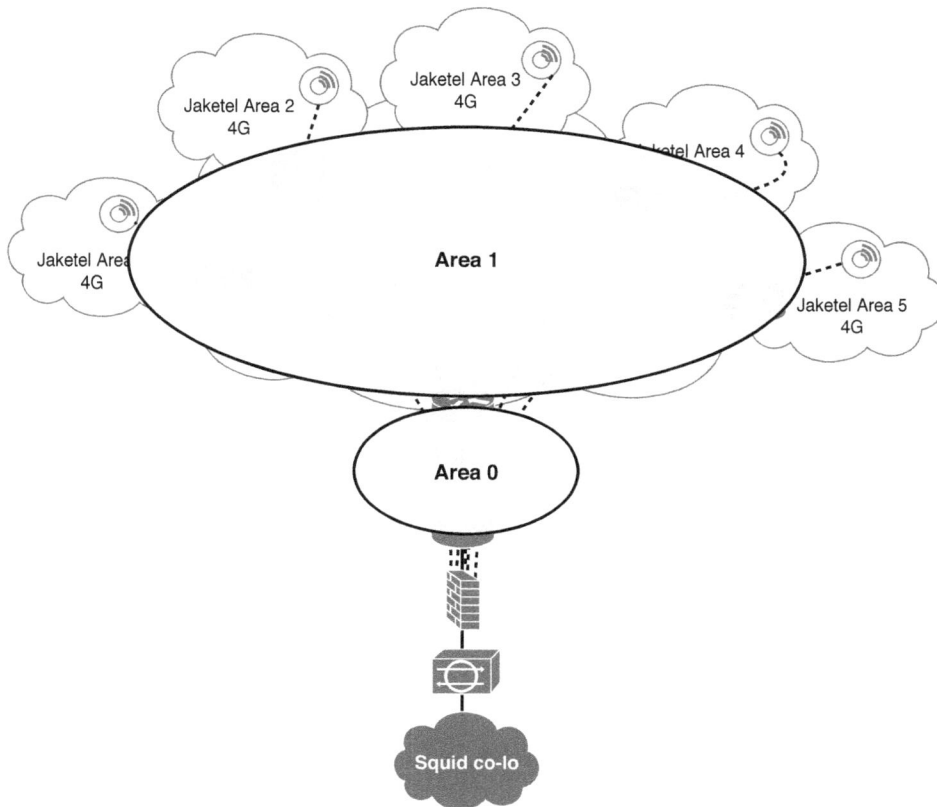

b.

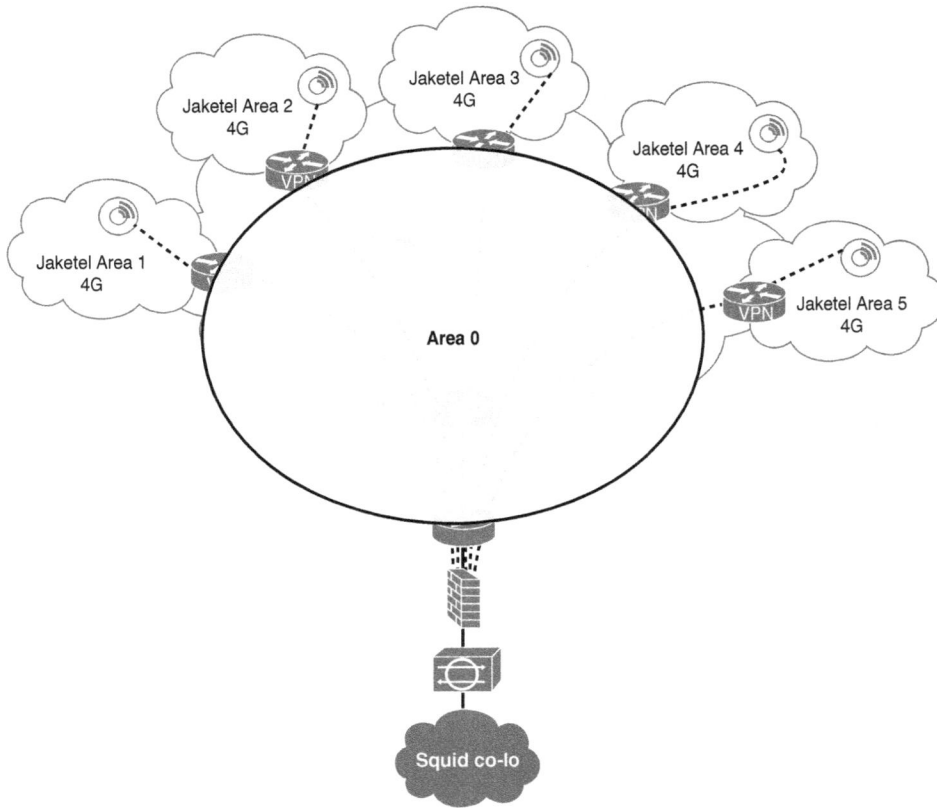

c.

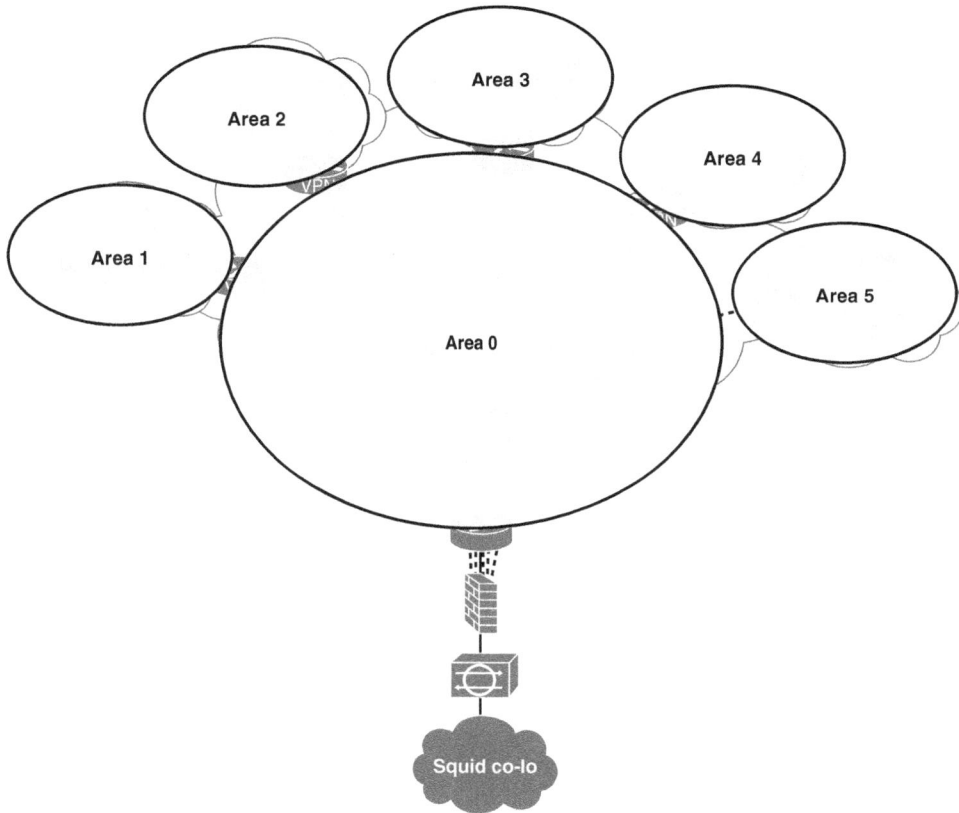

d.

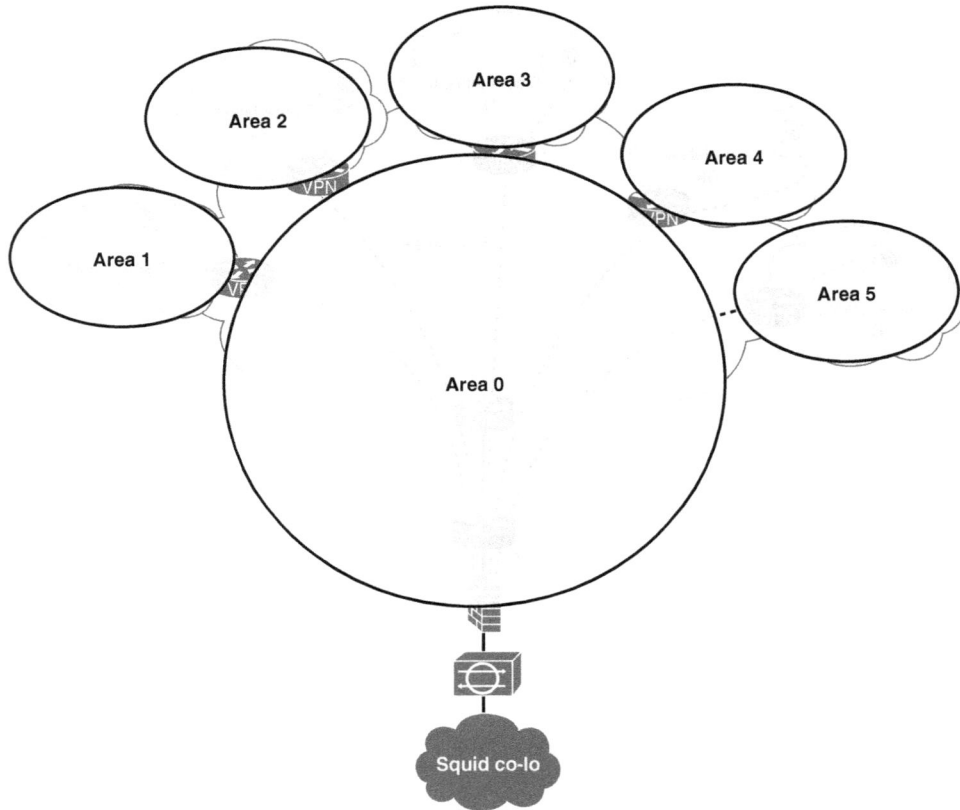

e.

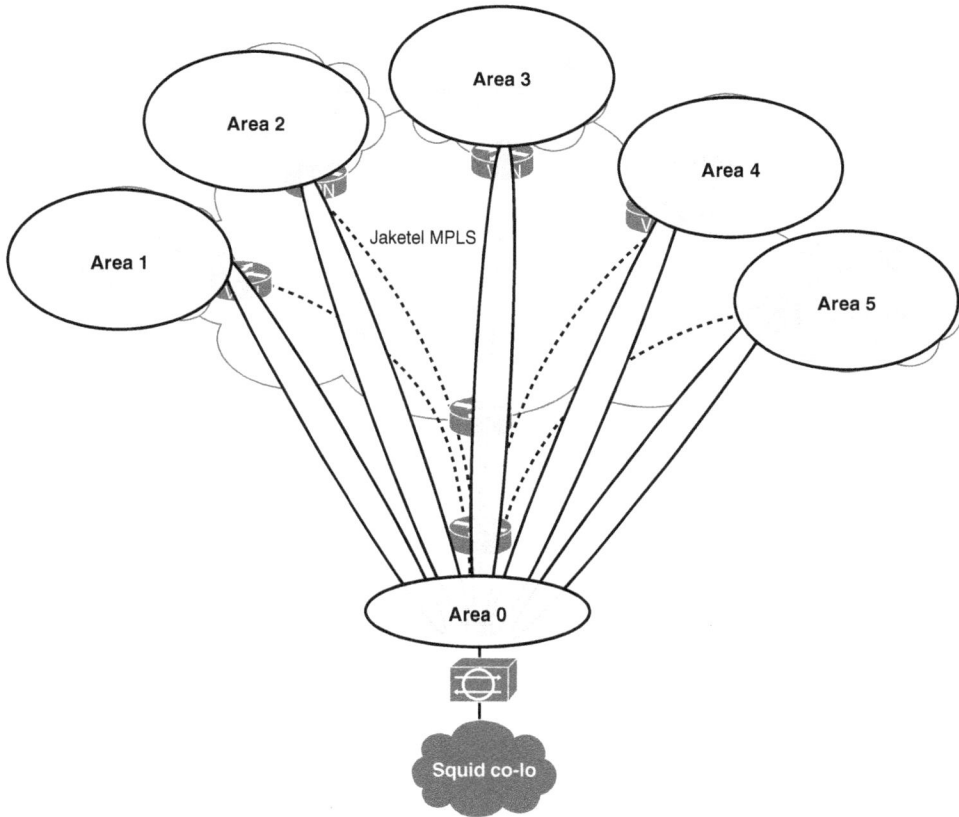

Question 15

If Squid decides to use separate OSPF areas per region, which area type should these areas be set to? (Choose one.)

a. Normal area

b. Stub area

c. NSSA

d. Totally stubby area

Question 16

What would be a good design choice to enhance default OSPF stability, efficiency, and convergence when Squid introduces future resilience and deploys dual ABR routers connecting into multiple regions/APNs?

    a. Configuring link-state incremental SPF

    b. Running multi-hop BFD over the VPN links

    c. Configuring the VPN links as point-to-point OSPF network links

    d. Configuring summarization of areas toward Area 0

Email #9

From: Mich Fara-Day

To: CCDE Candidate

Subject: OSPFv3 Areas and IPv6 Prefix Allocation

Hi.

Thanks for your help with the OSPF WAN design. We decided to go with totally stubby areas and the topology outlined below. I was a little confused with underlays and overlays but understand where the ABRs are best positioned for us to scale.

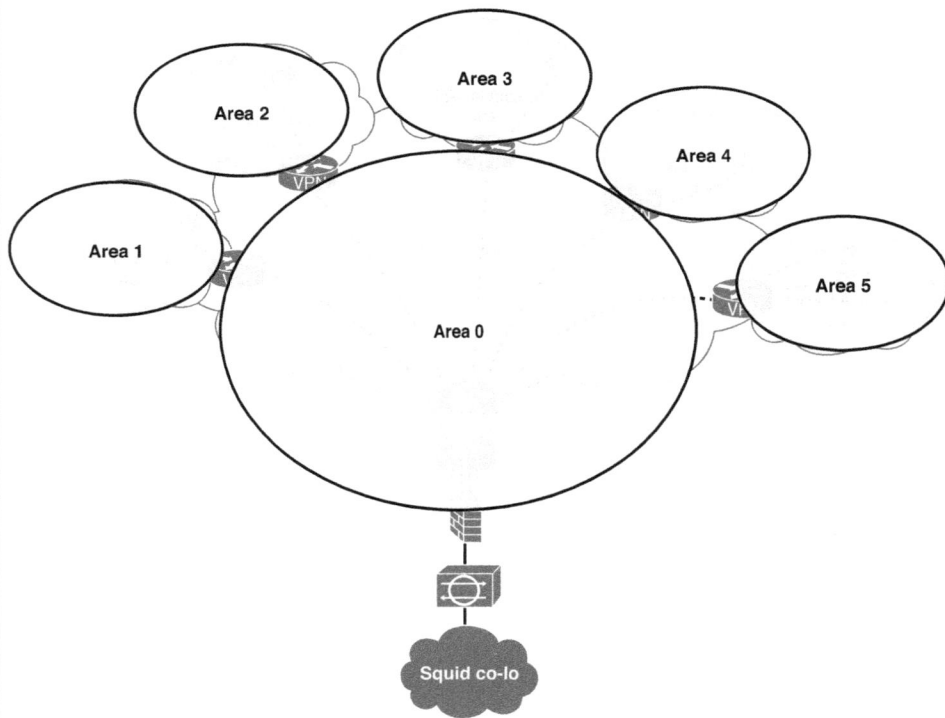

We just received our prefix back from RIPE that Jaketel has passed onto us. It got me thinking, what the hell happened to IPv5? Anyways, here it is:

2022:ccde::/32

Jaketel advised that, with such a large prefix, we would benefit from configuring summarization in the network—can you let me know how we should do that?

Rgds,

Mich Fara-Day
CTO Squid Energy

Question 17

Which of the following options provides optimal summarization for Squid from each OSPF area detailed within the OSPF topology in the email? (Choose one.)

a. Summarize at the region level on the ABR /32s

b. Summarize at the region level on the ABR /40s

c. Summarize at the region level on the ABR /48s

d. Summarize at the region level on the ABR /56s

e. Summarize at the APN level on the ABR /40s

f. Summarize at the APN level on the ABR /48s

Question 18

Squid has decided to summarize at the region level on the ABRs using /40 prefixes to cover all APNs and associated meter /64 prefixes with a single summary statement per ABR for the entire region. Which of the following ranges should be used for the five regions for the UK deployment of smart meters? (Choose one.)

a.

Region 1 (OSPF area 1) – 2022:ccde::/40

Region 2 (OSPF area 2) – 2022:ccde:0100::/40

Region 3 (OSPF area 3) – 2022:ccde:0200::/40

Region 4 (OSPF area 4) – 2022:ccde:0300::/40

Region 5 (OSPF area 5) – 2022:ccde:0400::/40

b.

Region 1 (OSPF area 1) – 2022:ccde::/40

Region 2 (OSPF area 2) – 2022:ccde:0001::/40

Region 3 (OSPF area 3) – 2022:ccde:0002::/40

Region 4 (OSPF area 4) – 2022:ccde:0003::/40

Region 5 (OSPF area 5) – 2022:ccde:0004::/40

c.

Region 1 (OSPF area 1) – 2022:ccde:0001::/40

Region 2 (OSPF area 2) – 2022:ccde:0002::/40

Region 3 (OSPF area 3) – 2022:ccde:0003::/40

Region 4 (OSPF area 4) – 2022:ccde:0004::/40

Region 5 (OSPF area 5) – 2022:ccde:0005::/40

d.

Region 1 (OSPF area 1) – 2022:ccde::/40

Region 2 (OSPF area 2) – 2022:ccde:0000:0001:/40

Region 3 (OSPF area 3) – 2022:ccde:0000:0002:/40

Region 4 (OSPF area 4) – 2022:ccde:0000:0003:/40

Region 5 (OSPF area 5) – 2022:ccde:0000:0004:/40

Email #10

From: Mich Fara-Day

To: CCDE Candidate

Subject: Application Load Balancing

Hi.

Thanks for summarizing! We're going to reserve the first subnet (2022:ccde:0000::/40) and then align with regions, so we will actually go with the following, which will aid in troubleshooting and allocation, and, above all, keep things simple!

Region 1 (OSPF area 1) – 2022:ccde:0100::/40

Region 2 (OSPF area 2) – 2022:ccde:0200::/40

Region 3 (OSPF area 3) – 2022:ccde:0300::/40

Region 4 (OSPF area 4) – 2022:ccde:0400::/40

Region 5 (OSPF area 5) – 2022:ccde:0500::/40

So we're looking good on the network; however, I've had the members of the application team in a workshop this morning, and they have explained to me that initially they believed the meters would be coming back to a central server system called SMARTS that would accommodate all the meters. We have planned sending their data every five to ten mins, at random intervals. Bit of a curveball—they have completed their own load testing in a lab environment and, when they scale the figures up, they believe the system will be overloaded. They have requested we provide some load balancing to spread the load to five separate servers behind a frontend VIP address that we push to the meters over an API through the encrypted links you have designed. They stated we could still run a single non-load-balanced system, but this would require serious upgrading of existing systems, and this would incur a three-month delay and cost would be double that of an appliance-based load-balanced solution with the additional lower spec servers. It's a little frustrating this late in the day to get this requirement, as we don't have the budget approved, and it will be difficult to get the sign-off for additional spend. They have told me it's effectively a simplex traffic flow from the meter to the VIP of the application, which registers power usage. Each data packet from the meter apparently includes the unique meter reference (customer ID) and required data in a UDP format that the application can then forward to backend systems, which are used to generate customer invoices.

The app guys went through some eventualities if the meter fails or has its IPv6 address changed for any reason, and apparently these are non-issues, as the unique meter reference (customer ID) is associated with the customer data and not the source IPv6 address. I've drawn up a picture they made up on my whiteboard. (I would have just sent you a photo of it, but as you know, app guys can't draw anywhere near as well as network guys.)

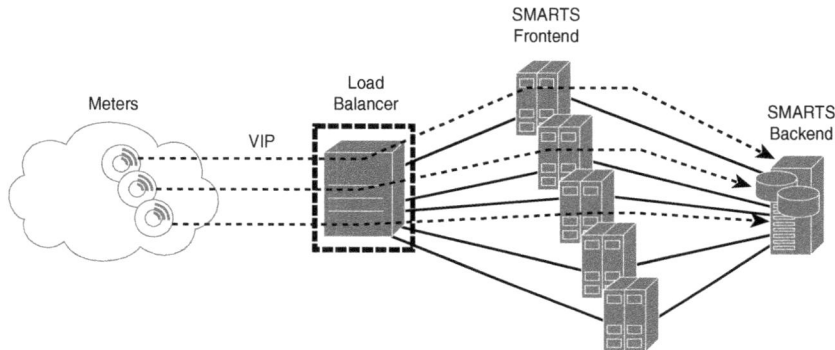

For your info, I've looked into the appliance-based load balancers the app guys mentioned from a well-respected vendor. They can scale to the number of required flows (they support stateful and non-stateful flows, and all features you would expect from a high-end load balancer). We are looking at and support IPv6. The resilience is stated as active/standby, so when one fails, the other takes over, but I think it could be better if we have to use them to have two VIPs that we push out to meters. Kind of alternate APNs or regions for one VIP and the other. This way, we could improve our scale and have the balancers backing each other up, so one is active for one VIP and one for the other while backing up each VIP. Alternatively, the switches in our DC apparently can also provide a basic non-stateful load-balancing mechanism called Traffic Scatter, providing frontend VIPs for L3 and L4 traffic at wire rate and just sending out to servers at the backend based on health/availability of the real server, as the dedicated load balancers do. It looks like they can scale, provide a resilient VIP service, and handle the numbers, and we don't need any license upgrade to enable this. It seems pretty basic in comparison, and they state it supports the VIP frontend, but only Direct Server Return. I need you to recommend which way to go, as this has to work Day 1, and we have to accommodate this change as quickly as we can.

Thanks!

Rgds,

Mich Fara-Day
CTO Squid Energy

Question 19

How can Squid accommodate the load-balancing requirement detailed in the email? (Choose one.)

a. Use the Traffic Scatter functionality in the existing switches in the DC

b. Use a pair of dedicated load balancer appliances with a single VIP in active/standby topology

c. Use a pair of dedicated load balancers with dual VIPs that provide resiliency for each other

d. Upgrade the system to the single non-load-balanced server to negate the requirement for load balancers

Email #11

Hi.

Thanks for the advice on the load balancing. Let's hope the scatter doesn't shatter under load! While you've been busy on the network design, I've had some questions come in from our engineering team about how we should go about setting up the home area network (HAN), which is associated to the smart meters. Obviously, we don't need to set up a network in every consumer's home. This is just the technology that the smart meter uses to communicate with a display unit that gives a real-time reading of the power usage that can be placed wherever the consumer chooses within their home. Apparently, we have options in how to deploy this communications link, which just piggybacks off the /64 IPv6 prefix the meter is assigned, so it's quite straightforward, I believe. (Famous last words!) We want to start a pilot, so if you can assist with the HAN info, that would be great.

Rgds,

Mich Fara-Day
CTO Squid Energy

Question 20

Assist Squid in deciding which is the optimal technology to use for the HAN between the smart meter and the display unit, which would be placed within the consumer's property to view real-time power usage provided by the smart meter. Fill in the protocol from the following list to match the associated distance for that protocol, as listed in the table.

Standard Zigbee 2.4GHz

Dual-band Zigbee 2.4GHz/868MHz

Bluetooth

Ethernet CAT5

2.4GHz Wi-Fi

Protocol	Distance
	100m
	Less than 20m
	Less than 10m
	Less than 30m
	50m

Question 21

Squid decided to implement a standard Zigbee service on the HAN network for the pilot and encountered interference in all areas of the pilot location and lower-than-expected range in areas of the pilot location that incorporated thicker-than-average walls. It is now concerned this could be representative of the user experience of the majority of consumers in the production rollout. Which of the following changes would you recommend in order to improve the HAN network usability while not introducing a management overhead on the running of the service? (Choose one.)

a. Change the Wi-Fi operating channel on consumers' home networks

b. Change the Zigbee operating channel on smart meters

c. Change Zigbee to 5G for the HAN rollout

d. Switch to dual-band Zigbee for the HAN rollout

e. Conduct a wireless survey in each consumer location and deploy the optimal technology based on the results

f. Switch to Bluetooth for the HAN rollout

Email #12

From: Mich Fara-Day

To: CCDE Candidate

Subject: Implementation

Hi.

Thanks for the advice on the HAN. We will get the team to complete the pilot on your recommendation of dual-band Zigbee. While the team finishes up, I need you to help with an implementation plan to enable our service. Let's get the service up and running!

Rgds,

Mich Fara-Day
CTO Squid Energy

Question 22

To assist Squid with delivery of its service, arrange the implementation tasks in sequence order:

Enable PKI infrastructure and application load balancing within Squid co-lo.

Install VPN edge routers in Jaketel regions and enable Jaketel MPLS service between regions to central PE.

Order Jaketel APN service and 4G SIM cards for smart meters.

Install CE router for Jaketel MPLS service within the co-lo.

Board smart meters to Squid's meter-reading application.

Install firewalls and IPS/IDS infrastructure devices within the co-lo.

Configure IPsec tunnels from firewalls to VPN routers.

Order MPLS connectivity from Jaketel to co-lo. Order smart meters/VPN routers/firewalls and IPS/IDS and PKI infrastructure from suppliers.

Configure the OSPF network from firewalls to region VPN router.

Email #13

From: Mich Fara-Day

To: CCDE Candidate

Subject: We're live!

Hi.

Thanks for your help. We're finally live! I was expecting the directors to be really excited this Monday morning, but they were fairly neutral about the whole thing, as it has been an expensive project. It definitely brought me down to earth after a long weekend, but we couldn't have done it without your help.

One thing we didn't fully consider, however, is if a customer migrates away from our service to another energy supplier. It appears that they cannot benefit from the government grant for the meter more than once, so they are stuck with the meter we provisioned on their behalf or will need to pay a premium when onboarded with a new supplier for a new meter. Can you have a think about how we can best migrate the meter onto a new provider's network so we have a process in place when this comes up?

Rgds,

Mich Fara-Day
CTO Squid Energy

Question 23

Which would be the best process for migration of a customer switching supplier and moving the smart meter away to a new supplier with minimal effort for Squid? (Choose one.)

a. Have the new supplier's onsite electrical engineer factory reset the smart meter and install a new SIM card configured for new supplier at time of cutover.

b. Apply a gateway between Squid's co-lo and major supplier networks to allow traffic to traverse between Squid and the new supplier's network for meter readings for migrated customers.

c. Mail out new 4G SIM cards for the consumer to swap over, which will be configured to connect to the new provider's smart meter network.

d. Provide Internet access to the Squid co-lo network or modify the private APNs to public APNs with local Internet access so new suppliers can route to the meters using the IPv6 globally unique addressing structure configured on the meters for direct meter reading access over an API call.

Email #14

From: Mich Fara-Day

To: CCDE Candidate

Subject: EVs

Hi.

The new system is working really well. We've managed to free up our field staff, etc., and automate a lot of deployment for consumers who are keen to get a smart-metered service. The board believes we now have the capacity to expand our offerings, so we're setting up some marketing to deploy our own EV charging points for vehicles at consumer locations. We see two types of customers—one already has the smart meter and we can offer incentives for them to buy a charging point from us, and one who doesn't use us as a supplier at all and we set them up from scratch. Either way, we need to have an option to connect each user type to our systems in the most cost effective manner.

The EV charging points have the same specification as the Zenith V3 meters we are using for WAN and HAN, and you should still have the specification if you need any data.

We envisage the EVs using the same application as the smart meters in the co-lo with identical traffic flow and security requirements.

Rgds,

Mich Fara-Day
CTO Squid Energy

Question 24

Which of the following options provide optimal connectivity for the new EV charging points to Squid's central system for billing for each customer type? (Choose two.)

a. Existing customers should have the EV charging point connected to the existing HAN provided for the smart meter using dual-band Zigbee for connectivity.

b. Existing customers should have the EV charging point use a new cellular connection within the same APN as the existing meter.

c. Existing customers should have the EV charging point use a new cellular connection within a separate Jaketel APN and new IPsec connection from the edge APN to the co-lo dedicated for aggregating charging point traffic to the co-lo.

d. New customers should have the EV charging point use a new cellular connection within the same APN as used for meters in the local area.

e. New customers should have the EV charging point use a new cellular connection within a separate Jaketel APN and a new IPsec connection from the edge APN to the co-lo dedicated to aggregating charging point traffic to the co-lo.

f. New customers should have the EV charging point use the consumer's own broadband connection over a Wi-Fi connection to connect to a newly provisioned Internet VPN service to access the Squid central systems hosted in a DMZ to maximize end-to-end security.

Question 25

If Squid creates a service for public EV charging points in public locations such as car parks and shopping malls, should the connectivity solution differ from a new customer EV charging point for a consumer? (Choose one.)

a. The solution should be identical.

b. The solution should be reevaluated for this use case.

Email #15

From: Mich Fara-Day

To: CCDE Candidate

Subject: EVs

Hi.

Thanks for your feedback on public charging. While we weigh everything, we are considering an option to allow users of public charging points to use a "call home" feature on the charging point to allow Squid help desk users to communicate directly with consumers who have difficulty entering credit card details on the system or who are having difficulty using charging apps compatible with the solution. Our devops team believes it can create an app for a consumer that can connect to the charger over Bluetooth and allow the user to talk directly to the help desk over our secure WAN network (a form of push to talk). This could be a great way to showcase our technology and innovation and increase our UX and customer service reviews. Devops thinks it can get a beta out in two weeks. We can modify a call center application to accept voice if we need to quickly, so we're keen to test this on a pilot as soon as we have the beta. For the pilot, we will connect the EV charger up identically as if it was a smart meter for a new customer and perform our testing.

We appreciate all of your help on the design, and we can carry on with the charging points when you move on!

Rgds,

Mich Fara-Day
CTO Squid Energy

Question 26

How would you recommend Squid facilitate the voice connectivity requirement for the pilot? (Choose one.)

a. Simply list a direct dial number and EV charging meter location code on the charger for the consumer to dial in to the call center with their own cell phone.

b. Set up a push-to-talk feature on the EV charger that piggybacks voice on the 4G SIM card to route voice over the Jaketel cellular connection as a normal cellular voice call, which is forwarded to the help desk.

c. Use a push-to-talk feature on the EV charger for a VoIP call that can be routed over the existing data network connectivity to the call center application within the Squid co-lo and prioritize voice traffic with DSCP EF.

d. Use a push-to-talk feature on the EV charger for a VoIP call that can be routed over the existing data network connectivity to the call center application within the Squid DC network, without any form of voice QoS.

Practice Lab 2 Debrief

This lab debrief section analyzes each question, showing you what was required and how to achieve the desired results. You should use this section to produce an overall score for Practice Lab 2.

Question 1

Which smart meter would you recommend to Squid to supply to end consumers? (Choose one.)

Requirements/constraints from supplied documentation:

The service is going to need to scale to a couple of million meters if our marketing team has done its homework correctly over the next five years. We have to assume we will migrate our current base of 300K customers gradually onto the smart meter program.

I don't know if these will connect back to us over a private WAN or the Internet, so at this phase I want to keep my options open and make sure we can support private and public addressing if need be.

I'll worry about the overall finance element, but you do need to keep this in mind as you don't have an open checkbook available. If you can save money where possible, then please do.

The price is right at £20 a unit, and the other one has some additional features at £28 a unit.

Both communicate to a basic display in the home to show current usage over a home area network (HAN) connection that is built into each device, which is included in the unit price.

We want to start the ordering process for a pilot ASAP, so please take a look at them.

a. SMARTS 2.0 meter

This is incorrect. There is some logic in thinking cheapest isn't going to be best, and you could always assume that there might be a specific reason to go for the more expensive product; otherwise, you wouldn't be asked. However, the real question is, why is one meter a better choice than the other? Which one actually meets the requirements? The service needs to scale to two million devices, and there is a requirement to support public and private IP addressing initially. It should be apparent that in this day and age you would have a real challenge to get this many public IPv4 addresses. If it was possible, it would more than likely wipe out the entire grant offered by the government. Without knowing anything about smart meters, you should find this question a simple one to start and secure a point to. You could argue that there is future IPv6 support on the roadmap for this particular meter, which would then support two million public IPv6 addresses, but you have no idea of when that will be, and an order needs to be placed ASAP for the pilot.

b. SMARTS 2.0 meter with dual-band optional upgrade

This is incorrect. It should make you think, what does this optional upgrade actually provide over and above the standard product? You probably don't know the specifics of a smart meter, and you shouldn't have to, as this can be viewed as a "black box" technology in reality. However, you should know that a dual-band radio option is really only going to provide some form of additional flexibility (possibly range or quality), but at this point in time you don't have specific details about why a dual-band option could be beneficial toward the hardware choice. The device would still be more cost effective than the Zenith, even with the additional £3 added, but there is no reason why the dual-band option makes this a good choice over and above the details provided in the explanation to Answer A.

c. Zenith V3 meter

This is correct. As detailed per the explanation for Answer A, the solution should scale to two million devices. As NAT is not supported, the only possibility is allocation of IPv6 addresses (public or private) due to the current exhaustion of IPv4 addresses. Smart meters are a classic Internet of Things (IoT) use case for IPv6 addressing due to the huge number of devices.

d. Zenith V3 meter with gas-metering software activation option

This is incorrect. There has been no requirement detailed at this point in time to provide support for gas metering in conjunction with electricity. Although this upgraded meter choice would function, it would be an unnecessary cost at this time. Should gas metering be required in the future, the activation could be carried out at that point in time, as it is a software activation as opposed to hardware feature, and it would then require replacement/site visit for an upgrade.

If you have answered this question correctly, you have scored one point.

Question 2

Which IP version should be deployed on the smart meters? (Choose one.)

Requirements/constraints from supplied documentation:

The service is going to need to scale to a couple of million meters over the next five years if our marketing team has done its homework correctly. We have to assume we will migrate our current base of 300K customers gradually onto the smart meter program.

I don't know if these will connect back to us over a private WAN or the Internet, so at this phase I want to keep my options open and make sure we can support private and public addressing if need be.

   a. IPv4

     This is incorrect. This question is really justification as to which meter type you selected. You could have also had a question asking why you selected this type of meter. Clearly IPv4 isn't going to scale to the requirement of two million devices if Squid wants to keep its options open going forward with a solution that could connect over the Internet.

   b. IPv6

     This is correct. As detailed in the explanation to Answer C in Question 1, IPv6 is a classic use case for IoT, and this would scale to two million publicly addressed devices.

If you have answered this question correctly, you have scored half a point.

Email #2

From: Mich Fara-Day

To: CCDE Candidate

Subject: Zenith WAN Options

Hi.

Thanks for selecting the Zenith smart meter. Our CFO wasn't really pleased we had to go with this one, but I explained we needed IPv6 support to make this scale. We're going to have to get these meters to communicate to our central DC facility over some form of WAN from a consumer's home location, which can be quite rural. I need you to come up with a recommendation of how we should achieve this. The facts I can gather from the meter company are as follows:

Typical IP packet size: **1000 bytes (includes IPsec overhead if used)**

IP protocol: **UDP**

Maximum packet per second rate (typically seen during firmware upgrades): **100**

Latency requirement normal operation: **Sub 80ms**

Power requirements: **10 watts**

WAN charges are relatively low with the cellular 2/3/4/5G network, ranging from 2G being the lowest cost to 5G being the highest cost.

Rgds,

Mich Fara-Day
CTO Squid Energy

Question 3

Based on the information supplied to date, which WAN technology would be most suitable for the meter rollout for Squid? (Choose one.)

Requirements/constraints from supplied documentation:

We're going to have to get these meters to communicate to a central facility or regional facilities and back to a central location WAN side from a customer's home location, which can be quite rural.

Typical IP packet size: **1000 bytes (includes IPsec overhead if used)**

IP protocol: **UDP**

Maximum packet per second rate (typically seen during firmware upgrades): **100**

Latency requirement normal operation: **Sub 80ms**

Power requirements: **10 watts**

WAN charges are relatively low with the cellular 2/3/4/5G network, ranging from 2G being the lowest cost to 5G being the highest cost.

I'll worry about the overall finance element, but you do need to keep this in mind, as you don't have an open checkbook available. If you can save money where possible, then please do.

a. 2G

This is incorrect. Aside from the fact that the 2G service is now considered legacy, the data rate required from the meter would not be possible. Taking the average packet size supplied (1000 bytes) with an average of 100 pps, this equates to a required bit rate of 800Kbps. The 2G network is generally known to only deliver up to 100Kbps, so 2G technology would not be suitable.

b. 3G

This is a suboptimal answer. 3G meets bandwidth requirements with a range of 200Kbps–2Mbps but is known to have a latency of less than 100ms. It's a little too close to the firm requirement of 80ms, so while it might work in the majority of implementations, 4G (Answer C) is a more reliable technology choice.

c. 4G

This is the optimal answer. 4G provides a bandwidth of 100Mbps–1Gbps and approximately 50ms latency. It is technology that provides wide coverage and will have a longer life cycle in comparison to 3G and 2G.

d. 5G

This is a suboptimal answer. The latency requirement and bandwidth do not justify the additional expense, which you have been asked to minimize. 5G would be a good technology choice for sub-10ms latency and up to 1Gbps bandwidth requirements.

e. Wireless mesh

This is incorrect. You have not been provided with any information in regard to a wireless mesh network. This would typically be more expensive than a cellular option and is unlikely to provide coverage in rural areas outside of cities. You would be making an assumption if you selected this option, which is a classic error in tackling the lab exam.

If you have answered this question correctly, you have scored one point.

Email #3

From: Mich Fara-Day

To: CCDE Candidate

Subject: Cellular Connectivity

Hi.

Historically, we've split the UK up into five different areas for marketing and service delivery/support. I think it makes sense if we create our new smart meter service in the same manner. I've decided to run with a 4G cellular service for WAN connectivity for the meters and have spoken to numerous cellular providers. A company called Jaketel offers 4G coverage to 94% of the UK and can provide us with data-only SIMs that we can fit into the smart meters we deploy. Jaketel stated it can configure multiple access point names (APNs) for us, which is the equivalent of a data service. This can be either private without access to the Internet or other Jaketel data subscribers or public with access to the Internet and other Jaketel data subscribers. Cost-wise, the private APN is marginally more expensive than the private. Jaketel also stated that in terms of IP address we are good with IPv6—either fixed (static), DHCP-based, or an SLAAC approach. The APNs Jaketel configures can fit into our five area footprint (there will be multiple APNs per area to assist with scale), and I'm told we can install our own equipment within its APNs to backhaul each area's traffic back to a central location. If I'm honest, this didn't mean a great deal to me other than coverage. I'm happy enough with 94% coverage, and I'm sure we can even extend some coverage in rural areas with additional antennas if really required and if we have to we can use a different supplier for the more complex installs, but we don't want to be seen to turn customers down. I do need you to evaluate the other aspects of the service though.

Rgds,

Mich Fara-Day
TO Squid Energy

Question 4

Which network APN mode should be selected for the 4G SIM network from Jaketel for the smart meter WAN network that will provide communications from the meters to a central location? (Choose one.)

Requirements/constraints from supplied documentation:

We're going to have to get these meters to communicate to our central DC facility over some form of WAN from a consumers' home location, which can be quite rural.

Jaketel stated it can configure multiple access point names (APNs) for us, which is the equivalent of a data service. It can be either private without access to the Internet or other Jaketel data subscribers or public with access to the Internet and other Jaketel data subscribers. Cost-wise, the private APN is marginally more expensive than the private. Jaketel also stated that in terms of IP address we are good with IPv6—either fixed (static), DHCP-based, or an SLAAC approach. The APNs Jaketel configures can fit into our five area footprint (there will be multiple APNs per area to assist with scale), and I'm told we can install our own equipment within Jaketel's APNs to backhaul each area's traffic back to a central location.

Squid is also wary of a well-publicized cyberattack on Ukraine's power network in 2015 and is adamant that it cannot find itself in that position.

a. Public APN

This is incorrect. Even though the public APN is marginally more cost effective, you haven't been informed of a requirement for the meters to be accessible on the Internet at this point in the network. You have, however, been informed of a historical cyberattack that Squid was adamant it wants to avoid. Having a public APN means the security of the overall system would be more complex and challenging in comparison to a private APN, which would natively offer more security.

b. Private APN

This is correct. The private APN option is marginally more expensive, but the additional security provided by not being accessible on the Internet directly from this zone makes this a good design choice due to a lack of requirements stating that Internet access is required at this point in the network. Even if the private APN is provisioned, the meters could still be accessible on the Internet if connectivity was provisioned from the central DC location and Squid had a later requirement for this. Provision of the private APN definitely reduces and helps mitigates the attack vectors in play.

If you have answered this question correctly, you have scored one point.

Question 5

Which type of IPv6 address assignment would you recommend for smart meters within the Jaketel APN? (Choose one.)

Requirements/constraints from supplied documentation:

Cost-wise, the private APN is marginally more expensive than the private. Jaketel also stated that in terms of IP address we are good with IPv6—either fixed (static), DHCP-based, or an SLAAC approach.

I'm happy enough with 94% coverage, and I'm sure we can even extend some coverage in rural areas with additional antennas if really required, and if we have to we can use a different supplier for the more complex installs, but we don't want to be seen to turn customers down.

a. Provider assigned (PA)

This is a suboptimal answer. PA ranges would potentially complicate the rollout if another supplier is used in conjunction with Jaketel for the harder-to-reach areas of the UK. The solution would still work with different ranges, but a PI assignment that each supplier could then use would provide additional flexibility.

b. Provider independent (PI)

This is optimal. As detailed in the explanation for Answer A, additional flexibility can be gained from the provision of a single address range that could potentially be used by multiple providers.

If you have answered this question correctly, you have scored one point.

Email #4

From: Mich Fara-Day

To: CCDE Candidate

Subject: IPv6 Address Allocation/Type

Hi.

I need your help to determine what type of IPv6 addressing we use on the smart meter network and how it should be allocated. We have to be able to route to the meters directly for software updates from our central DC. All we need to do for ID is to be able to know which IPv6 address belongs to which customer at their physical address location. To do this, we can allocate an IPv6 address prior to installation time before the meter is shipped to the installers that we can allocate centrally, or I'm told we can use DHCPv6 within each APN in Jaketel. When the meter has an IPv6 address and calls home, it registers its IPv6 address with the central application with a site ID that references the customer address, so we're covered either way. We're also thinking of registering each meter on its own /64 segment to give us some segmentation between devices and scale for the future. (Yeah I know, that's a lot of scale!)

Rgds,

Mich Fara-Day
CTO Squid Energy

Question 6

Which IPv6 address type should be used for the smart meter that would provide as minimal administrative overhead as possible? (Choose one.)

Requirements/constraints from supplied documentation:

We have to be able to route to the meters directly for software updates from our central DC. All we need to do for ID is to be able to know which IPv6 address belongs to which customer at their physical address location. To do this, we can allocate an IPv6 address prior to installation time before the meter is shipped to the installers that we can allocate centrally, or I'm told we can use DHCPv6 within each APN in Jaketel. When the meter has an IPv6 address and calls home, it registers its IPv6 address with the central application with a site ID that references the customer address, so we're covered either way.

Would provide as minimal administrative overhead as possible.

  a. Global Unicast Address (GUA)

  This is correct. A GUA from the 2003::/3 range will be globally routable and allow Squid to access the smart meter for readings and software updates from its remote DC. Being globally routable also provides additional flexibility should additional external connectivity be required in the future. This may allow a customer to access a different supplier from Squid, for example, without having to replace or reconfigure the meter or without using a form of NAT, which is not compatible with the meter according to the specification provided.

  b. Link Local (LLA)

  This is incorrect. An LLA fe80::/10 type of address is adequate for traffic that is self-contained within a single prefix area or link, but the smart meters are required to be accessed remotely for the data readings and software updates from the central DC. LLA would, however, definitely simplify address allocation by use of EUI-64 interface ID generation. You may have selected this option due to minimizing administrative overhead, but it's not going to allow routing off net, as per the requirements, so it's not a valid choice. If you feel you are being led by a question, just ensure that the requirements are being met prior to committing to it.

If you have answered this question correctly, you have scored one point.

Question 7

Squid has chosen to use Global Unicast Addressing (GUA) because it didn't want the meters to provision their own IPv6 addresses and needed to route to them from their DC location. Which address allocation mode should be used for the smart meter IPv6 addressing? (Choose one.)

Requirements/constraints from supplied documentation:

All we need to do for ID is to be able to know which IPv6 address belongs to which customer at their physical address location. To do this, we can allocate an IPv6 address prior to installation time before the meter is shipped to the installers that we can allocate centrally, or I'm told we can use DHCPv6 within each APN in Jaketel. When the meter calls home, it registers its IPv6 address with the central application with a site ID that references the customer address, so we're covered either way.

We're also thinking of registering each meter on its own /64 segment to give us some segmentation between devices and scale for the future. (Yeah I know that's a lot of scale!)

a. Manual configuration

This is incorrect. Clearly it's possible to manually configure the meters centrally and ship them out, but the logistics would not be efficient, tying everything up. It's far simpler to aim for a zero-touch deployment model, allowing for any unconfigured meter to be shipped to site or taken to site by an engineer. Similarly, the engineer deploying the meter could enter an address at time of installation, but again more logistics to line up, and this engineer would typically be an electrically trained engineer versus an IT engineer, as he would have to deploy the meter in line with the electrical supply being metered. If you did select this answer, your punishment may be to configure the two million smart meters yourself, just to gain a better understanding of the effort involved.

b. Stateless autoconfiguration

This is incorrect. This would be SLAAC-based stateless autoconfiguration based on RA advertisements, with a prefix being issued by a router on the segment and then the meter provisioning its own address matched with that prefix. The process would work, as it is detailed that a user ID is matched to an IPv6 address, so Squid doesn't actually need to allocate exact host addressing, but Squid has also stated it expects to use a /64 per smart meter. This would mean the company needs a locally connected router to each /64 segment in order for the RA to function. It seems a little far-fetched for this to function correctly at the scale being discussed (if all meters were provisioned within the same or limited number of /64 segments, then this approach would work well).

c. Stateful autoconfiguration

This is correct. Stateful autoconfiguration for IPv6 is DHCPv6 and would be the optimal choice for provisioning addresses within an IoT environment due to the sheer scale of hosts. In this scenario, the DHCPv6 servers could reside within the service provider's network or back in Squid's DC and reachable via DHCP relay from the cellular APNs.

If you have answered this question correctly, you have scored one point.

Question 8

If Squid has decided to use stateful autoconfiguration with DHCPv6 servers based in Jaketel APNs, how long would you recommend the lease be set for? (Choose one.)

a. One day

This is incorrect. It's a good choice for a hot desk or wireless network, but a static meter would not need to refresh its lease on a daily basis. There would be a great deal of unnecessary cumulative traffic generated for a daily lease for all meters.

b. One week

This is incorrect. As per the explanation for Answer A, there is still little benefit to be achieved by extending the lease period to one week.

c. One month

This is optimal. The previous answers are too short a lease period, and Answer D (one year) is arguably too long.

d. One year

This is a suboptimal answer. A lease could actually extend to 135 years on some systems, if required, but one year would generally be considered too long a period, even for a static device that, in theory, may need to change suppliers at some point.

If you have answered this question correctly, you have scored half a point.

Email #5

From: Mich Fara-Day

To: CCDE Candidate

Subject: IPv6 Address Block

Hi.

Thanks for the info on addressing. We've evaluated your responses and decided to run with PI GUAs issued by DHCPv6. If we need to run with other providers, it will provide some additional flexibility. I need to request a block of addresses from Jaketel, which I guess goes to RIPE on our behalf on the PI side, so I could use your help in requesting a large enough block. This is what we've determined so far:

1. We have five regions/areas, as you know, but we want to have the ability to scale to 256 max if we expand into Europe in the future.

2. We want to have the ability to have up to 256 APNs in each region.

3. We want to run up to 65,000 smart meters per APN.

4. We want each smart meter to have an individual /64 prefix.

5. Smart meters use a form of unnumbered IPv6 addressing from their main /64 prefix over the APN, so we don't need to worry about any prefixes for the APN/WAN. The /64 prefix will also be used for the HAN for displays and any other devices that require access to the meter or further connectivity to our systems.

Rgds,

Mich Fara-Day
CTO Squid Energy

Question 9

Which size IPv6 prefix should be requested from RIPE for Squid's smart meter roll out? (Choose one.)

Requirements/constraints from supplied documentation:

1. We have five regions/areas, as you know, but we want to have the ability to scale to 256 max if we expand into Europe in the future.

2. We want to have the ability to have up to 256 APNs in each region.

3. We want to run up to 65,000 smart meters per APN.

4. We want each smart meter to have an individual /64 prefix.

5. Smart meters use a form of unnumbered IPv6 addressing from their main /64 prefix over the APN, so we don't need to worry about any prefixes for the APN/WAN. The /64 prefix will also be used for the HAN for displays and any other devices that require access to the meter or further connectivity to our systems.

a. /24

This is incorrect. See the explanation for Answer B for details.

b. /32

This is correct. Referring to the following figure, the allocation is simpler if you work from right to left (host to network) of the 128-bit block. You are informed the meters require a /64 prefix (it still sounds absurd that a device or a VLAN can be allocated twice the size of the entire IPv4 address space, but these are the requirements). You need 65,000x /64s per APN, so an APN will require an additional 16 bits, which takes you to a /48 from the /64 starting point. You require 256 APNs per region, so this equates to a further 8 bits, taking you to a /40, and 256 regions are required, so a final additional 8 bits is required, taking you to a /32. This shouldn't be a difficult question and doesn't require detailed knowledge of IPv6; however, it can be challenging and easy to make an error if you are under a time constraint, so it's well worth practicing with address scheme scenarios prior to the CCDE lab so you can tackle a question like this with ease.

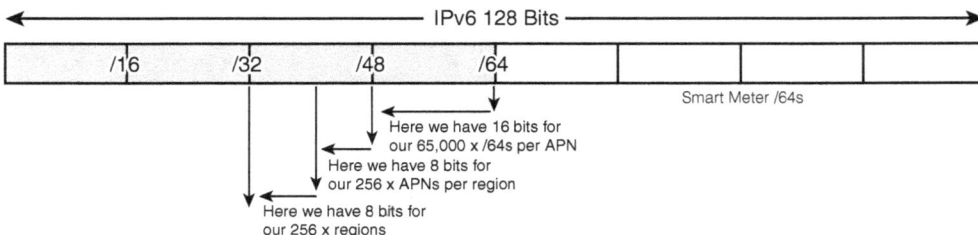

IPv6 128 Bits

/16   /32   /48   /64

Smart Meter /64s

Here we have 16 bits for
our 65,000 x /64s per APN

Here we have 8 bits for
our 256 x APNs per region

Here we have 8 bits for
our 256 x regions

c. /40

This is incorrect. See the explanation for Answer B for a detailed explanation.

d. /48

This is incorrect. See the explanation for Answer B for a detailed explanation.

e. /60

This is incorrect. See the explanation for Answer B for a detailed explanation.

If you have answered this question correctly, you have scored one point.

Email #6

From: Mich Fara-Day

To: CCDE Candidate

Subject: WAN to Central Location Design

Hi.

Marketing worked out that we will need to scale to 400,000 customers per region/area, which is formed with multiple APNs. Jaketel apparently runs its own MPLS network also and has priced up a way of backhauling aggregated APN traffic onto our central location.

I did read about an Internet-based attack in the Ukraine power network some time ago, and that cannot be permitted here, so I'll need you to make it as secure as possible. Therefore, everything should be encrypted outside of our own DC. I was informed that we can use a DHCPv6 option in the offer to the smart meters that gives the meters the ability to connect to a remote IPsec peer of our choice that we configure on the DHCPv6 server. Hopefully, we can make use of this feature. If you can absorb the information below and then get started on a design, that will allow us to connect the smart meters to the cellular network and then onto a DC, which is likely going to be a co-located area where we can rent some rack space in London and where we will install the associated compute environment. I'm just not convinced our own DC is up to this. I've discussed some of the security aspects with our security leads, and they have requested we run an appliance-based IPS/IDS that can monitor the traffic flow into the co-lo before it reaches the compute environment to enhance security over and above a perimeter firewall, which will also be required in front of the connection to the meters.

As mentioned previously, Jaketel said we can connect our own infrastructure devices within each region in order to connect back to a central location. These devices will effectively have a logical connection into each APN provisioned within that region. Jaketel is going to provide a Layer 3 MPLS VPN for us to assist with backhauling WAN cellular traffic to the central location, which will be our co-lo, and we can just connect up a local 10Gbps fiber connection into our co-lo area, as a Jaketel PE is conveniently sited in the same co-lo building.

In terms of infrastructure devices at our disposal, we have 10Gbps routers with six interfaces and 10Gbps VPN routers with four interfaces. The VPN routers are capable of terminating 500,000 VPNs connections, and we have firewalls that are VPN compatible with 4x 10Gbps interfaces and can also terminate up to 500,000 VPNs. The smart meters will connect to the Jaketel APN on bootup thanks to their SIM card and a preconfigured APN on the Jaketel side. Also, as mentioned, we can preload some configuration to point to a remote VPN of our choice to make use of Jaketel's IPsec feature using DHCPv6 options. Oh, and the IPS/IDS device—due to the number of flows that can go through it, the price is eye-watering. I need you to use as few of these as possible, and they have 2x 10Gbps interfaces (an in and an out, so they work in series). All routers and firewalls can run OSPF and BGP with dual-stack IPv4 and IPv6, and we calculate the overall peak aggregate traffic load into the co-lo would not exceed 6Gbps.

Rgds,

Mich Fara-Day
CTO Squid Energy

Question 10

Design the WAN connectivity in order to provide IPv6 connectivity from the smart meters back to the co-located environment. Your design should use single infrastructure devices and connections at this point in time; resilience can be addressed at a later stage. Add the required infrastructure devices, as shown in the following diagram key, as required, and use 10Gbps Ethernet connections or IPsec tunnels. Any infrastructure device placed within the MPLS network can be assumed to have a 10Gbps direct connection to the MPLS network without the need to specifically add it within the diagram.

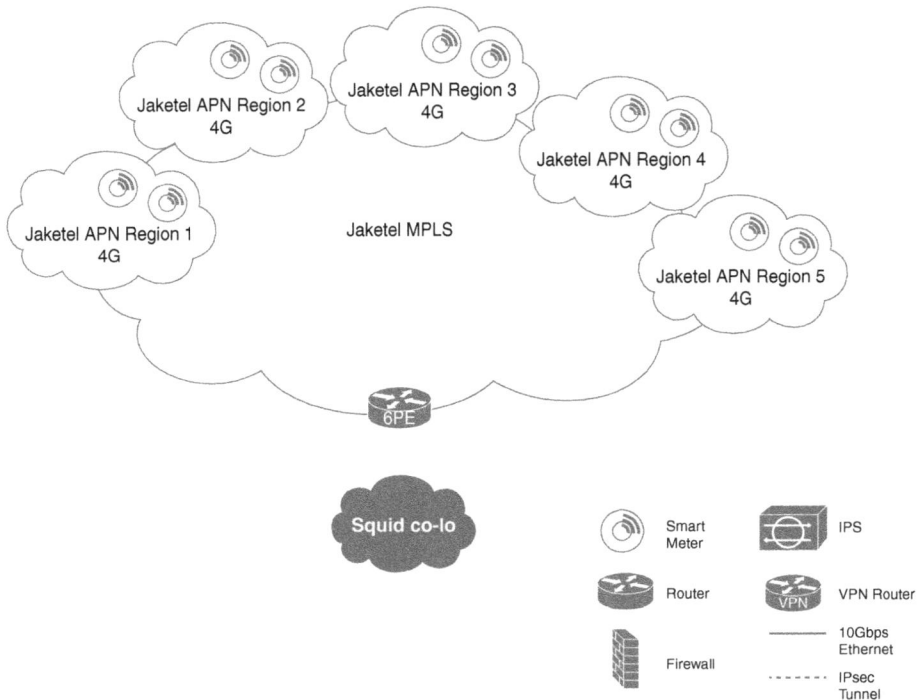

Requirements/constraints from supplied documentation:

The APNs Jaketel configures can fit into our five area footprint (there will be multiple APNs per area to assist with scale), and I'm told we can install our own equipment within Jaketel's APNs to backhaul each area's traffic back to a central location.

Marketing worked out that we will need to scale to 400,000 customers per region/area, which is formed with multiple APNs. Jaketel apparently runs its own MPLS network also and has priced up a way of backhauling aggregated APN traffic onto our central location.

We have reserved some space in a co-lo in central London where I'd like you to bring all the smart communication network back to.

I did read about an Internet-based attack in the Ukraine power network some time ago, and that cannot be permitted here, so I'll need you to make it as secure as possible.

Therefore, everything should be encrypted outside of our own DC. I was informed that we can use a DHCPv6 option in the offer to the smart meters that gives the meters the ability to connect to a remote IPsec peer of our choice that we configure on the DHCPv6 server. Hopefully, we can make use of this feature. If you can absorb the information below and then get started on a design, that will allow us to connect the smart meters to the cellular network and then onto a DC, which is likely going to be a co-located area where we can rent some rack space in London and where we will install the associated compute environment.

Run an appliance-based IPS/IDS system that can monitor the traffic flow into the co-lo before it reaches the compute environment to enhance security over and above a perimeter firewall, which will also be required in front of the connection to the meters.

As mentioned previously, Jaketel said we can connect our own infrastructure devices within each region in order to connect back to a central location. These devices will effectively have a logical connection into each APN provisioned within that region. Jaketel is going to provide a Layer 3 MPLS VPN for us to assist with backhauling WAN cellular traffic to the central location, which will be our co-lo, and we can just connect up a local 10Gbps fiber connection into our co-lo area, as a Jaketel PE is conveniently sited in the same co-lo building.

In terms of infrastructure devices at our disposal, we have 10Gbps routers with six interfaces and 10Gbps VPN routers with four interfaces. The VPN routers are capable of terminating 500,000 VPNs connections, and we have firewalls that are VPN compatible with 4x 10Gbps interfaces and can also terminate up to 500,000 VPNs. The smart meters will connect to the Jaketel APN on bootup thanks to their SIM card and a preconfigured APN on the Jaketel side. Also, as mentioned, we can preload some configuration to point to a remote VPN of our choice to make use of Jaketel's IPsec feature using DHCPv6 options. Oh, and the IPS/IDS device—due to the number of flows that can go through it, the price is eye-watering. I need you to use as few of these as possible, and they have 2x 10Gbps interfaces (an in and an out, so they work in series). All routers and firewalls can run OSPF and BGP with dual-stack IPv4 and IPv6, and we calculate the overall peak aggregate traffic load into the co-lo would not exceed 6Gbps.

The following figure details the required WAN connectivity. The main constraint is to use the minimal number of IPS/IDS devices, which really shapes the design and can be achieved with a single IPS/IDS device (remember you have not been asked to provide a resilient service at this point in time). In order to use a single IPS/IDS device, a single firewall would be required, as the IPS/IDS device only has a 10Gbps input and output. In order to use a single firewall, the smart meters cannot terminate IPsec connections directly to the firewall, as it can only accommodate 500,000 VPN connections. The smart meters would need to connect to a VPN router within the region/area of the APNs, which can accommodate up to 500,000 VPN connections. This VPN router would terminate the IPsec sessions to the meters and aggregate all of the meters' traffic back to the co-lo over a single IPsec VPN connection to a co-lo firewall, which is required to provide perimeter security into the co-lo. The design is very simple, with the Jaketel MPLS service providing connectivity between each region and the central co-lo with hierarchy providing scale and modularity.

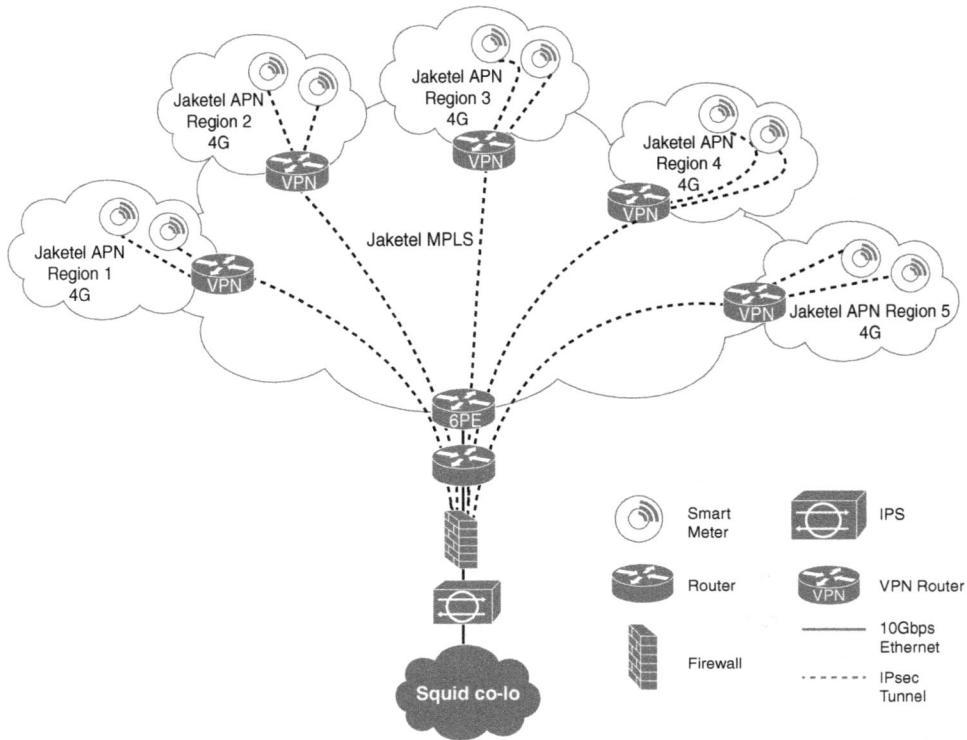

Alternative design options could use the perimeter firewall in the co-lo to terminate IPsec VPN connections directly from the smart meters; however, this would require multiple firewalls to scale, as each firewall is only capable of terminating up to 500,000 VPN connections, and up to two million connections could be required if 400,000 meters were connected in each region/area. This would require four separate firewalls, which would then require four IPS/IDS devices to connect to them, making the price significantly higher than the design detailed previously. The design may offer more overall throughput, but you are informed a maximum of 6Gbps is required. Similarly, you could use 4x VPN routers in the co-lo to terminate the IPsec connections direct from the meters if connectivity was provided over the MPLS network, but this would also result in an increase in the number of firewalls and IPS/IDS appliances.

This type of question can be extremely complex, as you need to fully understand the requirements, and there are a huge number of variables in play. It is really worth absorbing from the information provided what is actually required, keeping the design as simple as possible, and using your design skills to provide scale and hierarchy in such a large IoT deployment.

If you have answered this question correctly, you have scored three points.

Email #7

From: Mich Fara-Day

To: CCDE Candidate

Subject: WAN to Co-lo Design

Hi.

Thanks for your help in the overall WAN design. We're going for the design outlined below. We can work out the resilience at a later date. We'll just double up on infrastructure and connectivity to ensure we have no single points of failure. The VPN routers placed within the APN regions terminate the IPsec VPN connections from the smart meters from their local APN, and then each region VPN router has L3 MPLS VPN connectivity through the central 6PE to the co-lo edge router to the central firewall. The firewall has an IPsec VPN connection to each region's VPN router, so all traffic is encrypted end-to-end and the IPS/IDS appliance is able to monitor all flows. We decided not to run the IPsec VPN tunnels direct from the meters to the firewall, as this approach didn't scale as well.

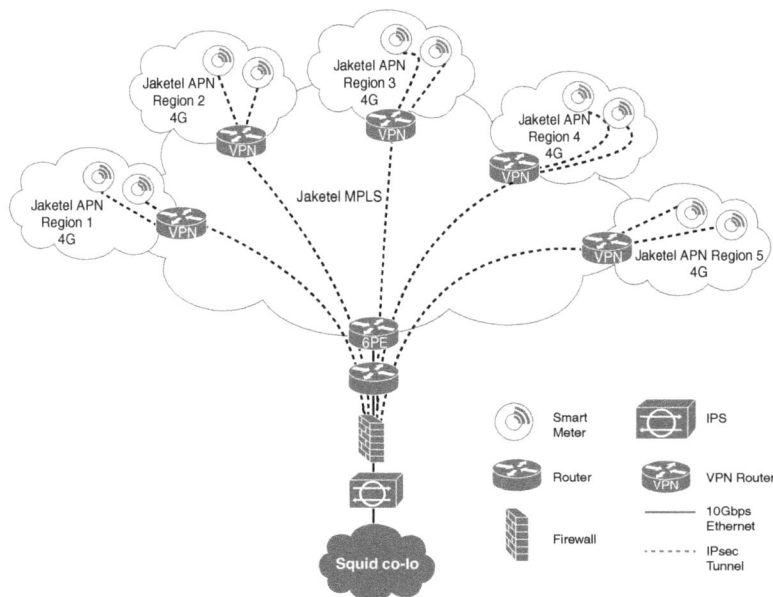

Rgds,

Mich Fara-Day
CTO Squid Energy

Question 11

As detailed in the email, Squid chose to run IPsec VPN connections from the smart meters to the region/APN edge VPN routers. How would you recommend the IPsec authentication be deployed for meters to VPN routers for maximum security and minimal administrative overhead? (Choose one.)

Requirements/constraints from supplied documentation:

Maximum security and minimal administrative overhead.

a. Certificate-based with self-signed X.509 certificates on smart meters

This is incorrect. While a self-signed certificate would potentially suffice in a private network, Squid has stated it requires maximum security. Certificates signed by a CA offer additional protection in comparison to self-signed certificates. There is also no detail of a PKI infrastructure with this option, so deploying the certificates (regardless of how they are signed) would be a challenge.

b. Certificate-based PKI infrastructure with a dedicated CA located within Squid's DC/co-lo

This is correct. PKI-issued certificates with a dedicated CA within Squid's DC/co-lo offer the most security of all options presented. Placing the CA in a private network would ensure it is protected from public access or DoS-type Internet-based attacks. Having a CA provides trust and offers a stronger level of authentication in comparison with self-signed certificates. Without a PKI, the issuing and revocation of certificates would be a significant challenge in an IoT environment of this scale.

c. Certificate-based PKI infrastructure with a shared CA located within the Internet

This is incorrect. Squid stated it requires maximum security. With a CA sited on the Internet, it could be vulnerable to attacks, and an additional risk is that the CA is shared in this option rather than dedicated, providing an additional level of risk to the service.

d. Manual pre-shared key configuration on IPsec peers

This is incorrect. While the option would be secure, it would be an administrative nightmare to deploy and modify keys at defined intervals at this level of scale.

If you have answered this question correctly, you have scored one point.

Question 12

As detailed in the email, Squid has chosen to run IPsec VPN connections from the region/APN edge VPN routers to the co-lo firewall to aggregate and encrypt meter traffic flowing into the co-lo. How would you recommend IPsec be deployed for VPN routers to the firewall for the five IPsec tunnels with maximum security and minimal administrative overhead? (Choose one.)

Requirements/constraints from supplied documentation:

Maximum security and minimal administrative overhead.

a. Certificate-based PKI infrastructure with a dedicated CA located within Squid's DC

This is the optimal answer. It makes more sense to recommend the same PKI infrastructure as recommended for the smart meters rather than having a manual process in place just for these separate connections. If these links failed due to key or certificate expiry, a complete APN region would be offline.

b. Manual pre-shared key configuration on IPsec peers

This is a suboptimal answer. If the five VPNs were the only IPsec VPNs, then, yes, this would make more sense for pre-shared keys, as setting up a PKI for five links wouldn't be efficient. However, as you should have recommended a PKI for the smart meters, it makes sense to utilize it also for these VPNs.

If you have answered this question correctly, you have scored one point.

Question 13

Squid has decided to implement certificates with a PKI infrastructure with a root CA in order for the smart meters to be authenticated and encrypt traffic. Which is the optimal method of provisioning the required certificates onto the smart meters?

Requirements/constraints from supplied documentation:

Certificates with a PKI infrastructure with a root CA.

Maximum security and minimal administrative overhead.

No TLS support.

a. SCEP

This is the optimal answer. Simple Certificate Enrollment Protocol (SCEP) can be used reliably with the PKI infrastructure that Squid is investing in with a root CA to issue certificates to the smart meters.

b. Embedded meter self-signed certificate

This is incorrect. Self-signed certificates can be used in closed IoT environments, but this would typically be a less secure approach in comparison to Answer A.

c. CMP

This is incorrect. The main function of Certificate Management Protocol (CMP) is certificate management in terms of revocation and status.

d. EST

This is incorrect. EST uses TLS as the transport security layer for certificate provision, and the smart meters do not natively support TLS.

If you have answered this question correctly, you have scored one point.

Email #8

From: Mich Fara-Day

To: CCDE Candidate

Subject: Dynamic Routing

Hi.

Thanks for your help with the security side, I'm going to get our security guys to fully design the PKI. It has occurred to me we don't have any routing defined for the WAN-to-co-lo design. I initially thought we'd just run static routes, but I'd rather run a dynamic routing protocol to provide additional flexibility and resilience as we scale out and add multiple routing devices to remove existing single points of failure. I was going to ask you to evaluate a bunch of protocols, but I'm going to save you the bother, as our team members only have experience with OSPF. It's going to be too much of a learning curve for them to learn a new protocol, so we'll just bump up their knowledge from V2 to V3 to accommodate the IPv6. I did ask them if we needed to bother with areas for the routing, and their eyes glazed over, so this one's on you. Can you have a think and let us know which OSPF design is going to be optimal for us? From the co-lo network we will just have a default route pointing to the co-lo edge firewall to reach the meters.

Rgds,

Mich Fara-Day
CTO Squid Energy

Question 14

Which of the following OSPF WAN designs would be most suitable for Squid to provide dynamic routing from the regions into the co-lo environment to discover IPv6 prefixes assigned to the smart meters? (Choose one.)

Requirements/constraints from supplied documentation:

I initially thought we'd just run static routes, but I'd rather run a dynamic routing protocol to provide additional flexibility and resilience as we scale out and add multiple routing devices to remove existing single points of failure.

In terms of infrastructure devices at our disposal, we have 10Gbps routers with six interfaces and 10Gbps VPN routers with four interfaces. The VPN routers are capable of terminating 500,000 VPNs connections, and we have firewalls that are VPN compatible with 4x 10Gbps interfaces and can also terminate up to 500,000 VPNs.

All routers and firewalls can run OSPF and BGP with dual-stack IPv4 and IPv6.

Provide dynamic routing from the regions into the co-lo environment to discover IPv6 prefixes assigned to the smart meters.

From the co-lo network, we will just have a default route pointing to the co-lo edge firewall to reach the meters.

a.

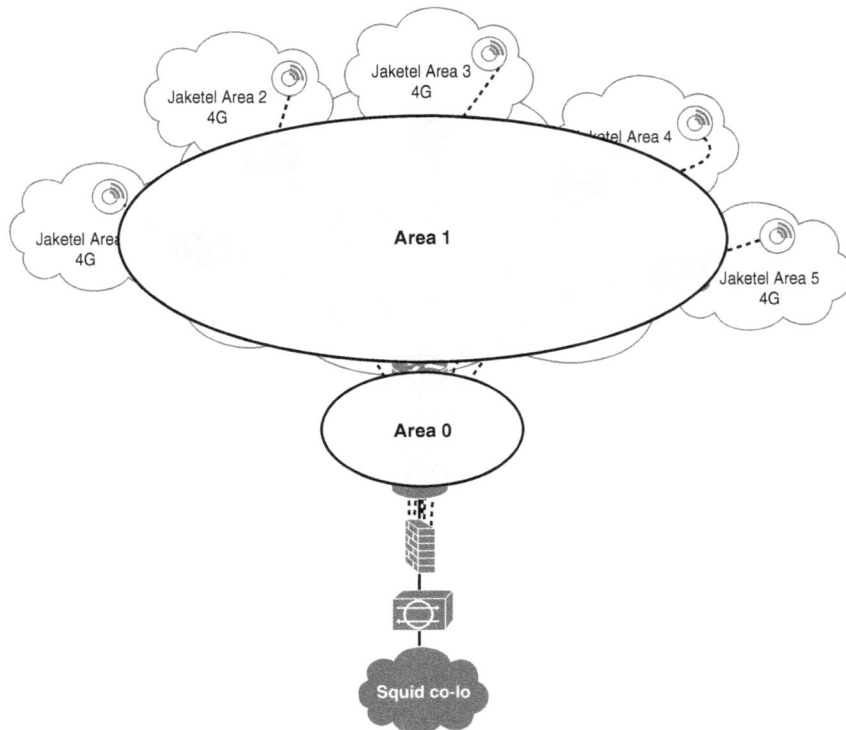

This is incorrect. This one can be ruled out quickly because Area 0 is provisioned between the Jaketel 6PE and the router terminating the connectivity into the co-lo. The overlay IPsec VPN traffic is running through these underlay devices. As such, they wouldn't have visibility of the prefixes assigned to each region/APN. The underlay is purely providing connectivity for the IPsec tunnels. OSPF terminates on the edge router in the co-lo in this option and not the firewalls where the IPsec VPN connectivity is provided from. As such, this has more use as an underlay network design and would assist in dynamically learning IPsec tunnel endpoints as opposed to IPv6 prefixes assigned to smart meters in each region.

b.

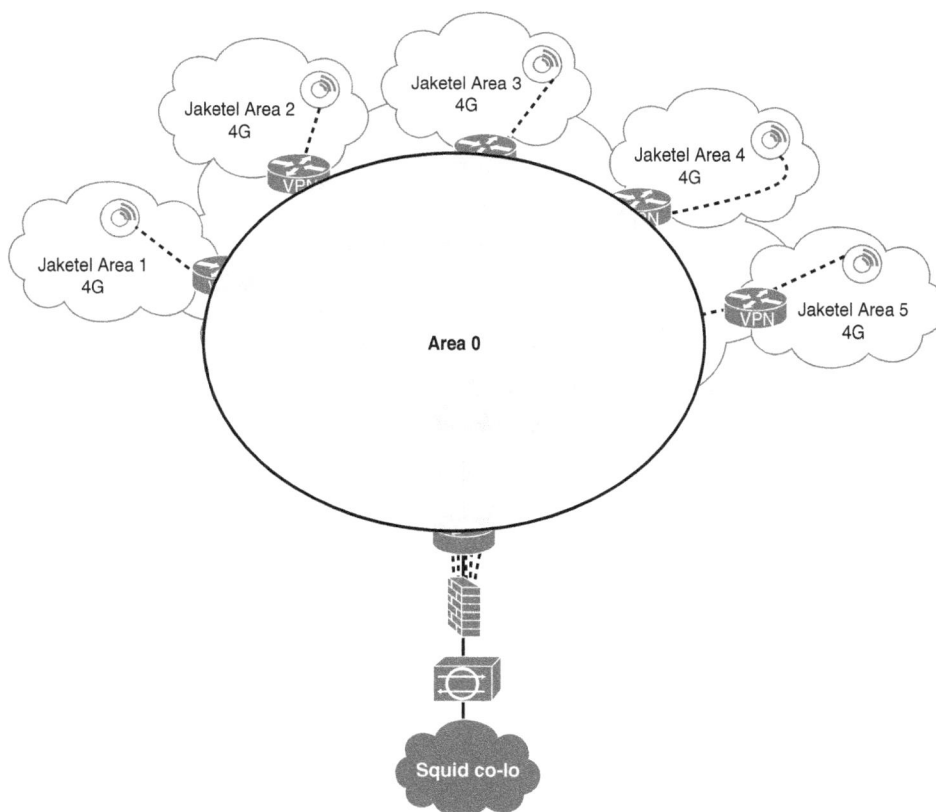

This is incorrect. This can also quickly be ruled out because a single Area 0 is provisioned throughout the entire network. This wouldn't facilitate summarization or scale. Similarly, the overlay IPsec VPN traffic is running through the underlay infrastructure devices. As such, they wouldn't have visibility of IPv6 prefixes assigned to the meters in each region, as OSPF terminates on the edge router in the co-lo and not the firewall, which is the IPsec VPN tunnel endpoint.

c.

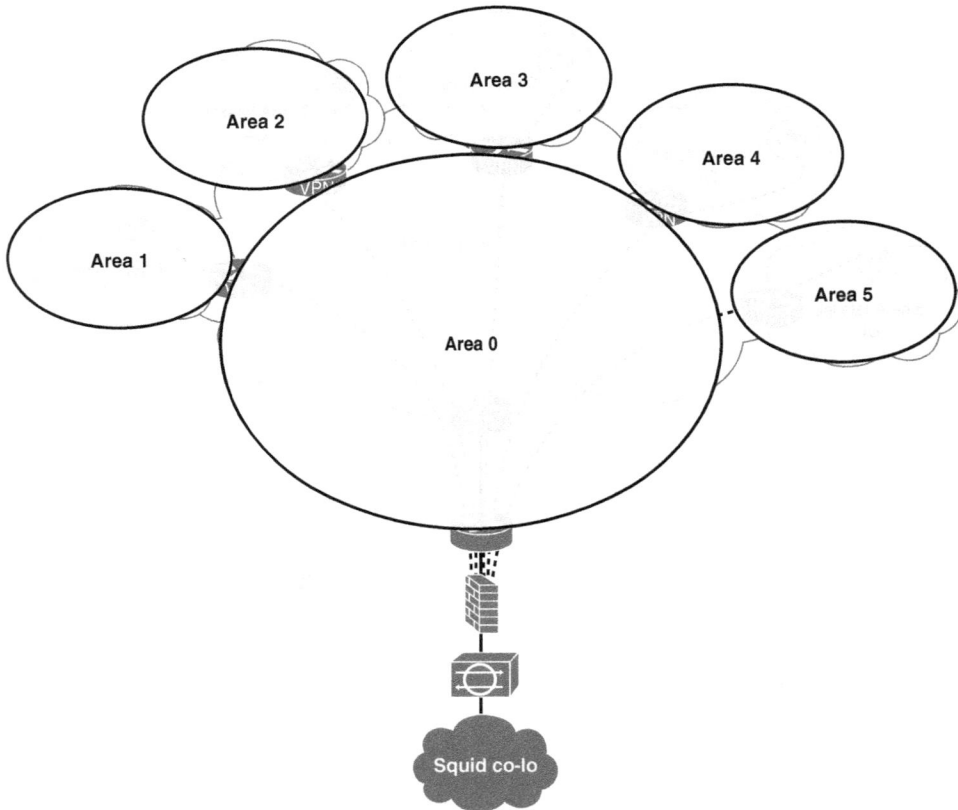

This is incorrect. Hierarchy has been introduced with separate areas per region, but the overlay IPsec VPN traffic is running through the underlay infrastructure devices. As such, they wouldn't have visibility of IPv6 prefixes assigned to the meters in each region, as OSPF terminates on the edge router in the co-lo and not the firewall, which is the IPsec VPN tunnel endpoint.

d.

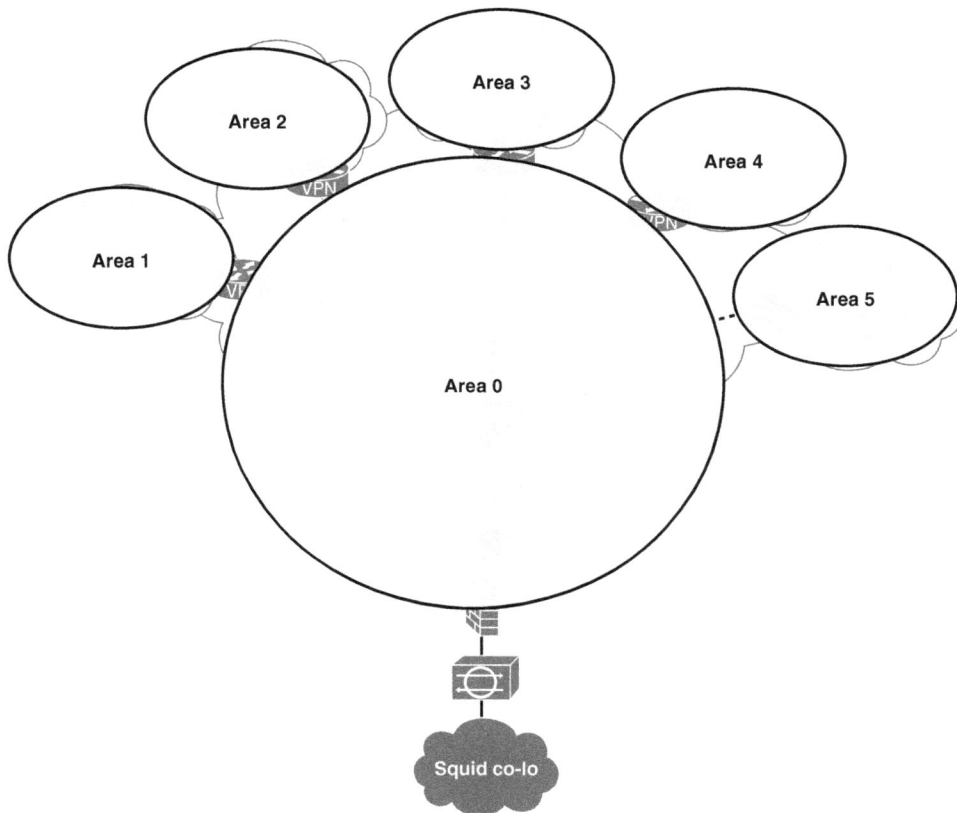

This is the optimal answer. Because the overlay IPsec VPN tunnels from the VPN edge routers in each region terminate on the co-lo firewall, the OSPF network needs to follow this overlay model in order to advertise the meter prefixes from each region. The OSPF areas follow the regions, allowing for hierarchy and facilitating summarization. The IPsec VPN region routers are a natural choice for ABRs where the summarization of each region/APN can occur. The underlay network wouldn't actually necessarily be running OSPF in this topology, and the co-lo firewall would simply need to be able to route to IPsec VPN tunnel endpoints, which are the VPN edge routers in the regions over the Jaketel MPLS network, which is effectively the underlay in this topology.

e.

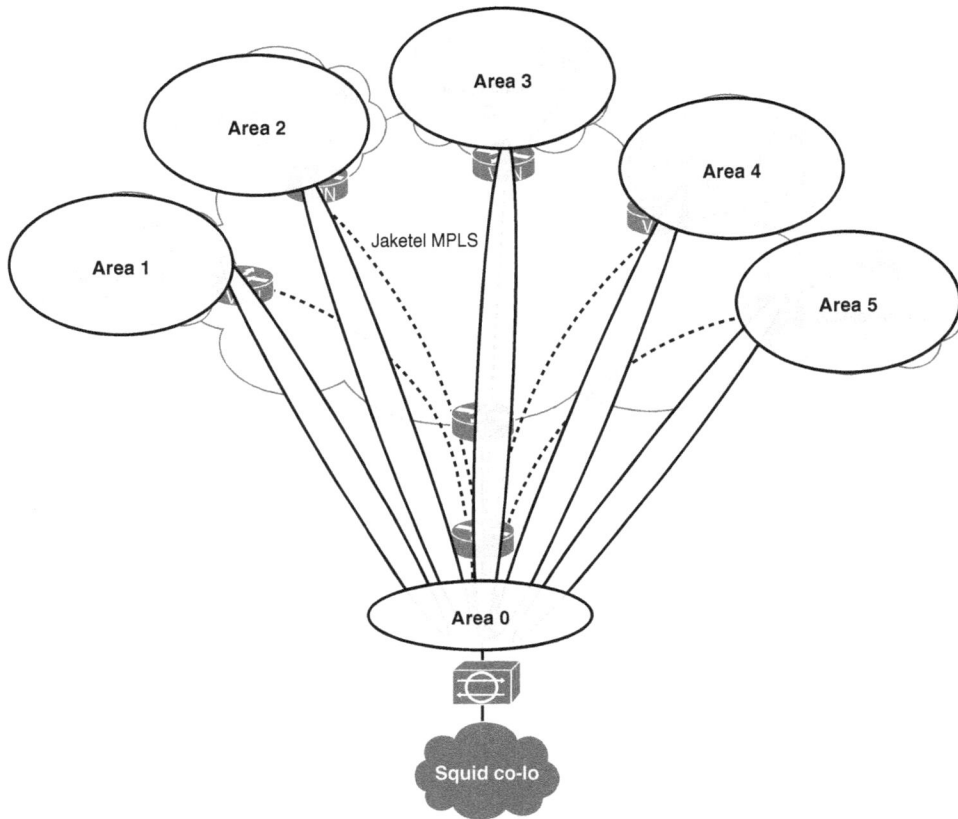

This is a suboptimal answer. This is very similar to Answer D in terms of overlay, but the co-lo firewall is now the ABR. The design choice here is, would you really want a firewall controlling the entire OSPF network and be responsible for summarization into and out of area? If the IPsec VPN tunnels terminated onto a high-powered router in the co-lo instead of the firewall, this might be a good design choice in comparison to Answer D.

Did this question really make you think about underlays and overlays and evaluate optimal ABR placement? If it did or if it has stimulated further research, then it has been a good exercise to go through to focus on the why, which is so crucial in the CCDE. If you have answered this question correctly, you have scored two points.

Question 15

If Squid decides to use separate OSPF areas per region, which area type should these areas be set to? (Choose one.)

Requirements/constraints from supplied documentation: N/A

a. Normal area

This is incorrect. A normal area would be a good choice for an area with multiple OSPF routers and flexibility for connectivity options going forward, but from the information presented to date, each area will not have any additional links to different networks and simply requires an ABR to reach Area 0 and the Squid co-lo area. A normal area will also have multiple LSAs propagated between the area and Area 0. As such, without further measures such as summarization, there is a distinct possibility that SPF (full or incremental) would be run more frequently than required based on a change outside of the local area.

b. Stub area

This is a suboptimal answer. A stub area is a good starting point for an area with no external connectivity and a ABR link into Area 0 with the known default route propagated from the ABR into the stub area. Type 3 LSA routes are, however, generated into a stub area, which wouldn't necessarily be required in the Squid OSPF topology, so Answer D is a better design choice here.

c. NSSA

This is incorrect. There is no requirement for redistribution from an external routing protocol requiring ASBRs within Squid's topology for the regions/areas.

d. Totally stubby area

This is the optimal answer. As detailed in the explanation to Answer B, a stub area suits this topology, but taking the default route concept one stage further and removing any summary LSA Type 3s (as well as Type 5s) into the area provides an efficient OSPF network and will reduce the SPF (full and partial) throughout the network by effectively reducing the state in the topology. In other networks, totally stubby areas can provide suboptimal routing to the ABR as a consequence of removing the Type 3 LSAs, but this wouldn't be an issue within Squid's topology, which would only really have a pair of ABRs in each region/area once resiliency was introduced (as opposed to having 50 OSPF routers within the area).

If you have answered this question correctly, you have scored one point. If you selected Answer B, award yourself half a point.

Question 16

What would be a good design choice to enhance default OSPF stability, efficiency, and convergence when Squid introduces future resilience and deploys dual ABR routers connecting into multiple regions/APNs?

Requirements/constraints from supplied documentation:

Enhance default OSPF stability, efficiency and convergence.

It sounds obvious, but the key to answering this and every question in the CCDE lab is a full understanding of the question. You are asked to enhance default stability, efficiency, and convergence. This question, then, is really about optimization of the OSPF network instead of asking how to purely provide fast convergence, for example.

a. Configuring link-state incremental SPF

This is incorrect. This feature builds on partial SPF runs and would just recalculate a part of a tree that has changed, enhancing convergence. This might be a good choice if you are informed of multiple SPF runs causing an issue, but this is not relevant in this scenario.

b. Running multi-hop BFD over the VPN links

This is incorrect. Multi-hop BFD could be a good design choice for VPN links provisioned in an overlay when part of the underlay failing might not signal to OSPF, and thus OSPF could not detect the failure and propagate the event in order to converge, but this option really only provides a convergence benefit.

c. Configuring the VPN links as point-to-point OSPF network links

This is incorrect. Configuring links as a point-to-point network type in OSPF is beneficial on broadcast media such as Ethernet, and this will enhance convergence as there would be no DR or BDR election; however, the VPN links would typically use tunnel interfaces with GRE to transport the required multicast for OSPF to function and would by default already be point-to-point network type links.

d. Configuring summarization of areas toward Area 0

This is correct. Summarizing at the ABRs would significantly reduce the LSA flooding. Also, the LSDB and routing tables would be reduced, which improves CPU utilization and memory usage. In comparison to the alternative options, the summarization provides benefits that will enhance the overall stability, efficiency, and convergence, and this is key to scaling within OSPF networks.

If you have answered this question correctly, you have scored one point.

Email #9

From: Mich Fara-Day

To: CCDE Candidate

Subject: OSPFv3 Areas and IPv6 Prefix Allocation

Hi.

Thanks for your help with the OSPF WAN design. We decided to go with totally stubby areas and the topology outlined below. I was a little confused with underlays and overlays but understand where the ABRs are best positioned for us to scale.

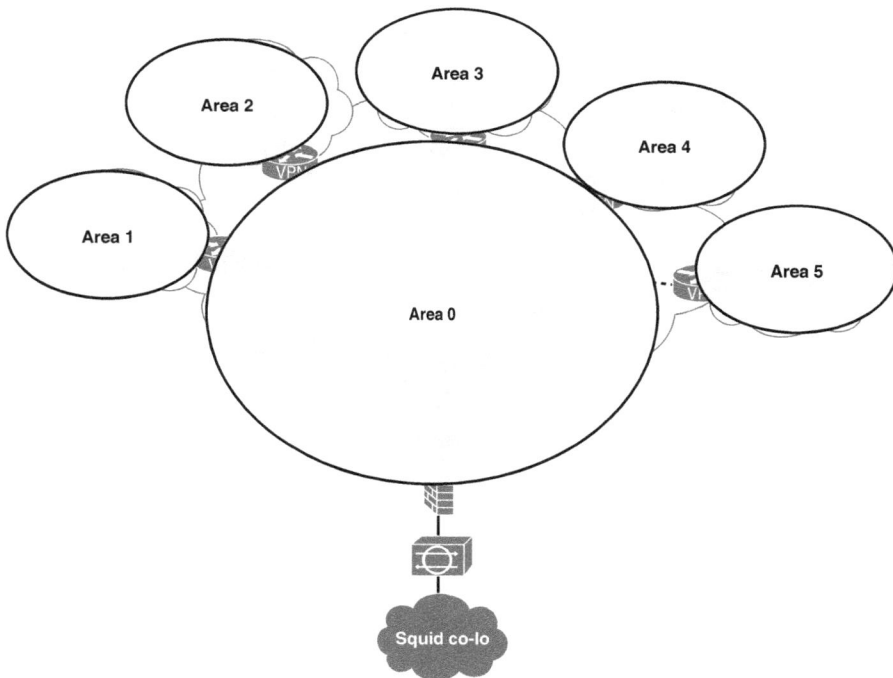

We just received our prefix back from RIPE that Jaketel has passed onto us. It got me thinking, what the hell happened to IPv5? Anyways, here it is:

2022:ccde::/32

Jaketel advised that, with such a large prefix, we would benefit from configuring summarization in the network—can you let me know how we should do that?

Rgds,

Mich Fara-Day
CTO Squid Energy

Question 17

Which of the following options provides optimal summarization for Squid from each OSPF area detailed within the OSPF topology in the email? (Choose one.)

Requirements/constraints from supplied documentation:

1. We have five regions/areas, as you know, but we want to have the ability to scale to 256 max if we expand into Europe in the future.

2. We want to have the ability to have up to 256 APNs in each region.

3. We want to run up to 65,000 smart meters per APN.

4. We want each smart meter to have an individual /64 prefix.

5. Smart meters use a form of unnumbered IPv6 addressing from their main /64 prefix over the APN, so we don't need to worry about any prefixes for the APN/WAN. The /64 prefix will also be used for the HAN for displays and any other devices that require access to the meter or further connectivity to our systems.

a. Summarize at the region level on the ABR /32s.

This is incorrect. This can quickly be ruled out because the whole allocation is /32, so summarization will need to be less than the entire /32.

b. Summarize at the region level on the ABR /40s.

This is correct. As per requirements, using 8 bits from 32 to summarize with a /40 will provide a range of 256 APNs (within a single region), which can cover 65,000 smart meters per APN. This ties in perfectly for summarization. One range command would be required on the ABR to cover the entire OSPF area.

c. Summarize at the region level on the ABR /48s.

This is incorrect. This can quickly be ruled out because a /48 summary would only cover one APN, with up to 65,000x /64 prefixes.

d. Summarize at the region level on the ABR /56s.

This is incorrect. This can quickly be ruled out because a /56 summary would only cover less than one APN, with up to only 256x /64 prefixes.

e. Summarize at the APN level on the ABR /40s.

This is incorrect. This can quickly be ruled out because a /40 would provide summarization of up to 16.7 million /64 meter prefixes and doesn't provide any summarization for regions or APNs.

f. Summarize at the APN level on the ABR /48s.

This is a suboptimal answer. A /48 does actually summarize the 65,000 smart meters in a single APN; however, if you have five APNs in a region, you would need 5x /48 summarization statements and would therefore need to manually add further statements if more APNs were added to the region, so this is not an optimal approach.

If you have answered this question correctly, you have scored one point. If you selected Answer F, award yourself half a point.

Question 18

Squid has decided to summarize at the region level on the ABRs using /40 prefixes to cover all APNs and associated meter /64 prefixes with a single summary statement per ABR for the entire region. Which of the following ranges should be used for the five regions for the UK deployment of smart meters? (Choose one.)

Requirements/constraints from supplied documentation:

We have five regions/areas, as you know, but we want to have the ability to scale to 256 max if we expand into Europe in the future.

a.

Region 1 (OSPF area 1) – 2022:ccde::/40

Region 2 (OSPF area 2) – 2022:ccde:0100::/40

Region 3 (OSPF area 3) – 2022:ccde:0200::/40

Region 4 (OSPF area 4) – 2022:ccde:0300::/40

Region 5 (OSPF area 5) – 2022:ccde:0400::/40

This is correct. This is the optimal summarization, and you should see that you can create up to 256 regions from this.

b.

Region 1 (OSPF area 1) – 2022:ccde::/40

Region 2 (OSPF area 2) – 2022:ccde:0001::/40

Region 3 (OSPF area 3) – 2022:ccde:0002::/40

Region 4 (OSPF area 4) – 2022:ccde:0003::/40

Region 5 (OSPF area 5) – 2022:ccde:0004::/40

This is incorrect. This is an example of /48 summarization and not /40.

c.

Region 1 (OSPF area 1) – 2022:ccde:0001::/40

Region 2 (OSPF area 2) – 2022:ccde:0002::/40

Region 3 (OSPF area 3) – 2022:ccde:0003::/40

Region 4 (OSPF area 4) – 2022:ccde:0004::/40

Region 5 (OSPF area 5) – 2022:ccde:0005::/40

This is incorrect. This is a further example of /48 summarization and not /40. It does tie in nicely with the OSPF area numbers, though, so you could end up being led to select this option if you're under time pressure.

d.

Region 1 (OSPF area 1) – 2022:ccde::/40

Region 2 (OSPF area 2) – 2022:ccde:0000:0001:/40

Region 3 (OSPF area 3) – 2022:ccde:0000:0002:/40

Region 4 (OSPF area 4) – 2022:ccde:0000:0003:/40

Region 5 (OSPF area 5) – 2022:ccde:0000:0004:/40

This is incorrect. This is an example of /64 summarization and not /40.

If you have answered this question correctly, you have scored one point.

Email #10

From: Mich Fara-Day

To: CCDE Candidate

Subject: Application Load Balancing

Hi.

Thanks for summarizing! We're going to reserve the first subnet (2022:ccde:0000::/40) and then align with regions, so we will actually go with the following, which will aid in troubleshooting and allocation, and, above all, keep things simple!

Region 1 (OSPF area 1) – 2022:ccde:0100::/40

Region 2 (OSPF area 2) – 2022:ccde:0200::/40

Region 3 (OSPF area 3) – 2022:ccde:0300::/40

Region 4 (OSPF area 4) – 2022:ccde:0400::/40

Region 5 (OSPF area 5) – 2022:ccde:0500::/40

So we're looking good on the network; however, I've had the members of the application team in a workshop this morning, and they have explained to me that initially they believed the meters would be coming back to a central server system called SMARTS that would accommodate all the meters. We have planned sending their data every five to ten mins, at random intervals. Bit of a curveball—they have completed their own load testing in a lab environment and, when they scale the figures up, they believe the system will be overloaded. They have requested we provide some load balancing to spread the load to five separate servers behind a frontend VIP address that we push to the meters over an API through the encrypted links you have designed. They stated we could still run a single non-load-balanced system, but this would require serious upgrading of existing systems, and this would incur a three-month delay and cost would be double that of an appliance-based load-balanced solution with the additional lower spec servers. It's a little frustrating this late in the day to get this requirement, as we don't have the budget approved, and it will be difficult to get the sign-off for additional spend. They have told me it's effectively a simplex traffic flow from the meter to the VIP of the application, which registers power usage. Each data packet from the meter apparently includes the unique meter reference (customer ID) and required data in a UDP format that the application can then forward to backend systems, which are used to generate customer invoices.

The app guys went through some eventualities if the meter fails or has its IPv6 address changed for any reason, and apparently these are non-issues, as the unique meter reference (customer ID) is associated with the customer data and not the source IPv6 address. I've drawn up a picture they made up on my whiteboard. (I would have just sent you a photo of it, but as you know, app guys can't draw anywhere near as well as network guys.)

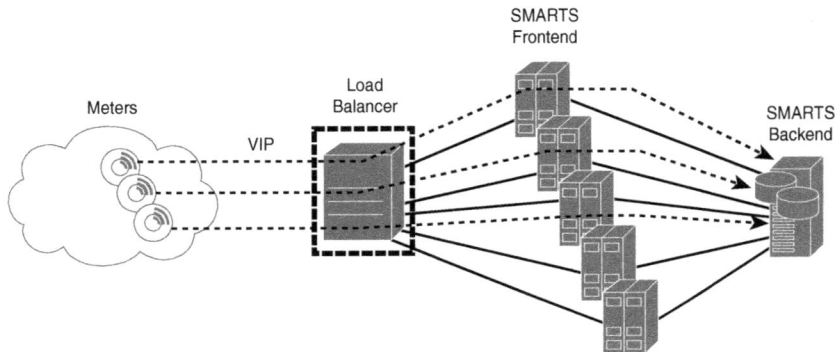

For your info, I've looked into the appliance-based load balancers the app guys mentioned from a well-respected vendor. They can scale to the number of required flows (they support stateful and non-stateful flows, and all features you would expect from a high-end load balancer). We are looking at and support IPv6. The resilience is stated as active/standby, so when one fails, the other takes over, but I think it could be better if we have to use them to have two VIPs that we push out to meters. Kind of alternate APNs or regions for one VIP and the other. This way, we could improve our scale and have the balancers backing each other up, so one is active for one VIP and one for the other while backing up each VIP. Alternatively, the switches in our DC apparently can also provide a basic non-stateful load-balancing mechanism called Traffic Scatter, providing frontend VIPs for L3 and L4 traffic at wire rate and just sending out to servers at the backend based on health/availability of the real server, as the dedicated load balancers do. It looks like they can scale, provide a resilient VIP service, and handle the numbers, and we don't need any license upgrade to enable this. It seems pretty basic in comparison, and they state it supports the VIP frontend, but only Direct Server Return. I need you to recommend which way to go, as this has to work Day 1, and we have to accommodate this change as quickly as we can.

Thanks!

Rgds,

Mich Fara-Day
CTO Squid Energy

Question 19

How can Squid accommodate the load-balancing requirement detailed in the email? (Choose one.)

Requirements/constraints from supplied documentation:

We have planned sending the meters' data every five to ten mins, at random intervals.

They have requested we provide some load balancing to spread the load to five separate servers behind a frontend VIP address that we push to the meters over an API through the encrypted links you have designed. They stated we could still run a single non-load-balanced system, but this would require serious upgrading of existing systems, and this would incur a three-month delay and cost would be double that of an appliance-based load-balanced solution with the additional lower spec servers.

We don't have the budget approved, and it will be difficult to get the sign-off for additional spend. They have told me it's effectively a simplex traffic flow from the meter to the VIP of the application, which registers power usage. Each data packet from the meter apparently includes the unique meter reference (customer ID) and required data in a UDP format that the application can then forward to backend systems, which are used to generate customer invoices.

The app guys went through some eventualities if the meter failed or has its IPv6 address changed for any reason and apparently these are non-issues, as the unique meter reference (customer ID) is associated with the customer data and not the source IPv6 address.

I think it could be better if we have to use them to have two VIPs that we push out to meters. Kind of alternate APNs or regions for one VIP and the other, and this way we could improve our scale and have the balancers backing each other up so one is active for one VIP and one for the other while backing each VIP up.

Alternatively, the switches in our DC apparently can also provide a basic non-stateful load-balancing mechanism called Traffic Scatter, providing frontend VIPs for L3 and L4 traffic at wire rate and just sending out to servers at the backend based on health/availability of the real server, as the dedicated load balancers do. It looks like they can scale, provide a resilient VIP service, and handle the numbers, and we don't need any license upgrade to enable it. It seems pretty basic in comparison, and they state it supports the VIP frontend, but only Direct Server Return. I need you to recommend which way to go, as this has to work Day 1, and we have to accommodate this change as quickly as we can.

a. Use the Traffic Scatter functionality in the existing switches in the DC

This is correct. You should have spotted that the Traffic Scatter function is perfect for the requirements, as well as being a zero-cost option that can forward at wire rate. There would be no changes required to the environment other than configuration of the load-balancing functionality. The fact that the meter flow is simplex (unidirectional) means there is no need for a fully stateful service, with any return traffic flowing back through the same application server because the service is only one way. Also, Direct Server Return (as opposed to through the VIP) isn't an issue for the meter, as it's UDP one-way, similar in operation to an SNMP trap, for example. Just fire and forget. The customer is also looking for a quick solution with minimal spend.

b. Use a pair of dedicated load balancer appliances with a single VIP in active/standby topology

This is incorrect. As well as not being the best choice, the customer has stated that if they went this route, they would want to run in an active/active topology if appliance-based load balancers were used.

c. Use a pair of dedicated load balancers with dual VIPs that provide resiliency for each other

This is a suboptimal answer. The solution would function, but it is not cost-effective and would take time to implement—it does match the operational mode the customer expects, however.

d. Upgrade the system to the single non-load-balanced server to negate the requirement for load balancers

This is incorrect. You are informed of financial and time constraints, which this option would incur and which the customer is keen to avoid on both counts.

If you have answered this question correctly, you have scored one point.

Email #11

From: Mich Fara-Day

To: CCDE Candidate

Subject: HAN Pilot

Hi.

Thanks for the advice on the load balancing. Let's hope the scatter doesn't shatter under load! While you've been busy on the network design, I've had some questions come in from our engineering team about how we should go about setting up the home area network (HAN), which is associated to the smart meters. Obviously, we don't need to set up a network in every consumer's home. This is just the technology that the smart meter uses to communicate with a display unit that gives a real-time reading of the power usage that can be placed wherever the consumer chooses within their home. Apparently, we have options in how to deploy this communications link, which just piggybacks off the /64 IPv6 prefix the meter is assigned, so it's quite straightforward, I believe. (Famous last words!) We want to start a pilot, so if you can assist with the HAN info, that would be great.

Rgds,

Mich Fara-Day
CTO Squid Energy

Question 20

Assist Squid in deciding which is the optimal technology to use for the HAN between the smart meter and the display unit, which would be placed within the consumer's property to view real-time power usage provided by the smart meter. Fill in the protocol from the following list to match the associated distance for that protocol, as listed in the table.

Standard Zigbee 2.4GHz

Dual-band Zigbee 2.4GHz/868MHz

Bluetooth

Ethernet CAT5

2.4GHz Wi-Fi

The protocols and associated distances are as follows:

Protocol	Distance
Standard 2.4GHz Zigbee	Less than 20m
Dual-band Zigbee 2.4GHz/868MHz	Less than 30m
Bluetooth	Less than 10m
Ethernet CAT5	100m
2.4GHz Wi-Fi	50m

If you have answered this question correctly, you have scored one point.

Question 21

Squid decided to implement a standard Zigbee service on the HAN network for the pilot and encountered interference in all areas of the pilot location and lower-than-expected range in areas of the pilot location that incorporated thicker-than-average walls. It is now concerned this could be representative of the user experience of the majority of consumers in the production rollout. Which of the following changes would you recommend in order to improve the HAN network usability while not introducing a management overhead on the running of the service? (Choose one.)

Requirements/constraints from supplied documentation:

Squid decided to implement a standard Zigbee service on the HAN network for the pilot and encountered interference in all areas of the pilot location and lower-than-expected range in areas of the pilot location that incorporated thicker-than-average walls.

Improve the HAN network usability while not introducing any management overhead on the running of the service.

Feature	Meter 2: Zenith V3
HAN Connectivity	Zigbee, dual-band Zigbee, Wi-Fi, Ethernet, Bluetooth

Dual-band Zigbee 2.4GHz/868MHz.

a. Change the Wi-Fi operating channel on consumers' home networks.

This is incorrect. While it might improve interference due to 2.4GHz Wi-Fi networks that could be overlapping with Zigbee, which operates in the same spectrum, it wouldn't solve the "thick wall" issue. Similarly, it's not a sound approach to expect your customers to work around the issue, and it's clearly going to introduce some admin overhead dealing with support calls only to have Squid's staff trying to guide the consumer through a raft of different Wi-Fi vendors' equipment in order to change channels.

b. Change the Zigbee operating channel on smart meters.

This is incorrect. While it might provide a better user experience by selecting a channel that doesn't have interference, this approach would involve administrative overhead for Squid's staff, which they are keen to avoid.

c. Change Zigbee to 5G for the HAN rollout.

This is incorrect. 5G is a WAN uplink option on the smart meter and not a compatible option for the HAN.

d. Switch to dual-band Zigbee for the HAN rollout.

This is correct. Dual-band Zigbee can operate with dual frequencies (2.4GHz and 868MHz). The 868MHz frequency will not overlap with 2.4GHz Wi-Fi networks and has the additional advantage of being more reliable through "thicker walls" due to the lower operating frequency.

e. Conduct a wireless survey in each consumer location and deploy the optimal technology based on the results.

This is categorically incorrect. This would cause huge administrative overhead and associated cost, which would result in a nonstandard rollout and thus create significant support and deployment issues.

f. Switch to Bluetooth for the HAN rollout.

Bluetooth might work around local interference issues, but the technology is only suited to very short distances. As such, it wouldn't cure the reported "thick wall" issue and would be a poor technology choice, which limits the display unit to extremely close proximity to the smart meter, and this would typically not be feasible in a real-world deployment.

If you have answered this question correctly, you have scored one point.

Email #12

From: Mich Fara-Day

To: CCDE Candidate

Subject: Implementation

Hi.

Thanks for the advice on the HAN. We will get the team to complete the pilot on your recommendation of dual-band Zigbee. While the team finishes up, I need you to help with an implementation plan to enable our service. Let's get the service up and running!

Rgds,

Mich Fara-Day
CTO Squid Energy

Question 22

To assist Squid with delivery of its service, arrange the implementation tasks in sequence order.

The correct order is as follows:

1. Order MPLS connectivity from Jaketel to co-lo. Order smart meters/VPN routers/ firewalls and IPS/IDS and PKI infrastructure from suppliers.

   Any lead-time-associated tasks have to be initiated within the first steps of the implementation plan. This task could also be Step 2.

2. Order Jaketel APN service and 4G SIM cards for smart meters.

   This task could also be Step 1, as it will incur some lead time.

3. Install VPN edge routers in Jaketel regions and enable Jaketel MPLS service between regions to central PE.

   This task must be completed after Step 1 and naturally occurs after Step 2.

4. Install CE router for Jaketel MPLS service within the co-lo.

   This task cannot be completed prior to Step 3 when the MPLS service is operational.

5. Install firewalls and IPS/IDS infrastructure devices within the co-lo.

   This task must be completed after Step 1. It could, however, be completed prior to Step 3 to ready the co-lo for external connectivity.

6. Enable PKI infrastructure and application load balancing within Squid co-lo.

   This task must be completed after Step 1 and must be completed prior to Step 7 to ensure the IPsec VPN connections can be established.

7. Configure IPsec tunnels from firewalls to VPN routers.

   This task must be completed after Step 1 and must be completed after Step 6 when the PKI infrastructure is live.

8. Configure the OSPF network from firewalls to region VPN router.

   This task must be completed after Step 1 and must be completed after Step 5 when the firewalls are live. It makes sense to configure the IPsec tunnels in Step 7 before enabling OSPF over them.

9. Board smart meters to Squid's meter-reading application.

   This step cannot be completed until all the other steps are completed when full network connectivity is provisioned between smart meters and the co-lo environment.

If you have answered this question correctly, you have scored 2 points. Partial marks can be awarded for specific sequencing.

Email #13

From: Mich Fara-Day

To: CCDE Candidate

Subject: We're live!

Hi.

Thanks for your help. We're finally live! I was expecting the directors to be really excited this Monday morning, but they were fairly neutral about the whole thing, as it has been an expensive project. It definitely brought me down to earth after a long weekend, but we couldn't have done it without your help.

One thing we didn't fully consider, however, is if a customer migrates away from our service to another energy supplier. It appears that they cannot benefit from the government grant for the meter more than once, so they are stuck with the meter we provisioned on their behalf or will need to pay a premium when onboarded with a new supplier for a new meter. Can you have a think about how we can best migrate the meter onto a new provider's network so we have a process in place when this comes up?

Rgds,

Mich Fara-Day
CTO Squid Energy

Question 23

Which would be the best process for migration of a customer switching supplier and moving the smart meter away to a new supplier with minimal effort for Squid? (Choose one.)

Requirements/constraints from supplied documentation:

Moving the smart meter away to a new supplier with minimal effort for Squid.

I did read about an Internet-based attack in the Ukraine power network some time ago, and that cannot be permitted here. I'll need you to make it as secure as possible; therefore, everything should be encrypted outside of our own DC.

a. Have the new supplier's onsite electrical engineer factory reset the smart meter and install a new SIM card configured for new supplier at time of cutover.

This is the optimal answer. Based on the alternatives, this requires the minimal amount of effort on Squid's part as it wouldn't need to send out an engineer and would simply need to offboard the customer on its system. The new supplier would pick up the overhead and deal with the commissioning of the meter onto its own network.

b. Apply a gateway between Squid's co-lo and major supplier networks to allow traffic to traverse between Squid and the new supplier's network for meter readings for migrated customers.

This is incorrect. If this was a separate enterprise that managed a single country-wide smart meter network that then partnered with major suppliers to access consumers' meters, this approach would be feasible; however, this is Squid's own private WAN, and there would be numerous security concerns with this approach.

c. Mail out new 4G SIM cards for the consumer to swap over, which will be configured to connect to the new provider's smart meter network.

This is incorrect—and Squid could end up with a lawsuit when the consumer accidently electrocutes themselves!

d. Provide Internet access to the Squid co-lo network or modify the private APNs to public APNs with local Internet access so new suppliers can route to the meters using the IPv6 globally unique addressing structure configured on the meters for direct meter reading access over an API call.

This is incorrect. Squid requires everything outside of its co-lo to be encrypted and does not want the meters to be visible on the Internet.

If you have answered this question correctly, you have scored one point.

Email #14

From: Mich Fara-Day

To: CCDE Candidate

Subject: EVs

Hi.

The new system is working really well. We've managed to free up our field staff, etc., and automate a lot of deployment for consumers who are keen to get a smart-metered service. The board believes we now have the capacity to expand our offerings, so we're setting up some marketing to deploy our own EV charging points for vehicles at consumer locations. We see two types of customers—one already has the smart meter, and we can offer incentives for them to buy a charging point from us, and one who doesn't use us as a supplier at all, and we set them up from scratch. Either way, we need to have an option to connect each user type to our systems in the most cost-effective manner.

The EV charging points have the same specification as the Zenith V3 meters we are using for WAN and HAN, and you should still have the specification if you need any data.

We envisage the EVs using the same application as the smart meters in the co-lo with identical traffic flow and security requirements.

Rgds,

Mich Fara-Day
CTO Squid Energy

Question 24

Which of the following options provide optimal connectivity for the new EV charging points to Squid's central system for billing for each customer type? (Choose two.)

Requirements/constraints from supplied documentation:

We see two types of customers—one already has the smart meter, and we can offer incentives for them to buy a charging point from us, and one that doesn't use us as a supplier at all, and we set them up from scratch. Either way, we need to have an option to connect each user type to our systems in the most cost-effective manner.

The EV charger points have the same specification as the Zenith V3 meters we are using for WAN and HAN, and you should still have the specification if you need any data.

We envisage the EVs to use the same application as the smart meters in the co-lo with identical traffic flow and security requirements.

Smart meters use a form of unnumbered IPv6 addressing from their main /64 prefix over the APN, so we don't need to worry about any prefixes for the APN/WAN. The /64 prefix will also be used for the HAN for displays and any other devices that require access to the meter or further connectivity to our systems.

We will get the team to complete the pilot on your recommendation of dual-band Zigbee.

a. Existing customers should have the EV charging point connected to the existing HAN provided for the smart meter using dual-band Zigbee for connectivity.

This is correct. You are informed the EV charging point has the same traffic flow requirements as the smart meter and can connect to the HAN using dual-band Zigbee as selected for the pilot. You are also informed that the /64 prefix assigned to the smart meter will also be used for the HAN and any other device that may require onward connectivity to the Squid systems. This is the most cost-effective solution for an existing customer by making use of existing connectivity.

b. Existing customers should have the EV charging point use a new cellular connection within the same APN as the existing meter.

This is incorrect. If a HAN was not available, however, then this would be applicable.

c. Existing customers should have the EV charging point use a new cellular connection within a separate Jaketel APN and new IPsec connection from the edge APN to the co-lo dedicated for aggregating charging point traffic to the co-lo.

This is incorrect. There is no benefit in creating a separate system when the security and traffic requirements for smart meters and EV charging points are identical. This would create additional complexity and cost.

d. New customers should have the EV charging point use a new cellular connection within the same APN as used for meters in the local area.

This is correct. Clearly a new customer will need cellular connectivity, and due to identical security and traffic flow requirements, there is no reason to create a new separate APN for EV charging points, and the existing APN created for smart meters should be utilized.

e. New customers should have the EV charging point use a new cellular connection within a separate Jaketel APN and a new IPsec connection from the edge APN to the co-lo dedicated to aggregating charging point traffic to the co-lo.

This is incorrect. There is no benefit in creating a separate system when the security and traffic requirements for smart meters and EV charging points are identical. This would create additional complexity and cost.

f. New customers should have the EV charging point use the consumer's own broadband connection over a Wi-Fi connection to connect to a newly provisioned Internet VPN service to access the Squid central systems hosted in a DMZ to maximize end-to-end security.

This is incorrect. Piggybacking onto a customer's Internet connection (assuming they even have one) is simply asking for trouble. Similarly, there is additional complexity for the new VPN and any systems required to terminate the traffic into a DMZ. Therefore, this answer can quickly be ruled out.

If you have answered this question correctly, you have scored one point.

Question 25

If Squid creates a service for public EV charging points in public locations such as car parks and shopping malls, should the connectivity solution differ from a new customer EV charging point for a consumer? (Choose one.)

Requirements/constraints from supplied documentation: N/A

a. The solution should be identical.

This is incorrect. You would really be making an assumption to state the solution would be identical for a public service. This would no longer be a known static consumer who has signed up to a service and would be multiple users using multiple payment types, which would typically require a different set of functional requirements, including PCI, and may require a dedicated WAN or DMZ. Remember, if you find you are having to make an assumption, then something is not right.

b. The solution should be reevaluated for this use case.

This is the correct answer. As detailed in the explanation for Answer A, this is a completely different use case, and it would be far safer to reevaluate rather than assume the existing system could be used.

If you have answered this question correctly, you have scored half a point.

Email #15

From: Mich Fara-Day

To: CCDE Candidate

Subject: EVs

Hi.

Thanks for your feedback on public charging. While we weigh everything, we are considering an option to allow users of public charging points to use a "call home" feature on the charging point to allow Squid help desk users to communicate directly with consumers who have difficulty entering credit card details on the system or who are having difficulty using charging apps compatible with the solution. Our devops team believes it can create an app for a consumer that can connect to the charger over Bluetooth and allow the user to talk directly to the help desk over our secure WAN network (a form of push to talk). This could be a great way to showcase our technology and innovation and increase our UX and customer service reviews. Devops thinks it can get a beta out in two weeks. We can modify a call center application to accept voice if we need to quickly, so we're keen to test this on a pilot as soon as we have the beta. For the pilot, we will connect the EV charger up identically as if it was a smart meter for a new customer and perform our testing.

We appreciate all of your help on the design, and we can carry on with the charging points when you move on!

Rgds,

Mich Fara-Day
CTO Squid Energy

Question 26

How would you recommend Squid facilitate the voice connectivity requirement for the pilot? (Choose one.)

Requirements/constraints from supplied documentation:

A company called Jaketel offers 4G coverage to 94% of the UK and can provide us with data-only SIMs that we can fit into the smart meters we deploy.

Our devops team believes it can create an app for a consumer that can connect to the charger over Bluetooth and allow the user to talk directly to the help desk over our secure WAN network (a form of push to talk). This could be a great way to showcase our technology and innovation and increase our UX and customer service reviews.

Devops thinks it can get a beta out in two weeks. We can modify a call center application to accept voice if we need to quickly, so we're keen to test this on a pilot as soon as we have the beta.

a. Simply list a direct-dial number and EV charging meter location code on the charger for the consumer to dial in to the call center with their own cell phone.

This is incorrect. It might be a simple solution, and possibly the most sensible, but it doesn't reflect the requirement to showcase Squid's innovation and desire to use its own network for the communication channel.

b. Set up a push-to-talk feature on the EV charger that piggybacks voice on the 4G SIM card to route voice over the Jaketel cellular connection as a normal cellular voice call, which is forwarded to the help desk.

This is incorrect. The 4G cellular service provisioned via Jaketel is data only, as detailed in previous exhibits.

c. Use a push-to-talk feature on the EV charger for a VoIP call that can be routed over the existing data network connectivity to the call center application within the Squid co-lo and prioritize voice traffic with DSCP EF.

This is a suboptimal answer. It might feel like the correct approach to mark voice traffic with EF, but this would only be of value if the entire WAN was configured with QoS and congestion was reported to be an issue within the network. Squid is looking to deploy the solution ASAP, and it would take time to deploy QoS through-out the WAN, if even feasible within the cellular areas.

d. Use a push-to-talk feature on the EV charger for a VoIP call that can be routed over the existing data network connectivity to the call center application within the Squid DC network, without any form of voice QoS.

This is the optimal answer. It meets the requirements to showcase innovation and would make use of the existing WAN network. There is no evidence that QoS is actually required for the pilot, and it would likely take more than two weeks to deploy QoS throughout the network, if it was even possible on the cellular network. Squid could evaluate the call quality during the pilot.

If you have answered this question correctly, you have scored one point.

Summary

Although this lab is primarily based on IoT, you can see that you don't actually need to be an expert in this field, as long as you have an understanding of the technology as outlined in the V3 Blueprint. You should be able to rely on your routing and core subject knowledge to be successful in this lab. IoT is fairly complex and covers a huge area of connectivity requirements, with scale and security at the forefront, so it's an ideal scenario for CCDE practice.

If you haven't worked on an IoT design previously, then hopefully you have gained some further insight and can research specific areas that may need strengthening. As per other labs it is crucial to connect with the scenario and get into the flow of it in order to be successful. If you do want to score yourself, there was a maximum of 28.5 points available in this lab. If you scored over 20 points (approx. 70%), you have a very good chance of being successful in your CCDE exam.

Chapter 3

CCDE Practice Lab 3: Bank of Jersey

Bank of Jersey

This final practice lab is the "area of expertise" module, which covers specific technology areas in conjunction with core module technologies. This would be the final lab exam in the afternoon session that you would select during the actual exam. The CCDE V3 areas of expertise are as follows:

- On-prem and Cloud Services

- Workforce Mobility

- Large-Scale Networks

This practice lab is based on the fictional company Bank of Jersey and has a combination of on-premises hosting and investigation into expansion of service hosting via cloud services.

Practice Lab Navigation

- Read, make notes, and highlight the background information for any relevant information, including constraints you feel might aid a design decision.

- Answer each question before you continue to the next question. Questions have been separated from each other, as additional information can be provided in subsequent questions.

- When you have completed a question, do not return to any previous questions, as you will not have this facility during the lab exam. You may, however, refer to any previous exhibit (email or diagram) that has already been provided.

- Take time to analyze the current environment. You need to absorb the current position and visualize any end goal by connecting with the scenario.

- Do not make assumptions, as all the required information has been provided in order to make an informed decision.

- Consider all information within the background documentation and new information provided by emails to make fact-based decisions.

- Think as an architect and not as a CCIE.

- Why? Focus on the *why*.

- Aim to complete the lab in a two-hour time frame. If you are unable to complete the lab in the recommended time frame, make a note of where you were at the two-hour point to gauge what your score would have been and then continue on with the lab until completion. Do not move on to the review section until you are finished to gain the maximum benefit from the practice lab experience.

Practice Lab

During this practice lab, you are the network architect for the Bank of Jersey.

Document 1: Company Background Information

The Bank of Jersey was formed in 1905 by the founders of the Royal Bank of London—UK. Jersey is located in the English Channel between the UK and France in the Channel Islands and was chosen by the founders as a location to leverage Jersey being a self-governing parliamentary democracy with Crown dependency on the UK. Jersey has its own independent administration as well as legal and financial systems, allowing it to operate separately from the UK, which does, however, provide defense for the island. Jersey enjoys a mature trade-free movement with the UK, which has proved to be mutually beneficial to both countries to date.

The Bank has capitalized over the previous 25 years on Jersey becoming one of the worlds' largest "off-shore" financial centers while the UK acts as a conduit for financial services. The island is not officially "tax free." However, prior to 2008, Value Added Tax was not applicable to goods and services, which enabled the Bank to attract major clients. Clients benefited from an effective European legal loophole that allowed them to legally access low-value consignment relief to establish tax-free fulfilment centers from the island. The UK damaged its relationship with the Bank of Jersey as a whole when the loophole was closed in 2012 and Value Added Tax was introduced on the island. This was attributable to 90% of the major clients exiting the island, and Jersey's economy suffered significantly as a result. The Bank invested heavily in its IT systems in 2011, and it was a major setback to lose multiple clients so soon after its investment, which failed to achieve ROI. The Bank has, however, benefited from a significant number of high-net-worth non-resident individuals with multicurrency accounts and a large number of European enterprises due to the long-standing "off-shore" status. Nevertheless, growth in each area has declined, and churn increased due to a recent European Union mandate on transparency, where account holders (both individuals and enterprises) by law have to declare financial holdings regardless of geographical location. This ensures local tax laws are being adhered to where the individual or enterprise resides. The Bank, unlike some competitors, has been extremely cooperative with the mandate and shared information freely to the authorities. Sharing of information has contributed to the decline in business to the point where the CEO has directly stated the Bank has now reached a position whereby to survive, it needs to disrupt European banks and offer an innovative low-cost banking solution to regain market share. The CEO initially wants to compete with UK high street banks, as the UK market would provide less complex penetration and then pivot into European markets with all of the associated Brexit complexities, which to a lesser extent will still apply to the Channel Islands. The CEO envisages an online-only banking product that will increase revenue significantly by scaling to an extensive base and could also become a conduit for high-value investment customers. The CEO has pledged a significant budget will be made available to ensure the Bank's IT systems can provide the necessary services, but only if an ROI can be proven within a one-year window.

The Bank has recently extended its presence in the Channel Islands by opening multiple branches in Guernsey, the adjacent Channel Island, where financial trading laws are identical. Guernsey also has a large campus location with a call center and training facility and, conveniently, a helicopter landing pad reserved for the CEO and premier clients by invitation.

Document 2: Network Information

The Bank of Jersey has an active DC in St Helier on the southern side of the island and a backup DC in Priory Inn, located 15 kms away on the northern side of the island. The network is composed of the following zones/areas:

1. BankExt network for external connectivity to ISP and third-party B2B connections.

2. BankDMZ network for hosting public-facing banking systems and employee RAS connectivity.

3. Banknet network for hosting of internal systems and corporate network connectivity for employees located in DC locations and remote branch/campus locations.

Services are spanned at Layer 2 in all zones, allowing VM migration and dynamic failover of services with a policy of no single points of failure within the network infrastructure. Even though Priory Inn was originally envisaged as a standby DC with full failover of systems and synchronous data replication of service between locations, both sites are running active services. The following figure details at a high level the primary Bank of Jersey network topology.

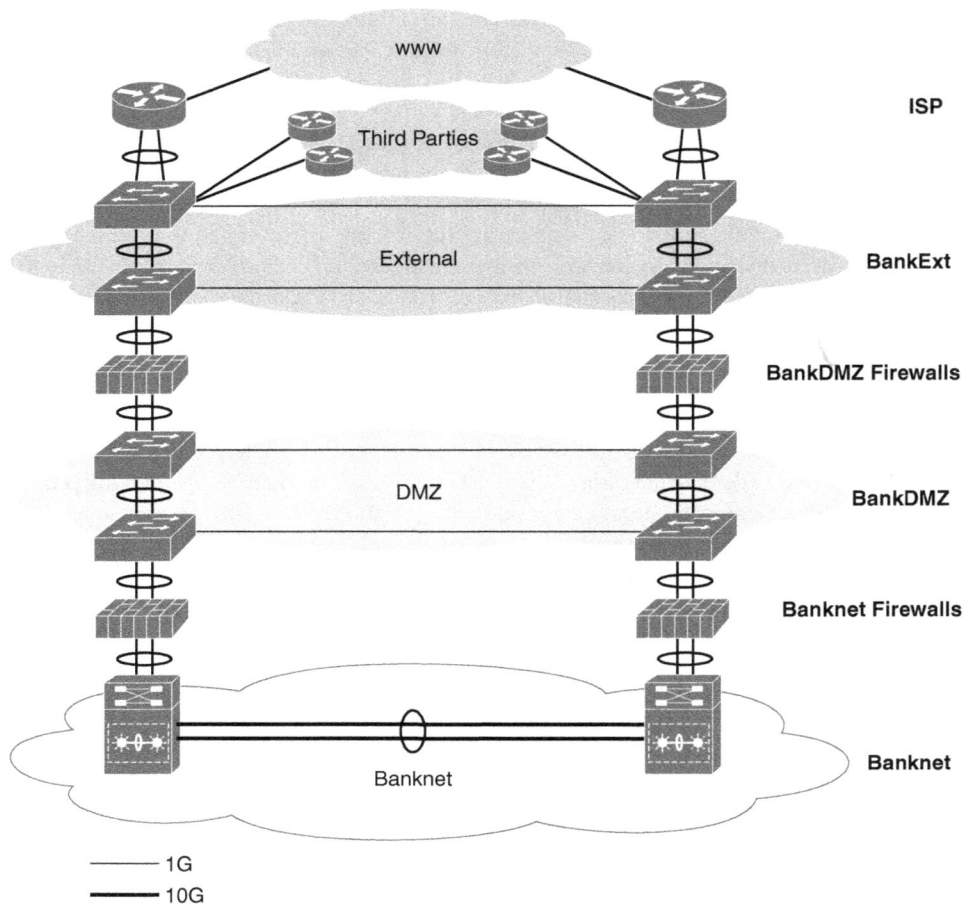

The specific networks/zones are described in further detail in the sections that follow.

BankExt Network

The external network is composed of a public-facing network, where ISP routers and third-party connection routers that provide market feeds and B2B connectivity are sited. Switches in the network are purely Layer 2 and propagate the local VLANs between DC locations, providing an active/standby facility for firewalls using VRRP and external routing to third parties using HSRP. Firewall state and high-availability VLANs are propagated between locations using non-IP-addressed VLANs. Third-party and B2B routing is static from the firewall to the HSRP addresses of routers, and multiple IPsec VPNs terminate on the external-facing firewalls for B2B connections over the Internet.

The following table details the VLANs in use within the BankExt network.

VLAN ID	Description
20	Third-party connectivity
21	ISP connectivity (public range)
22	External firewall state
23	External firewall HA
24	External management

The primary location for all devices on the BankExt network is the St Helier DC. In the event of a firewall failure in the St Helier location, the backup stateful firewall takes over service in the Priory Inn DC, the ISP routers and third-party routers for services such as SWIFT and Reuters remain active in St Helier, and cross-site routing is maintained until the firewall can be restored. If the entire St Helier site fails, all services dynamically fail over to the Priory Inn location. VLANs are trunked to the BankExt firewalls over EtherChannels. 802.1w STP is utilized on the Layer 2 1Gbps links between DC locations in a default configuration to ensure a loop-free topology between locations.

The uplink to the ISP from the BankExt network is 2Gbps from each location within an EtherChannel configuration. For egress traffic from the Bank, a default route is used within the network to point to the HSRP address of the ISP routers with the HSRP active ISP router sited in St Helier. For ingress traffic to the Bank, the ISP uses AS Path pre-pending on the Priory Inn router to ensure all traffic is routed by default toward St Helier from the Internet.

Security policy dictates that external connections are permitted only to flow into or through the BankExt network to the BankDMZ network and not into the Banknet network.

BankDMZ Network

Switches within the BankDMZ network are purely Layer 2 and propagate the local VLANs between DC locations, providing an active/standby facility. A firewall sandwich topology is created within the BankDMZ network with different vendor firewalls from the BankExt network, but providing the same VRRP and state failover characteristics. A Remote Access Services (RAS) VPN concentrator is terminated in a dedicated VLAN for employee remote access within the zone. The BankDMZ network hosts public-facing production and non-production services in a mix of load-balanced and non-load-balanced services from load balancers that are also located within the BankDMZ network. Dedicated VLANs provide frontend VIP connectivity for the load-balanced services. Backend VLANs provide direct server access for non-load-balanced services and connectivity for the backend servers for the load-balanced services within the network. VLANs are trunked to the BankDMZ firewalls over EtherChannels. 802.1w STP is utilized on the Layer 2 1Gbps links between locations in a default configuration to ensure a loop-free topology between sites.

The following table outlines the VLANs in use within the BankDMZ network.

VLAN ID	Description
12	RAS VPN
13–20	Public production services – VIP frontend
21–30	Public production services – server VLANs
31–38	Public non-production services – VIP frontend
39–50	Public non-production services – server VLANs
99	DMZ firewall state
100	DMZ firewall HA
101	DMZ management

Banknet DC Network

The internal DC network and DCI are primarily Layer 2 with Multi Chassis EtherChannel (MEC) technology upgraded from a legacy spanning tree topology. Services are spanned at Layer 2 between DCs, providing the facility for VM migration and dynamic failover of service. The DC LANs are connected over a 20Gbps DCI MEC between the core switches. The core switches provide Layer 2 aggregation for server and user access within each DC and all Layer 3 HSRP gateway access between locations. Multi-area OSPF is used to route between DCs over the DCI for nonspanned VLANs and to provide a backup between locations in the event of a WAN failure at either DC location.

There are approximately 200 VLANs in use within the DCs, with the majority of VLANs spanned between locations, with a limited number of local VLANs in each DC.

Synchronous data replication is used for the Bank's mainframe systems running active in St Helier and standby in Priory Inn, connected to a separate SAN, which requires 2ms (millisecond) or less RTT for successful write replication using FCoIP over the Banknet network between systems in each DC.

The compute environment is primarily VM, with a large number of legacy bare-metal servers present. IP voice call managers and appliance-based load balancers connect directly into the core network switches.

The following figure outlines the DC networks.

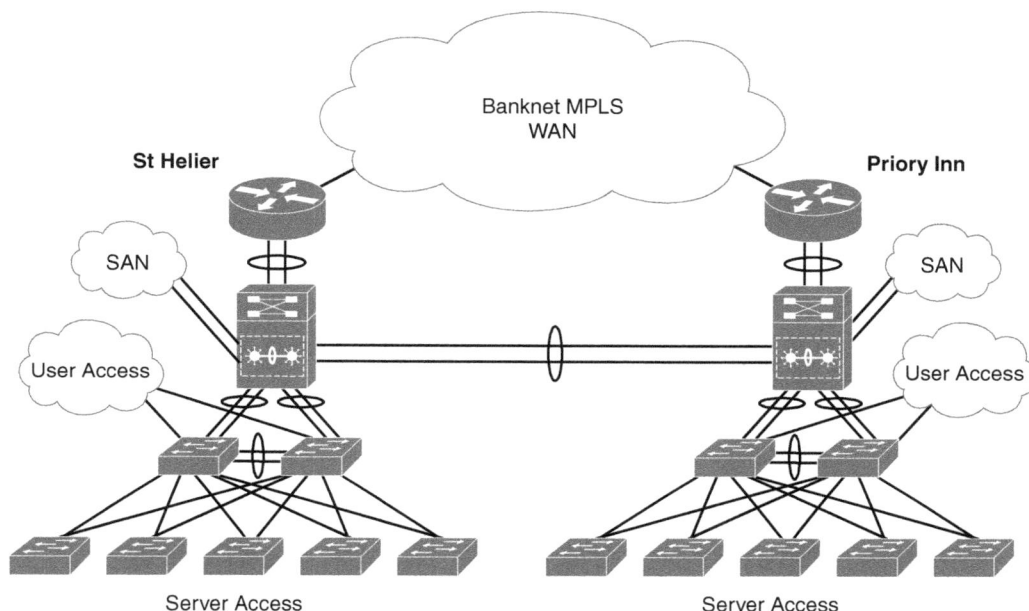

Banknet WAN

The internal WAN network is provided by Jerseytel, with a single Layer 3 MPLS VPN connecting all branch and campus locations to the DC locations. Jerseytel individual CE routers connect to each DC LAN side using dual 1Gbps interfaces connected in an EtherChannel, providing 2Gbps to the DC at each location and 1Gbps uplink to the Jerseytel network. DC prefixes are advertised to the MPLS network using eBGP from each DC, with MED values set to ensure the MPLS network sends all traffic to the DC prefixes via the active St Helier DC location. Traffic egressing each DC from spanned VLANs to the WAN uses the St Helier WAN connection due to St Helier being the HSRP active location for the spanned VLANs. Remote branch and campus locations are dual-homed to the MPLS WAN, with connection speeds varying depending on the size and requirements of each location. All links are configured for load sharing. QoS is configured on the network with four classes for voice traffic, mission-critical applications, transactional data, and a default class.

The WAN provides access for the Guernsey head office in St Andrew, which acts as hub site for Guernsey traffic with dual-routed submarine circuits to Jersey.

The following figure illustrates the WAN network.

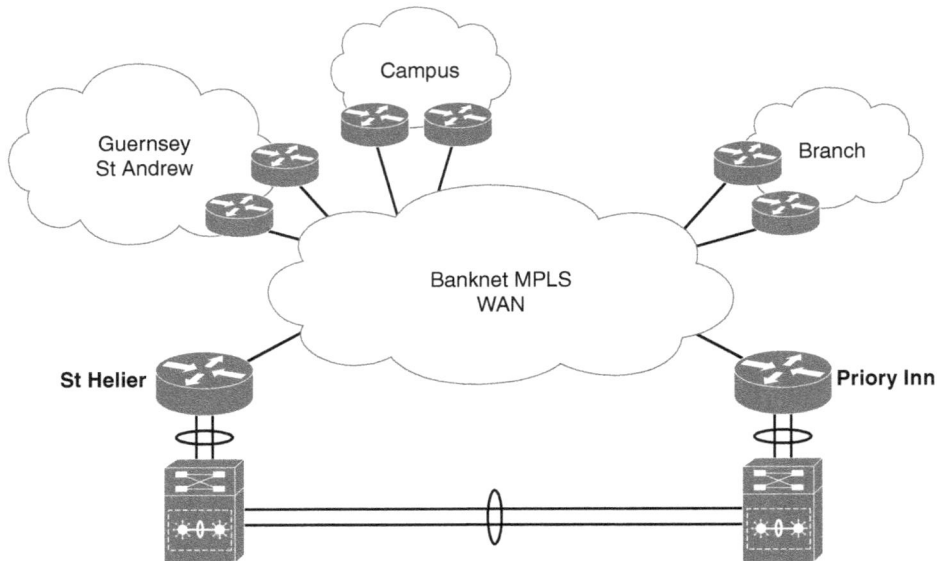

Branches and Campus Locations

There are 22 branch locations throughout the Channel Islands, with 13 located in Jersey. Each branch consists of dual-MPLS connections, typically with 10Mbps connections and dual Layer 2 switches connected together with no single points of failure. Each branch switch contains four VLANs configured with the MPLS CE router as the DGW for each VLAN with ATM cash machine network, Banknet VLAN for local banking systems, and an employee access VLAN and Voice VLAN for VoIP handsets. Campus locations have additional MPLS bandwidth (depending on headcount) with Layer 3 collapsed core and Layer 2 switches dual-homed to the collapsed core throughout the campus with PoE.

OSPF is used for campus MPLS network sites to route to the dual CE routers and advertise local VLANs.

Network Management

All management tools that access the infrastructure are sited in a separate Ethernet out-of-band management network that spans both DCs. Firewalls are used between the tools VLAN and multiple VLANs that connect to the management ports of infrastructure. The firewall connects to the production Banknet network in order to provide access to remote WAN locations. The Bank has a policy that only management tool hosts can connect to the infrastructure based on IP address and specific management protocols.

Document 3: Relevant Information

The network and DCI are primarily Layer 2 with MEC technology (virtual switching with multi-chassis EtherChannel capability) upgraded from a legacy spanning tree topology, which was attributed to a major outage within both data centers in 2018. This made international press headlines, and the banking regulator was involved, which led to investment of the MEC infrastructure for mitigation. After the MEC technology installation, no additional problems have been encountered, but the IT staff is not confident that the Layer 2 risk has been fully mitigated.

The Bank of Jersey wants to enable its IT systems to offer the online-only account the CEO envisages; however, investigation of capabilities of the network and compute infrastructure has shown upgrading IT systems will be required in order to reliably support the new product launch.

The Bank recently commissioned a group of financial IT consultants for two weeks to officially investigate its current IT systems and to make recommendations with the goal of enhancing resiliency and availability and to be able to determine what would be required to host the new innovative online-only accounts. Their findings are summarized as follows:

1. The existing business continuity plan does not cover natural events such as flooding, changing weather patterns, unprecedented seismic events, and extreme flooding due to rising sea levels.

2. There is possible disruption to key business activities, including facilities and workspace, infrastructure and IT systems, and supply chain based on finding one.

3. There is no system in place to account for staff in the event of a natural disaster.

4. Compute systems are installed on an ad-hoc basis, with lack of strategy and with minimal scale on a project-by-project basis.

5. Storage and replication systems are approaching end of life.

6. ATM cash machine systems run legacy networking protocols with non-DNS addressing applications.

7. The RAS system offers access for only up to 50% of the workforce and is connected only in the primary DC.

8. Public-facing IP ranges are exhausted.

9. Current ISP BW is saturated with long lead times on BW (which will require new circuits to increase).

10. No packet scrubbing is employed on ISP connections. A previous DDoS outage could have been averted with appropriate systems in place.

11. Third-party connections have limited security employed.

12. Networking infrastructure is approaching end of life and is at capacity, not allowing growth or performance required for new initiatives.

13. There is no dedicated test or pre-production network facility. There is a risk to the production network by implementing services without testing them in isolation prior to delivery.

14. The standby DC is running active VMs and is therefore not a standby DC. Risk and suboptimal traffic flow are highly likely.

15. The Banknet network is implicitly open, with branch users able to access all DC resources and remote branches.

16. The network relies on legacy spanning tree in multiple areas/zones.

17. There is not an effective system in place for vulnerabilities checking and staging of complex changes.

18. Configuration management systems are proprietary, and code is not maintained.

19. SNMP data is not effectively managed, and there is no capacity management in place.

20. There are no testing procedures in place to regularly test resilient services.

Email #1

From: Tim Jacobson

To: CCDE Candidate

Subject: Consultant Findings for Banknet

Hi.

Welcome aboard. You've joined the team at an exciting time, and we look forward to using your experience. Hopefully you have read through the information provided to you to get yourself up to speed.

As you would have seen, we have had the findings published from the UK consultants. The CTO was expecting some issues but wasn't prepared for the number of issues we ultimately need to address. I've just had a one-to-one with him, and his main focus will be on providing business continuity successfully following the recommendations in order to build an architecture capable of delivering our new initiative of the new online account initiative, which we are going to call "Channel." Ultimately, it appears we are going to require a new DC location and will mean moving away from the existing facility in Priory Inn (we may be able to use a separate new enhanced facility in the Priory Inn area, however) while we maintain a presence in St Helier. I need you to help recommend the best possible new location. You'll find below some locations that the CTO has been investigating with associated costs. We appreciate that this is going to be a large invest-ment and that our existing technology is unlikely to be fit for this purpose, so we will also look at providing a new DCI network between locations as well as a new DC LAN in each location. The CTO has advised we should be looking to provide double the previous bandwidth between locations for our Banknet network, which includes the replication of systems. So the A end location can remain at the St Helier DC, and we're going to con-tinue to use synchronous replication for our systems and main banking application. The CEO has insisted we use Jerseytel for connectivity (I'm pretty sure he plays golf with the Jerseytel CEO and he banks with us). We were advised we would need a minimum of two diversely routed circuits to ensure there are no single points of failure (all circuits will be "wires/fiber only" without SP infrastructure with exception to MPLS circuits, and these will be provided with a managed CPE device). So, to reiterate, this is purely for Banknet. We'll sort out the BankExt and BankDMZ networks once we determine the best course of action for Banknet.

Here's the circuit info (costs are per circuit/channel):

New Circuit Type	B End Location	CAPEX	OPEX per annum	Contract Term
100G Ethernet Metro	New Priory Inn Jersey	£50K	£45K	36 months
40G Ethernet Metro	New Priory Inn Jersey	£35K	£35K	36 months
10G DWDM Channel	New Priory Inn Jersey	£5K	£15K	24 months
10G MPLS L2 or L3 VPN Circuit	New Priory Inn Jersey	£5K	£20K	12 months
100G Ethernet Metro	St Andrew Guernsey	£50K	£45K	36 months
40G Ethernet Metro	St Andrew Guernsey	£35K	£35K	36 months
10G DWDM Channel	St Andrew Guernsey	£5K	£15K	24 months
10G MPLS L2 or L3 VPN Circuit	St Andrew Guernsey	£5K	£20K	12 months
10G DWDM Channel	Portsmouth UK	£10K	£15K	36 months
10G MPLS L2 or L3 VPN Circuit	Portsmouth UK	£12K	£18K	36 months

This is a map of Jersey with St Helier and Priory Inn areas. As you know, it's quite a small island (approximately 15 km wide).

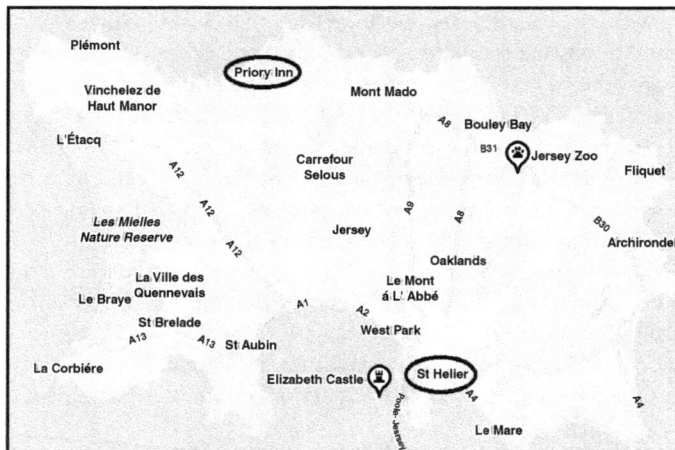

Here are the other options in Guernsey (Channel Islands) and Portsmouth (UK), with approximate distances.

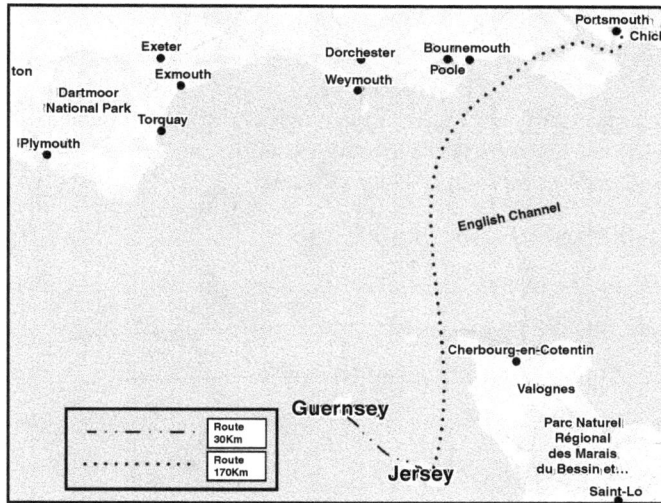

Rgds,

Tim Jacobson
Network Manager
Bank of Jersey

Lab Questions

Question 1

Which circuit type and new DC location provides the most suitable option for the Bank, with minimal cost for the new DC location? (Choose one option from A–D for the circuit type and one option from E–G for location.)

a. Dual 100G Ethernet metro circuits

b. Dual 40G Ethernet metro circuits

c. Multiple 10G DWDM channels

d. Multiple 10G MPLS (L2 or L3 VPN) circuits

e. Priory Inn Jersey

f. St Andrew Guernsey

g. Portsmouth UK

Email #2

From: Tim Jacobson

To: CCDE Candidate

Subject: New DC

Hi.

Thanks for your recommendation. The CTO has investigated the options and looked at your findings and has a preference for Guernsey using 100Gbps circuits, but the hosting company in Portsmouth has offered us a great incentive to use its location going forward. This, paired with the enhanced geographical separation it offers, makes it look like an attractive option. The hosting company has said it can light up additional channels really quickly if we go with its DWDM option, providing us with what we need for Day 1 and future scale.

Rgds,

Tim Jacobson
Network Manager
Bank of Jersey

Question 2

Are there any potential issues with using Portsmouth as a location for the backup DC? (Choose one.)

a. Excessive latency for replication requirements

b. Data sovereignty

c. Data governance

d. High opex if further DWDM channels are required

Email #3

From: Tim Jacobson

To: CCDE Candidate

Subject: New DC

Hi.

Just to let you know, we've been investigating Portsmouth as a possible DC location in more detail, and the CTO has checked and can confirm that there are no data sovereignty issues with using the UK. We've been supplied with the fiber run map for two fully resilient circuits that we can run DWDM channels on (attached). Looks like this could be a good option, but we'd appreciate if you could check it out prior to signing any orders.

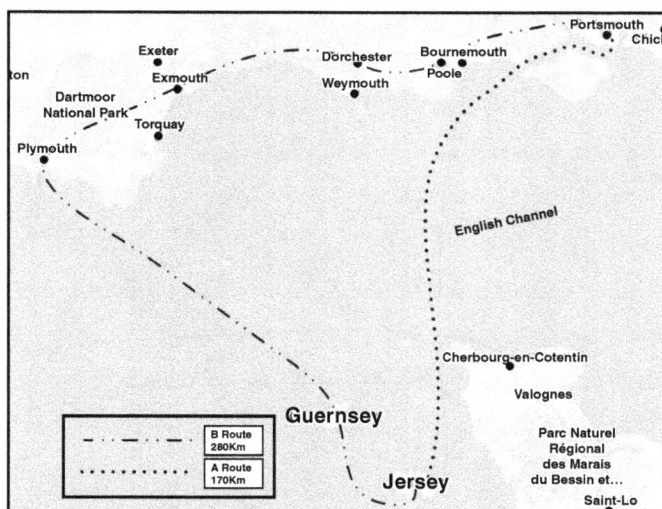

Rgds,

Tim Jacobson
Network Manager
Bank of Jersey

Question 3

Based on the new information supplied for the DWDM circuits, is there any risk associated with the Portsmouth location being selected as a standby DC location for the Bank of Jersey? (Choose one.)

a. Yes

b. No

Question 3.1

If you answered Yes to Question 3, what is the potential issue with Portsmouth as a location? (Choose one.)

a. The latency requirement for the synchronous replication is likely to be exceeded with one fiber route.

b. If load sharing over the DWDM channels/circuits, there will be out-of-order TCP packets due to the circuit distances and resulting latency differences between them.

Email #4

From: Tim Jacobson

To: CCDE Candidate

Subject: New DC and Legacy Issues

Hi.

Good spot on the potential replication issue on the B route to Portsmouth. That route worked out to be 280 km, and using a rough calculation of 1ms per 100 km for a round trip, we would have been just over our limit for the replication application. I've taken your information to the CTO and had a session with him. We were lucky enough to be able to get the CEO on a video session, and the new direction is to revert to Guernsey as a location and use dual 100Gbps links as they offer great performance and scale. He's going to clear it with the banking regulators and provide some of the information about our actual physical location in Guernsey being high enough above sea level to not be a risk of flooding, etc., and ensure we have sufficient geographical separation for business continuity. The circuits are more expensive, but the CEO is comfortable we can secure the budget based on the additional scale and performance that they provide.

Before we get started on the new technology required to deliver the network, we have a couple of issues we need to solve in the existing network. We can work around the majority of issues that have been identified and just make sure we are covered on the new network for those. However, the main ones we need to address immediately are:

1. The BankExt and BankDMZ networks are running hot. We need to find a way to increase bandwidth between locations, as STP is blocking one of our cross-site links within each network. We can invest, if required, but we just don't expect to be in that location for more than eight months, but we will need to get the available 2Gbps between sites for each network. I've checked out the switches, and they are pretty basic, but we can enable some other features by upgrading the licenses, or we can look at new switches and circuits if we absolutely have to. I will leave it to you to investigate the following information, which is the same for the switches in both BankExt and BankDMZ:

License upgrade Bronze: Voice VLANs, PVLANs, evaluation license free for 12 months

License upgrade Silver: Layer 3 functionality and dynamic routing enabled for £2K per switch

License upgrade Gold: Stacking capability and QoS for £5K per switch

New 1Gbps circuit: 36-month term, £2K per circuit

2. We've had an issue with one of our third-party B2B connections. Their router sited in our St Helier DC on VLAN2 was effectively running at 100% CPU, and it wasn't able to pass traffic. Investigation on their side suggests it was the subject of an attack from an address that isn't within our DC ranges. I can only assume it originated from one of the other third-party connections, and we don't have the tooling in place to investigate. They have had to apply an infrastructure ACL as a countermeasure but are insisting we need to protect them also. I need you to come up with an easy-to-manage solution to help. The network team doesn't have time to make small adjustments every time a third party wants to make changes.

Rgds,

Tim Jacobson
Network Manager
Bank of Jersey

Question 4

In order to address the bandwidth limitation in the BankExt and BankDMZ network, which is the optimal option? (Choose one.)

a. Upgrade switch licenses to Silver and enable Layer 3, convert the Layer 2 circuits to Layer 3, and run ECMP between locations and tunnel Layer 2.

b. Move the second Layer 2 circuit into the primary switch to form an EtherChannel to double the bandwidth.

c. Add one 1Gbps circuit to one of the cross-site switch pairs in each network and form an EtherChannel on one cross-site switch pair.

d. Upgrade switch licenses to include stacking capability and form a virtual stack, making the topology nonblocking.

e. Add one 1Gbps circuit to each of the cross-site switch pairs in each network and form an EtherChannel on each cross-site switch pair.

f. Configure VLAN load balancing.

Email #5

From: Tim Jacobson

To: CCDE Candidate

Subject: New DC and Legacy Issues

Hi.

Thanks for the suggestion to simply load-balance VLANs on the links. I will get our engineers to modify the STP priorities per VLAN to adjust the topologies! I thought we might need to invest in some new licenses to enable other features, but that would be wasted money, so we can keep the licensing as is.

Rgds,

Tim Jacobson
Network Manager
Bank of Jersey

Question 5

In order to address the third-party router issue for routers connecting to VLAN2 in the BankExt network, what would a prerequisite be in order to mitigate further attacks? (Choose one.)

a. Enable Bronze evaluation licensing on the switches.

b. Create an ACL per third party on the BankExt switches, allowing only traffic from that third-party IP range into the BankExt network switches.

c. Create an ACL per third party on the BankExt switches, blocking traffic from that third-party IP range into other third parties on the BankExt network switches.

d. Create a firewall rule blocking any third party from communicating directly to another third party.

Question 5.1

If you selected Answer A in Question 5, please validate you answer. (Choose one.)

a. The Bronze license will allow you to run PVLANs.

b. The license will allow you to apply ACLs on the switches.

Question 5.2

If you selected Answer B in Question 5, please validate you answer. (Choose one.)

a. The ACL will block communication between third parties on the switch.

b. The ACL will only allow communication from the defined third party to the Bank.

Question 5.3

If you selected Answer C in Question 5, please validate you answer. (Choose one.)

a. The ACL will block communication between third parties on the switch.

b. The ACL will only allow communication from the defined third party to the Bank.

Question 5.4

If you selected Answer D in Question 5, validate you answer. (Choose one.)

a. The firewall will block communication between third parties on the switch.

b. The firewall will only allow communication from the defined third party to the Bank.

Email #6

From: Tim Jacobson

To: CCDE Candidate

Subject: New DC Separation Technology

Hi.

Thanks for sorting out the issues. So, since we have decided on Guernsey as our new secondary DC location, we have ordered dual 100Gbps circuits from St Helier, which will be delivered with complete resilience. With all of the work going on, we've completely neglected the fact up to now that we should also provision dual circuits for our BankExt network and BankDMZ network. The costs are actually looking very prohibitive to provision an additional four circuits, so I'd like you to investigate alternative options so we can run all networks over the dual 100Gbps circuits. There will be a huge amount of capacity with the new circuits and the potential to save a significant amount of shareholders' funds if we can offer separation in a way that will keep the regulators happy.

Rgds,

Tim Jacobson
Network Manager
Bank of Jersey

Question 6

Complete the following table to assist the Bank of Jersey with its assessment of potential technologies to provide separation and connectivity of cross-site BankExt, BankDMZ, and Banknet networks over the dual 100Gbps DCI links being provisioned between St Helier and Guernsey DCs. Place an X in each cell if the technology per row offers the features detailed in the columns.

Technology	Offers Layer 2 separation between different Bank of Jersey networks	Offers Layer 3 VRF separation between Bank of Jersey networks	Offers ability to transport <20 VLANs between dual locations at Layer 2	Offers ability to scale to transport >200 VLANs between dual locations at Layer 2	Offers flexibility to transport multiple VLANs between more than two locations at Layer 2
QinQ					
VXLAN EVPN Multipod					
VXLAN EVPN Multisite					
VRFs and 802.1Q (VRF Lite)					
MPLS Layer 3					
H-VPLS					

Email #7

From: Tim Jacobson

To: CCDE Candidate

Subject: New DC Separation Technology

Hi.

Thanks for the info. I've had time to go through this, but I need you to recommend the right technology for separation of networks that provides us the flexibility to run an additional DC in conjunction to St Helier and Guernsey if we need to in the future. I don't know right now if we want to—I just don't want to limit ourselves to having to change the technology if we do decide to at a later date. The technology would need to provide separation of all of our networks combined on one effective network and should be compatible with what technology we use to actually provision ports in each network. I need you to be confident the technology can also limit our failure domain to a single DC if we have any Layer 2 type issues, even though we still need to propagate Layer 2 between DCs. As mentioned, we have a preference for separation without having to buy additional circuits for BankExt and BankDMZ DCIs. (I've sounded out Security, and they aren't too happy. However, if we can prove physical and logical separation, they said we are compliant with the security policy.)

Rgds,

Tim Jacobson
Network Manager
Bank of Jersey

Question 7

Which of the following technologies is best suited to provide connectivity between St Helier and the new DC location in Guernsey for the Bank based on its requirements for new networks and use of dual 100Gbps circuits? (Choose one.)

a. QinQ

b. H-VPLS

c. VXLAN EVPN multipod

d. VXLAN EVPN multisite

Question 8

Bank of Jersey decided to run VXLAN EVPN multisite technology to provide flexibility for the future and to run multiple network overlay instances over a Layer 3 fabric. What is a recommended approach for the deployment to provide separation of legacy network zones to meet the Security department's requirement? (Choose one.)

a. Provision of separate spines and leaf switches per network zone

b. Provision of separate underlay fabric per network zone

c. Provision of separate overlay per network zone

d. Provision of separate overlay and leaf switches per network zone

Email #8

From: Tim Jacobson

To: CCDE Candidate

Subject: VXLAN EVPN Multisite

Hi.

Thanks for your recommendation. Let's go ahead and run an EVPN VXLAN multi-site infrastructure to support all of our three network zones between St Helier and Guernsey as separate overlays on one underlay fabric. We are unlikely to need the ability to run more than two data centers, but if we can introduce the flexibility in the initial design, then this would be a real bonus, and I prefer the separation benefits multi-site brings. I've been looking at appropriate network hardware (leaf and spine switches) for the new network, including differences between licensing, and can't comment on all the technical features other than we will want to run vPC (virtual port-channel/multi-chassis EtherChannel), as each of our servers will be dual-homed and we have no plans for running multicast in the overlay. If things change, we can always go ahead and pay for a license upgrade in situ, but I need your help in selecting hardware and licensing. So see what you can do to keep costs as low as possible. 100Gbps optics, for example, are running at £2000 vs. £1500 for 40Gbps each. I definitely want the fabric to be non-blocking for the uplinks on the 1Gbps leaf switches, even if we have a single spine switch failure, for example. Don't worry about the costs of the actual switches, as these are fairly standard. Just select what we need to create the network.

Switch types available:

48x 10Gbps-based leaf switches

128x 10Gbps-based leaf switches

48x 1Gbps leaf switches

48x 40/100Gbps spine switches

Spines can support 40Gbps or 100Gbps on each port, depending on optics purchased. The spines are actually from a different vendor than the leafs, as they were significantly cheaper than the leaf vendor's spines, but they are compatible, don't have a license option, and seem to come with an enterprise edition as standard that covers every feature listed on each license type of the leafs.

We will need some border leaf switches dedicated for services for each zone, such as load balancers and zone firewalls. The DCI links can be terminated on border leaf switches also. Border leaf switches can be 48x 10Gbps leaf switches that we purpose as border leafs—I will need you to determine which license is required for them.

All leaf switch options come with six uplink ports onboard and just require the necessary optics purchased to enable the ports (as per the spine ports, they will operate at 40Gbps or 100Gbps, depending on which optics are inserted).

Optics: 40Gbps optics are £1.5K and 100Gbps optics are £2K.

Silver Leaf License Features (included in switch purchase price):

OSPF

IS-IS

MP-BGP

VXLAN

EVPN multipod

EVPN multisite

vPC (multi-chassis EtherChannel)

MACSEC

IPsec

GETVPN

GRE

Multicast

Automation suite (OpenConfig, IETF, native)

Gold Leaf License Features (additional £2K per switch):

OSPF

IS-IS

MP-BGP

VXLAN

EVPN multipod

EVPN multisite

vPC (multi-chassis EtherChannel)

MACSEC

IPsec

GETVPN

GRE

Multicast

vPC (multi-chassis EtherChannel) fabric peering

Tenant routed multicast

Automation suite (OpenConfig, IETF, native)

Streaming telemetry

Here are the latest computer hardware device counts required for Day 1 (per DC):

Network	Servers/devices @ 1Gbps port speed	Servers/devices @ 10Gbps port speed
BankExt	26	—
BankDMZ	32	22
Banknet	92	182

Rgds,

Tim Jacobson
Network Manager
Bank of Jersey

Question 9

Draw out the physical topology of the required EVPN VXLAN network infrastructure for one DC to consolidate the BankExt, BankDMZ, and Banknet networks to support Day 1 services in the most cost-effective manner. Use as many leaf switches, border leaf switches, and spine switches as necessary, based on the requirements provided, and select the most appropriate optic speed and count.

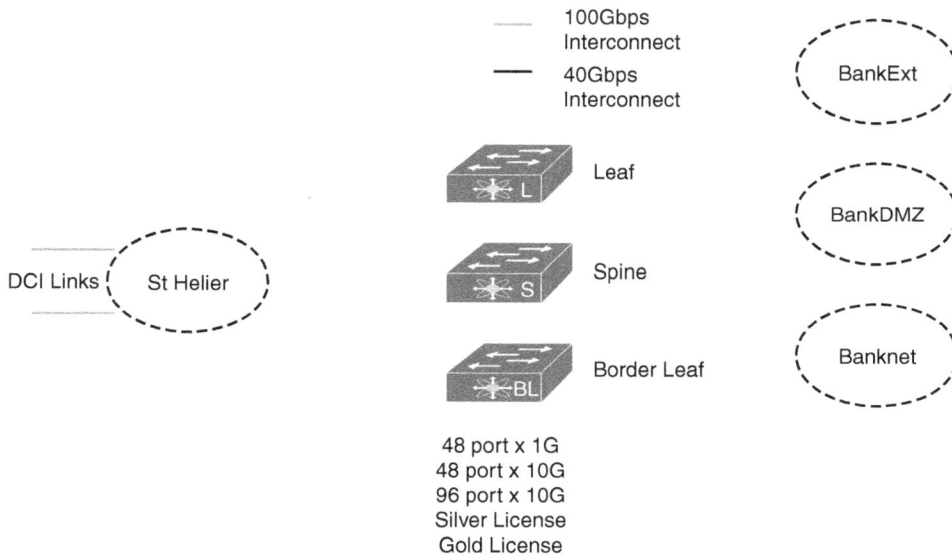

100Gbps
Interconnect

40Gbps
Interconnect

Leaf

Spine

Border Leaf

48 port x 1G
48 port x 10G
96 port x 10G
Silver License
Gold License

BankExt

BankDMZ

Banknet

DCI Links   St Helier

Question 10

The VXLAN design was submitted to an Architectural Review Board within the bank, and a comment was documented that suggested super-spines would be required within the design in order to provision the BankExt, BankDMZ, and Banknet networks over the same fabric. What would your response be to the comment? (Choose one.)

a. Super-spines would be required based on supplied requirements and can be formed by adding two further spines per DC connecting directly to the planned new spines.

b. Super-spines would not be required based on supplied requirements.

Email #10

From: Tim Jacobson

To: CCDE Candidate

Subject: New Design

Hi.

Thanks for the design. I've got one of the guys to document it. He initially thought we could reduce leaf count by consolidating some of the BankExt and BankDMZ ports into the same device and allocate ports per VRF, but I told him Security requested physical and logical separation. We can obviously do this if we use distinct switch pairs per environment for physical separation and use the underlay fabric for the logical separation and tunnel VXLAN over the top per environment. The vPC fabric peering enabled by purchase of the Gold license has saved a good sum and reduced the optic and fiber patch requirements between leaf switch pairs considerably in order to provision server resiliency per leaf switch pair. I hadn't realized initially we would need a set of border leaf switches per environment/network zone, but it makes sense if we apply services for each zone such as firewalls or load balancers on a single pair of border leaf switches, then we wouldn't meet our security requirement of providing physical separation between network zones. It seemed to make sense to connect the DCI links into the Banknet border leaf switches, as we have the majority of services running on this network, and this does ensure logical separation between zones, as it's all VXLAN overlay by the time traffic flows over the DCI links.

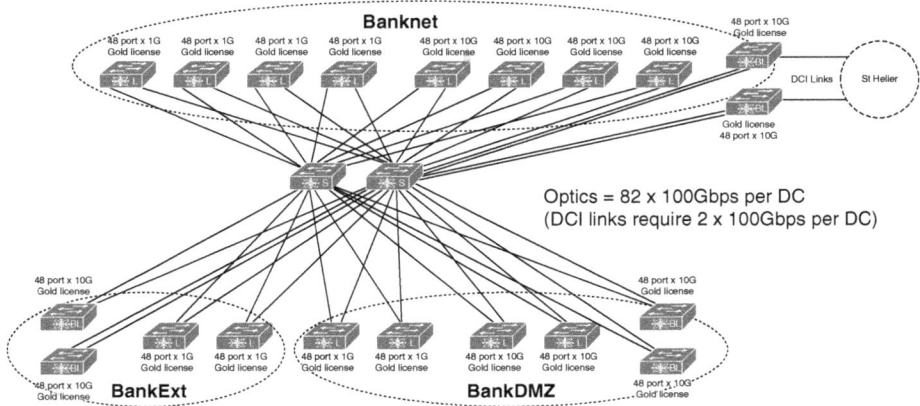

We will connect up the management ports on all of the new switches, which have a dedicated management VRF, and drop these into our dedicated management network that the team has already built out using legacy infrastructure.

We will connect up all circuits and required firewalls for each environment onto the dedicated border leaf switches per zone and assign them to the required VRFs when we build this out.

Rgds,

Tim Jacobson
Network Manager
Bank of Jersey

Question 11

If the Bank of Jersey's Security department changed policy and decided to permit BankExt networks and BankDMZ to share the same physical leaf switches and then applied configuration mitigation for Layer 2 security to block access between networks, is there a further issue that would need to be rectified for this change in policy? (Choose one.)

a. Yes

b. No

Question 11.1

If you chose Yes for Question 11, please validate your answer. (Choose one.)

a. Overlapping VLAN numbers exist between network zones. There would be an issue allocating a VLAN to a unique VNI per network.

b. Overlapping VLAN numbers exist between network zones. This would mean multi-destination BUM (broadcast unknown multicast) traffic destined from one network would be received on the other network also.

Question 11.2

If you chose No for Question 11, please validate your answer. (Choose one.)

a. Configuring features such as VLAN hopping mitigation would provide sufficient control.

b. The firewalls required between networks would provide sufficient control.

Question 12

Complete the following table to assist Bank of Jersey engineers in creating VNIs for the BankExt, BankDMZ, and Banknet networks. Create any VNID using seven digits, with the last four digits used for VLAN numbers.

Network Zone	VLAN	VNI
BankExt	20	
BankExt	21	
BankDMZ	20	
BankDMZ	21	
Banknet	20	
Banknet	21	

Email #11

From: Tim Jacobson

To: CCDE Candidate

Subject: Multi-Destination BUM Traffic

Hi.

As we get closer to implementing the network design, we've been looking into the specifications of how VXLAN will work, and it appears we need a design decision based on the multi-destination BUM (broadcast unknown unicast and multicast) traffic using ingress replication or multicast mode in the underlay. The leaf switches can run either mode, so what do you recommend for our setup?

Rgds,

Tim Jacobson
Network Manager
Bank of Jersey

Question 13

Do you have sufficient information to make a design decision for multi-destination BUM traffic forwarding to run using multicast or ingress replication for the new network? (Choose one.)

a. Yes

b. No

Question 13.1

If you answered Yes for Question 13, which replication mode would you select for multi-destination BUM traffic? (Choose one.)

a. Ingress replication

b. Multicast replication in the underlay

Question 13.2

If you answered No for Question 13, what further information do you require? (Choose one.)

a. Additional leaf switch CPU utilization for predicted traffic baseline for ingress replication

b. Which multicast modes are possible for multicast forwarding in the underlay

Email #12

From: Tim Jacobson

To: CCDE Candidate

Subject: Multi-Destination Replication Mode Info

Hi.

So the ingress replication mode for multi-destination BUM traffic we are told will increase CPU by only 5% based on our anticipated throughput, and the maximum it could reach is an additional 10%. The multicast mode of replication in the underlay will increase at a fixed additional 3% using BiDir or ASM.

Rgds,

Tim Jacobson
Network Manager
Bank of Jersey

Question 14

The Bank has decided to implement multicast replication for BUM traffic based on a clear CPU reduction in comparison to ingress replication rather than request a design recommendation. When it comes to implementation, however, what would be a benefit of using BiDir as opposed to ASM for the underlay multicast protocol to transport BUM traffic between VTEPs across each DC? (Choose one.)

a. BiDir does not require a rendezvous point.

b. BiDir offers native resilience.

c. BiDir uses out-of-band signaling between the receiver and the group it requires to join, making it more scalable, and there is no requirement for pruning multicast trees.

d. BiDir drastically reduces the mroute state in the network.

Email #13

From: Tim Jacobson

To: CCDE Candidate

Subject: Pre-Production Banknet Network

Hi.

We've almost fallen down the same hole as before in the legacy network, providing the Banknet as a single network with production and pre-production services as called out by the consultants. I need you to work out how we can provide a pre-production environment within Banknet that can communicate without any policy control to the production environment within Banknet, typically within the same VLAN. Unfortunately, due to legacy reasons, we have some prod and pre-prod compute services running on the same VLANs, and the server guys are telling me it would take six months to re-address and make the required application changes, and that's too long. We want to offer the best possible protection between environments, so a Layer 2 type STP issue or broadcast issue in pre-prod can't affect prod.

Rgds,

Tim Jacobson
Network Manager
Bank of Jersey

Question 15

How can Banknet production and pre-production compute services be provisioned on the new network, providing mitigation from Layer 2 broadcast type events in either network propagating into each other? (Choose one.)

a. Create separate production and pre-production overlay VRFs in VXLAN and use route-leaking between VRFs for communication.

b. Create separate production and pre-production overlay VRFs in VXLAN and use route-leaking and NAT between VRFs for communication.

c. Create separate production and pre-production overlay VRFs in VXLAN and use a routed firewall between VRFs for communication.

d. Create separate production and pre-production overlay VRFs in VXLAN and use a transparent firewall between VRFs for communication.

e. Group compute production infrastructure onto specific VTEP leaf pairs and pre-production compute onto other pairs with Storm-Control configured on leaf uplinks.

Email #14

From: Tim Jacobson

To: CCDE Candidate

Subject: Implementation

Hi.

Thanks for the info. We will create some compute PODs with separate production and pre-production PODs with our leaf pairs. It should look like this:

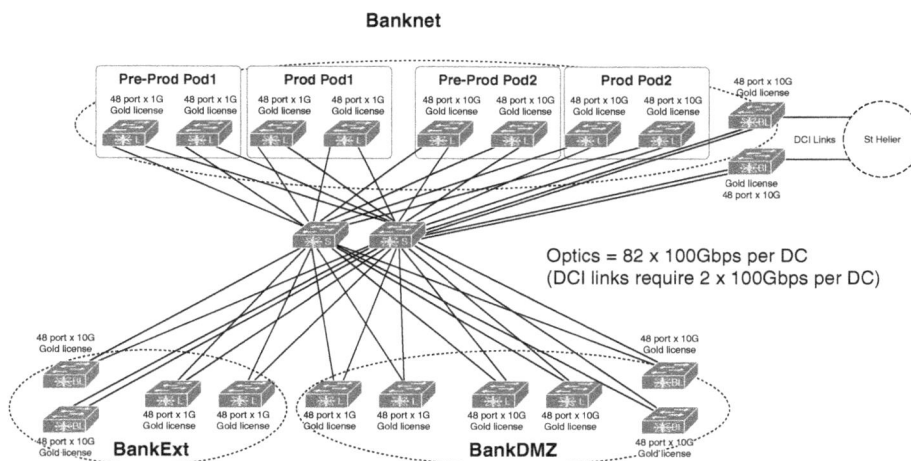

By the way, Jerseytel has informed us the DCI circuits are now in place. Apparently, it was a simple job of splicing in a few locations, as it had fiber in the ground and between Jersey and Guernsey Islands already. We are all tested, error free, and latency is good, so we will have no issues with our replication. We need you to plan the migration of services to the new DC while we wait for the network infrastructure to be delivered from the UK. Internet and WAN circuits have been ordered for the new DC and will be here in time for migration. (We don't need new circuits for St Helier. We can just re-patch these from legacy to new networks at time of migration.)

Rgds,

Tim Jacobson
Network Manager
Bank of Jersey

Question 16

Place the following implementation/migration steps in order to allow the Bank of Jersey to migrate to the new network infrastructure (not all steps are required).

Configure VLAN translation for overlapping VLANs on each network on leaf switches.

Connect Layer 2 trunk from legacy Banknet network to new Banknet border leaf switches in St Helier, connect Layer 2 trunk from legacy BankDMZ network to new BankDMZ border leaf switches in St Helier, and connect Layer 2 trunk from legacy BankExt network to new BankExt border leaf switches in St Helier.

Shut down Internet/WAN circuit(s) in Priory Inn.

Enable new Internet/WAN circuit(s) in new Guernsey DC and migrate St Helier Internet/WAN circuit(s) in St Helier.

Connect Layer 3 routing links from legacy Banknet network to new Banknet border leaf switches in St Helier.

Install spine switches in each DC.

Enable Anycast gateways in VXLAN for Banknet VLANs.

Install leaf switches in each DC and configure separate VRFs for BankExt, BankDMZ, and Banknet networks within VXLAN.

Migrate inner and outer FWs and RAS infrastructure to VXLAN network on appropriate border leaf switch.

Shut down HSRP gateways in the legacy Banknet network for each VLAN.

Install border leaf switches and enable DCI circuits in each DC, and test between DCs on the Banknet border leaf switches.

Migrate physical compute environment from St Helier and Priory Inn to new DCs.

Email #15

From: Tim Jacobson

To: CCDE Candidate

Subject: Implementation/Migration Update

Hi.

The migration went really well. I got our guys to script the larger number of VLANs we migrated in Banknet in terms of shutting down and re-enabling the Layer 3 side, and we literally had a 1 second blip per VLAN. The users didn't even notice, and we had no related tickets, which was great news. However, good news is usually accompanied with bad, unfortunately. We've had the regulators in post-migration, and we walked them through the new design and what we have accomplished. While their overall impression was positive in regard to the new network and improvements to our business continuity, they have made the following comments:

1. The infrastructure that connects to the production compute environment is not physically protected. We need a cage around it to ensure that nobody who has access to the DC in general can, without restriction, connect devices into the production switches and potentially compromise service.

2. Although not a current legality, we would expect you to encrypt DCI traffic leaving your premises.

3. Also not a current legality, but Banknet WAN and DC are implicitly open. We expect DC services to be protected behind a firewall from the WAN.

Please ensure you are compliant with point number 1 within four weeks and have a plan in place for points 2 and 3, as legislation could change with short notice.

We will need to resolve these matters. For point 2, we are OK on the WAN, as all WAN traffic into the DC uses HTTPS or traffic encrypted at the application layer, but we do know the DCI link will carry some unencrypted traffic.

Rgds,

Tim Jacobson
Network Manager
Bank of Jersey

Question 17

The financial regulator has stated that all of the Banknet network-specific switches that serve the production environment should be placed into a protective caged environment to ensure they are protected from unauthorized access. Highlight on the supplied network diagram where the cage should extend to.

Banknet

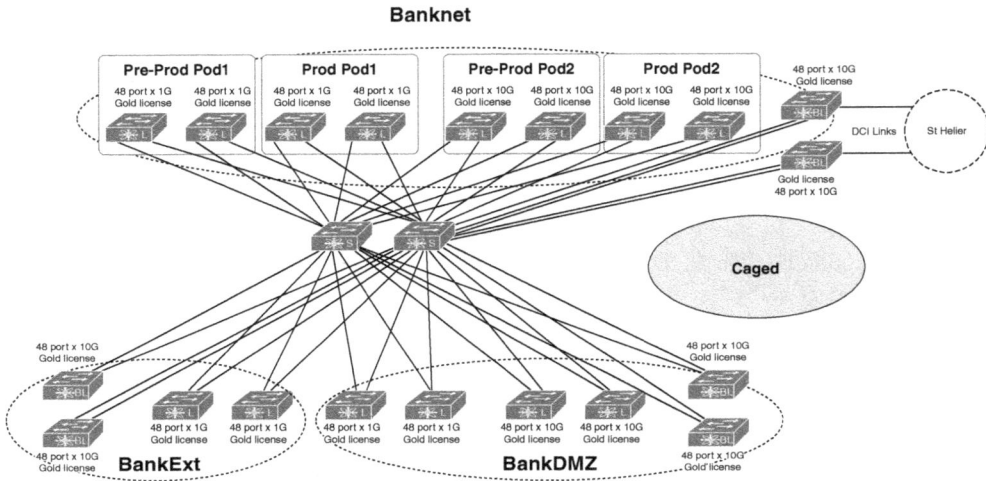

Question 18

If the Bank of Jersey were to encrypt traffic over the DCI links, which technology would you recommend that would be compatible with OSPF if this IGP was used in the underlay fabric? (Choose one.)

    a. GETVPN

    b. IPsec

    c. MACSEC

    d. GRE/IPsec

Email #16

From: Tim Jacobson

To: CCDE Candidate

Subject: Perimeter FW

Hi.

So, as you are aware, the auditors have raised a concern that the Banknet network is implicitly open once you are connected to the WAN, and they are recommending we place perimeter protection around our applications in the DCs. Ideally, I would like to add a firewall in each branch location, but unfortunately that isn't going to happen. We can get budget for DC/WAN perimeter firewalls (I want to do this with the minimal number possible, as they are expensive) because we want to future-proof it by investing in firewalls with a next-generation feature set. The firewalls we want to use have 10Gbps throughput, so they are fine for the WAN, which connects at 10Gbps into the service provider's network. The firewalls need a dedicated Layer 2 connection between them for state and high availability. They need to support transparent and Layer 3 routed mode. For high availability, they need to support active/standby, where in the event of a failure, the standby device takes over the active IP address and only the active IP address is configured on each firewall. In terms of routing, they can run static routing, OSPF, or iBGP, which is great, as we need the solution to still allow for the dynamic routing from the WAN into the DC. In terms of current setup, we have dual P2P /30 links (on contiguous prefixes) between the WAN CE on each site to the border leafs and eBGP between the borders and the MPLS CEs. I'm told all devices support L2 EtherChannel, and as you know, we can run vPC multi-chassis EtherChannel on the borders if required at L2, but they don't support L3 EtherChannel. In the event of a failure scenario (which could mean failing over between DCs due to a firewall or WAN failure), we need existing sessions to be maintained. We don't have a clue at this point what we should be setting the rule base to initially, so this is more of a tick-in-the-box exercise, and we will come back to define policy once we are able to monitor and baseline flows using some tooling. We can add different prefixes if required into the topology over and above the existing /30s in use, and I have a preference for simplicity with minimal change to the existing environment.

I'll obviously need your help to design this!

Rgds,

Tim Jacobson
Network Manager
Bank of Jersey

Question 19

Which of the following designs would be optimal for the Bank to control north/south flows into the DCs for Banknet services from the WAN? (Choose one.)

a. The firewalls should be deployed in routed mode. The WAN routers should connect directly into a single firewall at each DC location using an L3 EtherChannel for the "outside interfaces." The firewall at each DC location should then connect to the Banknet border leaf switches using an L3 EtherChannel (vPC) for the "inside interfaces." BGP should be configured on the firewalls for routing into and out of the DCs, and a Layer 2 VXLAN should be provisioned between DCs for firewall state connectivity, allowing one firewall in one DC location to be active and one to be standby.

b. The firewalls should be deployed in routed mode. The WAN routers should connect directly into a single firewall at each DC location using an L3 EtherChannel for the "outside interfaces." The firewall at each DC location should then connect to the Banknet border leaf switches using an L3 EtherChannel (vPC) for the "inside interfaces." BGP should be configured on the firewalls for routing into and out of the DCs, and a Layer 2 VXLAN should be provisioned between DCs for firewall state connectivity, allowing both firewalls to operate in a cluster mode.

c. The firewalls should be deployed in transparent mode. The WAN routers should connect directly into a single firewall at each DC location using an L2 EtherChannel for the "outside interfaces." The firewall at each DC location should then connect to the Banknet border leaf switches using an L2 EtherChannel (vPC) for the "inside interfaces." A Layer 2 VXLAN should be provisioned between DCs for firewall state connectivity, allowing one firewall in one DC location to be active and one to be standby. eBGP peering between the WAN routers and border leaf switches would remain as is due to the transparent configuration.

d. The firewalls should be deployed in routed mode. The WAN routers should connect into the border leaf switches at each DC location using an L2 EtherChannel. The firewalls at each DC location should then connect to the Banknet border leaf switches using an L2 EtherChannel (vPC) with separate VLANs used for the "inside interfaces" and "outside interfaces." Static routing should be used on the firewalls with DC routes pointing toward the border leafs and WAN routes pointing toward the WAN. Layer 2 VXLANs should be provisioned between DCs for firewall state connectivity—the "inside interface" VLAN and the "outside interface" VLAN allowing one firewall in one DC location to be active and one to be standby in the remote DC. Multihop eBGP should be configured between the WAN routers and border leaf switches.

e. The firewalls should be deployed in transparent mode. The WAN routers should connect directly into a single firewall at each DC location using an L2 EtherChannel for the "outside interfaces." The firewall at each DC location should then connect to the Banknet border leaf switches using an L2 EtherChannel (vPC) for the "inside interfaces." A Layer 2 VXLAN should be provisioned between DCs for firewall state connectivity, allowing one firewall in one DC location to be active and one to be standby.

Email #17

From: Tim Jacobson

To: CCDE Candidate

Subject: Auto m8?

Hi.

You will be glad to hear the firewall implementation has been planned. Thanks for your assistance!

Just when I thought our guys were gaining confidence with the new network, we've had a serious issue. They were making a change on the production network last night, migrating some of the servers responsible for the applications serving the ATM cash machines from the legacy network, and they ended up causing an outage in the entire ATM network. We had some unhappy customers who were unable to withdraw cash, but the damage was limited due to being an early morning change and backing it out quickly when they realized what had happened. The RCA shows some changes missed out on the border leaf switches and some configuration not being accepted correctly. I went through the detail and couldn't believe the amount of configuration required for the actual change for VXLAN parameters. The guys apparently scripted it due to the size and complexity and ended up creating the issue themselves! We simply cannot find ourselves in this position again. I have read that the infrastructure is compatible with network programmability, and I'd like you to look into how we can set up some automation to eliminate human error and introduce efficiencies. We can also enable the telemetry functionality that they have and move away from SNMP possibly. I have a couple of developers I can bring in from the dark side (application developers), when required, who can code. They can work with the network team to define what is required, so maybe we can start our own devops team if this works out. I've got Yin and Yang stuck in my head for some reason after my first conversation with the developers—can you believe one of them is called Jason! Anyway, have a think and let me know how you believe we should begin.

Rgds,

Tim Jacobson
Network Manager
Bank of Jersey

Question 20

In order to initiate automation, the developers need to know which individual YANG model to use for the new infrastructure. Which of the following models would be optimal? (Choose one.)

   a. Native

   b. OpenConfig

   c. IETF

   d. Mix of models

Question 21

In order to deploy the automation, the developers have recommended an OpenDaylight platform to use as a resilient SDN controller and portal for network programmability of the VXLAN infrastructure within the management network. Complete the following table in order that a project task list can be generated to deliver automation for the network infrastructure.

	OpenDaylight Controller	Spine Switches	Leaf Switches	DC1 Management Network	DC2 Management Network	Management Network Firewall
Task Required	Check the box below if the task is required on the devices/locations above.					
Enable Netconf/ Restconf.						
Enable REST API.						
Install SDN controller.						
Enable SSH TCP port 22 access from controller.						
Enable Netconf TCP port 830 access from controller.						
Enable Restconf TCP port 443 access from controller.						

Question 22

The Bank of Jersey wants to simplify multiple/recurring API calls from the SDN controller to individual devices for configuration and management purposes while keeping the required authentication as simple and secure as possible. Which authentication method should the Bank choose? (Choose one.)

   a. Basic Authentication (native)

   b. API Key – String

   c. API Key – Request Header

   d. API Key – Cookie

   e. Custom token

Question 23

The Bank is wary of atomicity, if one or both of the OpenDaylight controllers fail within the production network. If the controllers fail (under steady state operation and not while performing configuration actions), then which of the following should be viewed as the "source of truth" for the valid configuration of an infrastructure device? (Choose one.)

a. The primary SDN controller's saved configuration of the infrastructure device

b. The secondary SDN controller's saved configuration of the infrastructure device

c. The infrastructure device itself

d. A previous day's backup configuration of the infrastructure device itself

Question 24

The Bank wants to leverage the new infrastructure's model driven telemetry (MDT) capability. If an existing network management tooling application was limited to XML encoding only and not HTTP for MDT support, which of the following would be compatible on the network infrastructure? (Choose one.)

a. Dial-out telemetry

b. Dial-in telemetry

c. NetFlow

d. IPFIX

Email #18

From: Tim Jacobson

To: CCDE Candidate

Subject: Cloud Info

Hi.

The automation looks really promising. I have our guys working with the developers to automate some of the scripted tasks they complete on a daily basis and provide a new methodology for troubleshooting. Our guys are learning about Python, and the developers are learning about network operations and configurations, so it really looks mutually beneficial to the teams. The new network is functioning well, and it has allowed us to upgrade our backend compute systems. We've met our obligations with the financial regulators and rectified the majority of previous issues identified by the consultants.

Yesterday I had a long workshop with the CTO and IT department heads. We've been discussing how we are going to host the new Channel account the CEO is so keen to launch. I had originally thought we would spin up the service in each DC on the new network now that we're ready, but we've been discussing cloud and how that may be beneficial depending on if Channel takes off and we struggle to scale the service or if it fails and we have to write off any associated expenditure wasted for running it on-premises. We managed to get a cloud architect from a well-respected cloud provider in the UK (Cloudhop) on a video link for a couple of hours in the afternoon to go over some options, which proved to be really useful. So I need your help to aid the decision-making process to determine if we do go in this direction. From the output of the day, we've put together some information that should help. The CTO stated we have a secured budget of £625K for 12 months of opex for the project, and we have sufficient network firewall and compute infrastructure after the recent upgrade if we need to stand up any services on the premises to support a cloud-based frontend or a complete on-premises hosting without any cloud. Additional capex might not be feasible to aid the project.

Here's what we covered in the session on the technical front:

1. Our on-premises database that we can stand up for Channel in the backend can handle 1000 transactions per second, and the cloud provider we have spoken to (Cloudhop) says it can match that if we need to use its cloud-based database instance. Each transaction is estimated to use approximately 10KB of data, and we want to be able to run at the 1000 transactions-per-second level. We've worked with marketing and calculated for Day 1 service we wouldn't expect any more than 1 million transactions per day, so let's base this as the worst case, but we need the ability to scale communications and compute to grow if this figure is exceeded dynamically, regardless of how the service is provisioned.

2. The service must be highly available, as it's a direct reflection on the Bank and we cannot allow any of the service to be compromised due to being accessible over the Internet. We will need to be able to upgrade available Internet access bandwidth within the space of a couple of days to be able to adjust to the demands of the system.

3. The application developers have stated the Channel service will be a typical load-balanced web frontend protected via a firewall, which is accessible from lightweight Channel apps (typically via a customer's smartphone) over the Internet. The web frontend communicates with the application via load balancers; the application then communicates directly with a database. The web frontend just needs to be accessible for Internet clients so it can be hosted in the cloud or on the BankDMZ network. The middleware with application and database can be either on-premises in Banknet or hosted in the cloud.

4. The replication of the database required for Channel will be handled by a direct SAN connection if running on the premises or handled directly within the cloud if running in the cloud, so we can assume that there is no requirement here for additional network connectivity.

5. Security has dictated for Channel that we want all traffic natively using SSL from the client (which will be offloaded on the load balancers), and we are going to use a host-based firewall system on the Channel compute environment wherever it is hosted so we can provide security in multiple layers.

6. If we do go with cloud, we can host the entire system (web frontend, application servers, and database) in the cloud. If we did host some of the service on the premises, we would need a firewall for access into DC services, and we can provide any on-premises compute equipment into a dedicated Channel VRF to host the service. Note that any link from the cloud would need to be encrypted into our DC(s), and they support only Direct Connect or exchange connections.

7. The latency between the application servers and the database should be <=1ms to provide the best CX journey.

Cloud charges are estimated at £50K per month for private cloud for IaaS network and compute resources and a direct-connect circuit back to each one of our DCs (primary link to St Helier and a backup link to Guernsey). There is a 60% discount available if we wanted to run the service in a public cloud; data transiting the cloud is subject to Direct Connect charges listed below.

Cloudhop Outbound Direct Connect Prices:

First 1GB per month: £10

Over 200GB per month: £5

Cloudhop has stated its private cloud option is its most secure option, with public cloud offering strong levels of security. Packet-scrubbing services prior to entry for DDoS mitigation are offered only with the private cloud option. Cloudhop can run IPsec encryption on the virtual routers and normal routing such as eBGP and even VXLAN multisite to emulate a VTEP, providing Layer EVPN Type 5 routing. RFC1918 addressing can be used on either cloud type. Both cloud offerings include Internet ingress and egress charges, but Direct Connect prices apply to any traffic that is required to be sent back into Banknet from Cloudhop's premises. Internet access speeds and services can be upgraded instantly for the private cloud offering via a portal and within two weeks for the public cloud offering via an online request system.

We're going to treat Channel as a 12-month pilot. Based on the success of the service, we can evaluate our options toward the end of the pilot in terms of scaling the system up or down. We just need to work out where and how to best host it.

Rgds,

Tim Jacobson
Network Manager
Bank of Jersey

Question 25

Complete the following table to allow the Bank to select the optimum hosting method for the Channel system. (Check all required items.)

Question	Options (place an X in the appropriate cell per question)				
Which is the most suitable hosting platform/location for Channel? (Base your selection on a combination of cost and technical feasibility.)	On-prem Jersey DC	On-prem Guernsey DC	Public cloud all services (Cloudhop)	Private cloud all services (Cloudhop)	Hybrid (private Cloudhop web frontend + Banknet on-prem database)
If the hybrid solution was chosen, what would the most suitable access method be between cloud and database infrastructures?	SD WAN Internet connection to Banknet from Cloudhop	Internet VPN to Banknet from Cloudhop	Direct Connect to Banknet to Cloudhop	Exchange connection to Banknet	Jerseytel L3 MPLS VPN to Banknet between Cloudhop and Banknet
If the database for Channel is located on-premises within the Bank's network, what would be the Day 1 minimum bandwidth required, from cloud provider to the Bank of Jersey DC(s)?	1Mbps	5Mbps	20Mbps	100Mbps	1Gbps
Day 1 minimum bandwidth required, from cloud provider to Bank of Jersey DC(s), if the web frontend, application servers, and database for Channel are located within the cloud?	0Mbps	5Mbps	20Mbps	100Mbps	1Gbps

Question 26

The Bank of Jersey decided to use a hybrid cloud model for Channel with the web frontend in a private cloud and the database within a dedicated Channel VRF within the DC VXLAN network in St Helier. Complete the illustrated design that follows by inserting the correct device icons into each environment to show where the individual devices/functionality should be provisioned for Channel, including where the application servers should be sited (redundancy is not required within the design at this point for the sake of clarity, but do show where load balancers / application delivery controllers would be required).

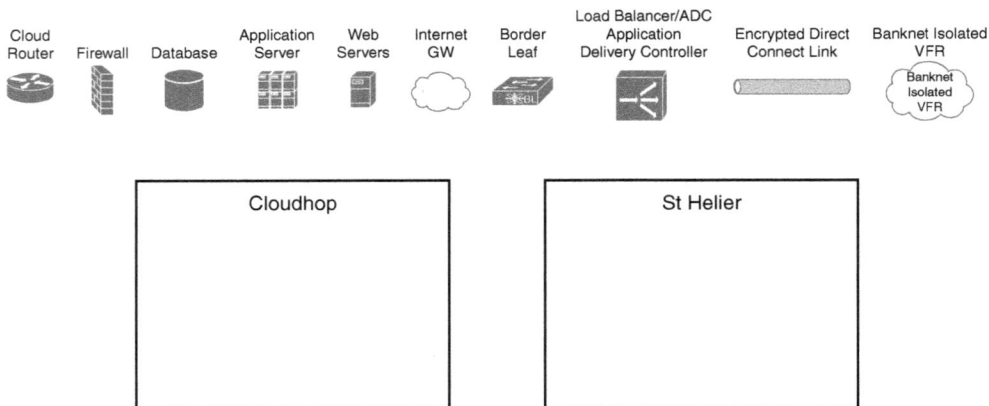

Question 27

The Bank of Jersey approved the hybrid cloud design illustrated in the diagram that follows to support Channel. Complete the table to assist in the implementation of the networking functionality in order to host the web frontend within the Cloudhop private cloud and application server and database functionality within the DC on-premises Channel VRF.

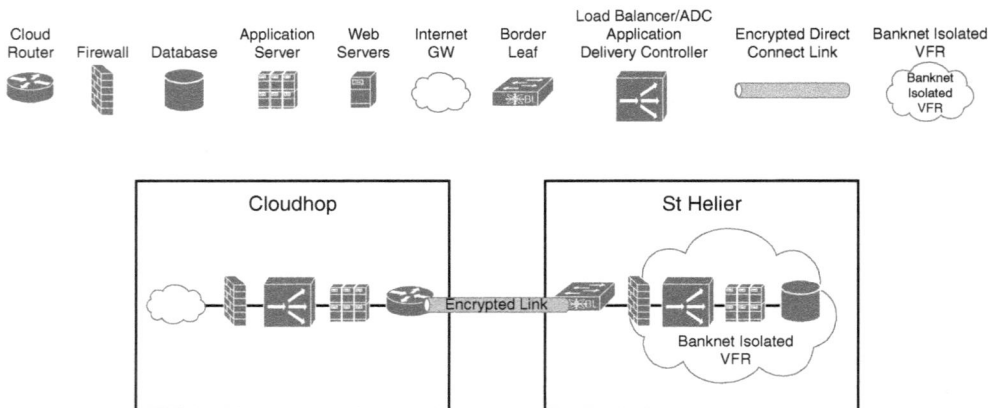

Mark within the table which feature is required for each device/area of the network.

Feature	Banknet Border Leafs	Cloudhop Router	Direct Connect Link	Cloudhop VPC
Extend OSPF underlay peering to advertise Banknet isolated VRF prefixes to Cloudhop.				
Configure eBGP peering to advertise Banknet isolated VRF prefixes to Cloudhop.				
Configure NAT for privately addressed database and application VLANs hosted within the isolated VRF.				
Enable Jumbo MTU support.				
Enable IPsec.				
Enable MACSEC.				
Extend Channel application and database VLANs over VXLAN to Cloudhop.				
Create new VLANs for hosting application servers and database server.				

Practice Lab 3 Debrief

This lab debrief section analyzes each question, showing you what was required and how to achieve the desired results. You should use this section to produce an overall score for Practice Lab 3.

Question 1

Which circuit type and new DC location provides the most suitable option for the Bank, with minimal cost for the new DC location? (Choose one option from A–D for the circuit type and one option from E–G for location.)

Requirements/constraints from supplied documentation:

The CTO has advised we should be looking to provide double the previous bandwidth at a minimum between locations.

The DC LANs are connected over a 20Gbps DCI MEC between the core switches.

An end location remains at St Helier DC, and we're going to continue to use synchronous replication for our systems and main banking application.

The existing business continuity plan does not cover natural events such as flooding, changing weather patterns, unprecedented seismic events, and extreme flooding due to rising sea levels.

Synchronous data replication is used for the Bank's mainframe systems running active in St Helier and standby in Priory Inn connected to a separate SAN, which requires 2ms (millisecond) or less RTT for successful write replication using FCoIP over the Banknet network between systems in each DC.

As detailed within the email, the DC location and circuit information is based purely on the Banknet network at this point in time, and BankExt and BankDMZ connectivity will be addressed subsequently. Current Banknet DCI connectivity is formed from dual 10Gbps links, and the CTO has requested double the previous bandwidth, so you will need at least 40Gbps made up from multiple 10Gbps circuits or single 40/100Gbps circuits. Synchronous replication will continue to be used, so the latency of fiber runs to the Portsmouth location is definitely worth consideration. The industry recognized rule of thumb is 1ms latency for 100 km round trip time (RTT). (Technology evolves rapidly but there isn't a great deal that can be enhanced with the speed of light at this point in time.) As such, at an approximate 170 km distance away, the Portsmouth location is within tolerance levels for the customer's application, which is stated as being 2ms. You may be tempted to dive in and start calculating costs, but this would take some unnecessary time and wouldn't actually provide you with a clear answer initially. Questions like this that have some cost element are generally worth starting by ruling out some distractors prior to any calculation, so it's worth narrowing down the options at this point based on best practice and the supplied constraints/requirements.

   a. Dual 100G Ethernet metro circuits

     This is a suboptimal answer. The optimal location is Portsmouth based on the geographical separation it provides, and 100G circuits are not available to Portsmouth.

   b. Dual 40G Ethernet metro circuits

This is also a suboptimal answer. The optimal location is Portsmouth based on the geographical separation it provides, and 40G circuits are not available to Portsmouth.

c. Multiple 10G DWDM channels

This is the optimal option. As the only circuit types available to Portsmouth are 10Gbps, then four circuits will be required, and some math comes into play to ensure the overall cost isn't an issue. 4x DWDM channels would cost £40K capex and £60K opex over the term (in total £100K). The MPLS circuits would be £48K capex and £56K opex over the term (in total £104K). DWDM is therefore marginally more cost effective than MPLS. A final comparison to determine which circuits would be optimal would involve double-checking the technology options. Here, the DWDM channels would provide more flexibility with the capability to trunk VLANs or route as required. The MPLS network could also provide L2 or L3 services, but there would be some assumptions around additional latency, and traffic engineering might be required in order to adhere to the latency requirement for replication. DWDM would therefore provide more flexibility and appears to meet all of the stipulated requirements. Ultimately, there isn't a compelling reason why you would choose a more expensive MPLS offering that might offer less flexibility.

d. Multiple 10G MPLS (L2 or L3 VPN) circuits

This is a suboptimal answer, as detailed in the explanation for Answer C.

e. Priory Inn Jersey

Jersey is actually not conducive as a second DC location based on the business continuity statement. There isn't a defined industry-stated distance required between DCs; however, for an island that is approximately 15 km wide, it probably makes sense to have the second location offshore. The consultants made a finding about this also, so you can actually rule out the new location in Priory Inn, and some geographical separation will be required.

f. St Andrew Guernsey

Guernsey is a reasonable candidate, being a separate island, and the costs are favorable, but the distance is still questionable for the true geographical separation required for business continuity. As such, this option is suboptimal.

g. Portsmouth UK

Portsmouth in the UK is the optimal choice for the physical location to provide the true geographical separation, and the latency over 170 km would be under the required 2ms RTT, as detailed previously. As the only circuit types available to Portsmouth are 10Gbps, then four circuits will be required.

Award yourself two points (one point per correct answer). If you selected suboptimal locations with associated speeds, then award yourself half a point per answer.

Email #2

From: Tim Jacobson

To: CCDE Candidate

Subject: New DC

Hi.

Thanks for your recommendation. The CTO has investigated the options and looked at your findings and has a preference for Guernsey using 100Gbps circuits, but the hosting company in Portsmouth has offered us a great incentive to use its location going forward. This, paired with the enhanced geographical separation it offers, makes it look like an attractive option. The hosting company has said it can light up additional channels really quickly if we go with its DWDM option, providing us with what we need for Day 1 and future scale.

Rgds,

Tim Jacobson
Network Manager
Bank of Jersey

Question 2

Are there any potential issues with using Portsmouth as a location for the backup DC? (Choose one.)

Requirements/constraints from supplied documentation:

None specifically. This is a best practice/industry standard practice item.

a. Excessive latency for replication requirements

This is a suboptimal answer. The distance from Jersey to Portsmouth is within tolerance of the synchronous replication latency limitation of 2ms (which would equate to an approximate maximum distance of 200 km), but it would be understandable if you did select this as a potential issue, as fiber runs are never typically as short as you might at first imagine. Award yourself half a point if you selected this as your answer.

b. Data sovereignty

This is the optimal answer. Although not a defined constraint, you do have some background information in regard to how the UK and Jersey operate at a fiscal level, but ultimately, they are separate countries and have separate governments. As such, data sovereignty laws could be different, and therefore the potential exists for issues in the way data is stored and handled between countries, so it's prudent to check whether this is an issue.

c. Data governance

This is incorrect. Data governance is policy around data such as departmental or organizational rules and is not a potential issue for the location.

d. High opex if further DWDM channels are required

This is incorrect. You have no compelling information stating that further channels will actually be required or that there will be a financial issue if they are.

If you have answered this question correctly, you have scored one point.

Email #3

From: Tim Jacobson

To: CCDE Candidate

Subject: New DC

Hi.

Just to let you know, we've been investigating Portsmouth as a possible DC location in more detail, and the CTO has checked and can confirm that there are no data sovereignty issues with using the UK. We've been supplied with the fiber run map for two fully resilient circuits that we can run DWDM channels on (attached). Looks like this could be a good option, but we'd appreciate if you could check it out prior to signing any orders.

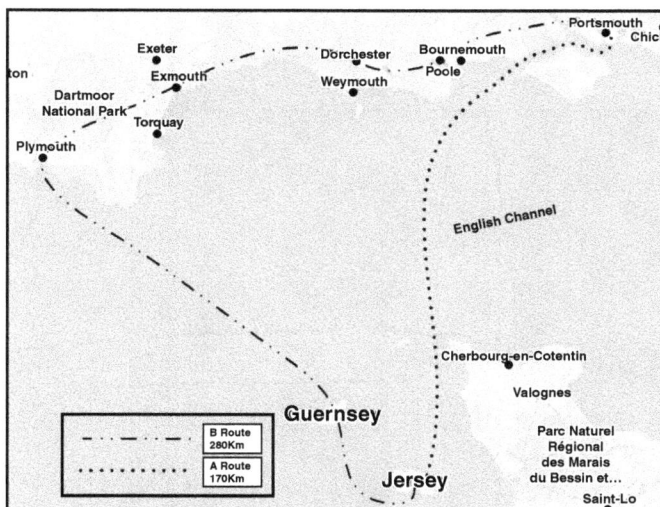

Rgds,

Tim Jacobson
Network Manager
Bank of Jersey

Question 3

Based on the new information supplied for the DWDM circuits, is there any risk associated with the Portsmouth location being selected as a standby DC location for the Bank of Jersey? (Choose one.)

Requirements/constraints from supplied documentation:

We're going to continue to use synchronous replication for our systems and main banking application.

Synchronous data replication is used for the Bank's mainframe systems running active in St Helier and standby in Priory Inn connected to a separate SAN, which requires 2ms (millisecond) or less RTT for successful write replication using FCoIP over the Banknet network between systems in each DC.

This is a validate-type question. When presented with this type of question, you will then be asked to validate your answer in a subsequent question. If you select the incorrect answer initially, you will not be able to score points for that question.

   a. Yes

   This is the correct answer. This reasoning is provided in the explanation for Question 3.1.

   b. No

   This is the incorrect answer. The reasoning is provided in the explanation for Question 3.2.

Question 3.1

If you answered Yes to Question 3, then what is the potential issue with Portsmouth as a location?

a. The latency requirement for the synchronous replication is likely to be exceeded with one fiber route.

As detailed in the explanation for Answer A in Question 2, there is a latency limitation of 2ms for the application, which would equate to a maximum approximate distance of 200 km. The B route for the fiber circuit to ensure diversity from the A route is shown as being 280 km, which would equate to a latency of approximately 2.8ms. As such, the B route is likely to be unsuitable for the Bank.

If you answered this question correctly, you scored one point.

b. If load sharing over the DWDM channels/circuits, there will be out-of-order TCP packets due to the circuit distances and resulting latency differences between them.

This does sound plausible, but typically load sharing would see an individual flow sent over a single circuit/channel and subsequent flows over a different circuit/channel. If per-packet load sharing was configured, then potentially there could be a problem, but generally it's the upper layers that put the stream together if packets arrive out of sequence. There isn't sufficient information supplied to state that this would actually be an issue, so in this case, you would be making an assumption. If you find yourself making assumptions during the exam, it's time to step back and further analyze the information you have been presented to ensure you haven't missed something.

If you answered No to Question 3, you score no points.

Email #4

From: Tim Jacobson

To: CCDE Candidate

Subject: New DC and Legacy Issues

Hi.

Good spot on the potential replication issue on the B route to Portsmouth. That route worked out to be 280 km, and using a rough calculation of 1ms per 100 km for a round trip, we would have been just over our limit for the replication application. I've taken your information to the CTO and had a session with him. We were lucky enough to be able to get the CEO on a video session, and the new direction is to revert to Guernsey as a location and use dual 100Gbps links as they offer great performance and scale. He's going to clear it with the banking regulators and provide some of the information about our actual physical location in Guernsey being high enough above sea level to not be a risk of flooding, etc., and ensure we have sufficient geographical separation for business continuity. The circuits are more expensive, but the CEO is comfortable we can secure the budget based on the additional scale and performance that they provide.

Before we get started on the new technology required to deliver the network, we have a couple of issues we need to solve in the existing network. We can work around the majority of issues that have been identified and just make sure we are covered on the new network for those. However, the main ones we need to address immediately are:

1. The BankExt and BankDMZ networks are running hot. We need to find a way to increase bandwidth between locations, as STP is blocking one of our cross-site links within each network. We can invest, if required, but we just don't expect to be in that location for more than eight months, but we will need to get the available 2Gbps between sites for each network. I've checked out the switches, and they are pretty basic, but we can enable some other features by upgrading the licenses, or we can look at new switches and circuits if we absolutely have to. I will leave it to you to investigate the following information, which is the same for the switches in both BankExt and BankDMZ:

License upgrade Bronze: Voice VLANs, PVLANs, evaluation license free for 12 months

License upgrade Silver: Layer 3 functionality and dynamic routing enabled for £2K per switch

License upgrade Gold: Stacking capability and QoS for £5K per switch

New 1Gbps circuit: 36-month term, £2K per circuit

2. We've had an issue with one of our third-party B2B connections. Their router sited in our St Helier DC on VLAN2 was effectively running at 100% CPU, and it wasn't able to pass traffic. Investigation on their side suggests it was the subject of an attack from an address that isn't within our DC ranges. I can only assume it originated from one of the other third-party connections, and we don't have the tooling in place to investigate. They have had to apply an infrastructure ACL as a countermeasure but are insisting we need to protect them also. I need you to come up with an easy-to-manage solution to help. The network team doesn't have time to make small adjustments every time a third party wants to make changes.

Rgds,

Tim Jacobson
Network Manager
Bank of Jersey

Question 4

In order to address the bandwidth limitation in the BankExt and BankDMZ network, which is the optimal option? (Choose one.)

Requirements/constraints from supplied documentation:

We need to find a way to increase bandwidth between locations, as STP is blocking one of our cross-site links within each network. We can invest, if required, but we just don't expect to be in that location for more than eight months, but we will need to get the available 2Gbps between sites for each network.

We can enable some other features by upgrading the licenses or look at new switches and circuits if we absolutely have to.

VLANs are trunked to the BankExt firewalls over EtherChannels. 802.1w STP is utilized on the Layer 2 1Gbps links between DC locations in a default configuration to ensure a loop-free topology between locations.

VLANs are trunked to the BankDMZ firewalls over EtherChannels. 802.1w STP is utilized on the Layer 2 1Gbps links between locations in a default configuration to ensure a loop-free topology between sites.

Services are spanned at Layer 2 in all zones, allowing VM migration and dynamic failover of services with a policy of no single points of failure within the network infrastructure.

   a. Upgrade switch licenses to Silver and enable Layer 3, convert the Layer 2 circuits to Layer 3, and run ECMP between locations and tunnel Layer 2.

This is incorrect. It sounds like the choice a CCIE might take for a challenge to transport Layer 2 over Layer 3. Although technically feasible, it's going to introduce complexity and changes into the environment, which translates to risk and outage. Layer 3 would require a Silver license upgrade for four switches per network, so £16K in total. Therefore, this should be an option to quickly rule out.

   b. Move the second Layer 2 circuit into the primary switch to form an EtherChannel to double the bandwidth.

This is incorrect. It would definitely provide the full 2Gbps between switches in a non-blocking EtherChannel, but it would create two single points of failure (the two connecting switches), which would not be acceptable.

   c. Add one 1Gbps circuit to one of the cross-site switch pairs in each network and form an EtherChannel on one cross-site switch pair.

This is incorrect and a distractor that should be easy enough to rule out right away. You are told that a solution is only required for up to eight months, and only to invest when necessary. This is going to take time and expense (£24K) to implement, with a three-year commitment, which would be challenging to justify.

d. Upgrade switch licenses to include stacking capability and form a virtual stack, making the topology non-blocking.

This is a suboptimal answer. Although it would definitely work, it could be considered more of a strategic longer-term fix. There is cost involved (£20K per network) to enable the stacking feature that could be avoided in Answer F. If you did select this answer, then award yourself half a point.

e. Add one 1Gbps circuit to each of the cross-site switch pairs in each network and form an EtherChannel on each cross-site switch pair.

Although this is incorrect, it would work, as STP could be configured to block the individual circuit and forward on the EtherChannel; however, as per the fourth email, you are told that a solution is required for up to eight months and to invest only when necessary. This is going to take time and expense to implement, with a three-year commitment, which would be challenging to justify.

f. Configure VLAN load balancing.

This simple solution is the correct answer. You may be asking yourself, why wasn't the Bank doing this before? I've included this to make a point and show that it is well worth taking a step back and evaluating the information you have in front of you and pairing it with your networking background. Not every question in the exam is going to be hard. You are informed that a default STP configuration is in place in each network. With VLAN load balancing configured within the topologies, both links could easily be forwarding on a per-VLAN basis to provide the required 2Gbps between locations. Quite often the best approach is simplicity. Simple just works, simple is easy to explain, and simple is easy to fix when things go wrong.

If you answered this question correctly, you scored one point.

Email #5

From: Tim Jacobson

To: CCDE Candidate

Subject: New DC and Legacy Issues

Hi.

Thanks for the suggestion to simply load-balance VLANs on the links. I will get our engineers to modify the STP priorities per VLAN to adjust the topologies! I thought we might need to invest in some new licenses to enable other features, but that would be wasted money, so we can keep the licensing as is.

Rgds,

Tim Jacobson
Network Manager
Bank of Jersey

Question 5

In order to address the third-party router issue for routers connecting to VLAN2 in the BankExt network, what would a prerequisite be in order to mitigate further attacks? (Choose one.)

Requirements/constraints from supplied documentation:

Investigation on their side suggests it was the subject of an attack from an address that isn't within our DC ranges. I can only assume it originated from one of the other third-party connections.

They have had to apply an infrastructure ACL as a countermeasure but are insisting we need to protect them also.

You need to come up with an easy-to-manage solution to help. The network team doesn't have time to make small adjustments every time a third party wants to make changes.

License Bronze: Voice VLANs, PVLANs, evaluation license free for 12 months

Switches in the network are purely Layer 2 and propagate the local VLANs between DC locations.

a. Enable Bronze evaluation licensing on the switches.

This is the correct answer. With the zero-cost license enabled, the PVLAN (private VLAN) feature will be available. This feature can then be configured for each third-party router port on the switch in VLAN2 to allow communication only with the firewall associated port on VLAN2 and not between router ports. This solution would be simple to manage and would not require any administration whenever there is an access change required by the third party (ACLs, for example, might require additional management administration to deal with changes).

b. Create an ACL per third party on the BankExt switches, only allowing traffic from that third-party IP range into the BankExt network switches.

This is incorrect and a quick one to rule out because the switches are operating in Layer 2 mode with a VLAN providing connectivity between the third-party routers and connected firewall that controls traffic entering and leaving the Bank. In theory, the switches could restrict traffic using VLAN ACLs (VACLs), but this isn't an available option, and it definitely wouldn't be a solution that would be manageable or meet the requirement to not make adjustments every time a third party wants to make a change.

c. Create an ACL per third party on the BankExt switches, blocking traffic from that third-party IP range into other third parties on the BankExt network switches.

This is incorrect and another quick one to rule out because the switches are operating in Layer 2 mode, as detailed in the explanation for Answer B.

d. Create a firewall rule blocking any third party from communicating directly to another third party.

This is incorrect. The firewall would not participate in any traffic flow between third-party router connections directed between third parties within the same VLAN (this would be Layer 2 traffic, which the firewall would not see).

If you answered this question correctly, you scored one point.

Another way you could deny third parties from communicating with each other in this scenario would be to terminate each third party onto a dedicated logical or physical interface on the firewall, but this simply doesn't scale. Converting the Layer 2 switch to Layer 3 and segmenting the third parties using different subnets and ACLs does work, but it doesn't scale. VACLs on the Layer 2 switch would function, but this would incur high management overhead if traffic flows change or even if the third-party routers are to be replaced. The simplest method is to run PVLANs and associate the firewall as a promiscuous port and only allow the third-party ports to communicate with the promiscuous port by configuring each third party as an isolated port, thereby blocking direct third-party-to-third-party communication over VLAN2 in this example.

Question 5.1

This is a validation of your understanding of Question 5, and you will only score a point if you correctly validate your answer. In the exam, you would simply be presented with one question dependent on your answer to the original question.

If you selected Answer A in Question 5, please validate you answer. (Choose one.)

a. The Bronze license will allow you to run PVLANs.

This is the correct answer. The license will allow you to apply PVLANs (private VLANs). This feature can then be configured to allow each third-party router port on the switch in VLAN2 to only allow communication with the firewall-associated port on VLAN2 and not between router ports without the need for specific ACLs.

b. The license will allow you to apply ACLs on the switches.

This is incorrect The Bronze license is not stated to enable ACLs. The switch would need to be operating in Layer 3 mode for ACLs to be applicable, which would require a Silver license.

If you answered this question correctly, you scored one point.

Question 5.2

If you selected Answer B in Question 5, please validate you answer. (Choose one.)

a. The ACL will block communication between third parties on the switch.

This is incorrect. The switches are operating in Layer 2 mode, with traffic flowing from the third-party connections into the firewall.

b. The ACL will only allow communication from the defined third party to the Bank.

This is incorrect. The switches are operating in Layer 2 mode, with traffic flowing from the third-party connections into the firewall.

Zero points.

Question 5.3

If you selected Answer C in Question 5, please validate you answer. (Choose one.)

a. The ACL will block communication between third parties on the switch.

This is incorrect. The switches are operating in Layer 2 mode, with traffic flowing from the third-party connections into the firewall.

b. The ACL will only allow communication from the defined third party to the Bank.

This is incorrect. The switches are operating in Layer 2 mode, with traffic flowing from the third-party connections into the firewall.

Zero points.

Question 5.4

If you selected Answer D in Question 5, validate you answer. (Choose one.)

a. The firewall will block communication between third parties on the switch.

This is incorrect. The firewall could only block communication between third parties if policy routing is used to forward traffic between third parties via the firewall.

b. The firewall will allow communication only from the defined third party to the Bank.

This would be the native behavior of the firewall rule base, but there are no points to be scored in Question 5.4.

Zero points.

Email #6

From: Tim Jacobson

To: CCDE Candidate

Subject: New DC Separation Technology

Hi.

Thanks for sorting out the issues. So, since we have decided on Guernsey as our new secondary DC location, we have ordered dual 100Gbps circuits from St Helier, which will be delivered with complete resilience. With all of the work going on, we've completely neglected the fact up to now that we should also provision dual circuits for our BankExt network and BankDMZ network. The costs are actually looking very prohibitive to provision an additional four circuits, so I'd like you to investigate alternative options so we can run all networks over the dual 100Gbps circuits. There will be a huge amount of capacity with the new circuits and the potential to save a significant amount of shareholders' funds if we can offer separation in a way that will keep the regulators happy.

Rgds,

Tim Jacobson
Network Manager
Bank of Jersey

Question 6

Complete the following table to assist the Bank of Jersey with its assessment of potential technologies to provide separation and connectivity of cross-site BankExt, BankDMZ, and Banknet networks over the dual 100Gbps DCI links being provisioned between St Helier and Guernsey DCs. Place an X in each cell if the technology per row offers the features detailed in the columns.

Technology	Offers Layer 2 separation between different Bank of Jersey networks	Offers Layer 3 VRF separation between Bank of Jersey networks	Offers ability to transport <20 VLANs between dual locations at Layer 2	Offers ability to scale to transport >200 VLANs between dual locations at Layer 2	Offers flexibility to transport multiple VLANs between more than two locations at Layer 2
QinQ	X	—	X	X	X
VXLAN EVPN Multipod	X	X	X	X	—
VXLAN EVPN Multisite	X	X	X	X	X
VRFs and 802.1Q (VRF Lite)	X	X	X	X	—
MPLS Layer 3	—	X	—	—	—
H-VPLS	X	—	X	X	X

This is seen as one of the harder question types in the exam by candidates, and it can be quite daunting to face with so many questions in effect. In reality, this is just a case of breaking up the overall question into line items and working your way through them independently. The question doesn't have specific constraints or requirements, so you will be relying purely on your technical knowledge to complete this one. You will definitely receive partial credit as it would be unrealistic to expect candidates to answer each item correctly. The technologies can be summarized as follows:

■ QinQ: Double-tagging of VLANs for scale and separation. A single VLAN could be allocated for each network in the Bank, and the separate VLANs in each network could be double-tagged with their respective carrier VLAN. Layer 2 separation between networks would be achieved, but the technology would rely on a Layer 2 trunk between locations with STP, which wouldn't offer Layer 3 VRF-type separation between networks, and additional technology or infrastructure would be required for this. The technology scales significantly and operates on a point-to-point and point-to-multipoint basis.

- VXLAN EVPN multipod: Layer 2 overlay on top of a Layer 3 underlay fabric using MAC in UDP encapsulation. The technology scales significantly and removes the knowledge that the phone will at some point ring at 3 a.m. with an STP disaster, as there is no longer a reliance on STP to extend Layer 2 between DCs. Layer 2 can be transported efficiently (including VLAN overlaps) with VNIs, and Layer 3 separation between networks can be provided by VRF in a similar function to Layer 3 MPLS VPNs with route distinguishers. Multipod can be seen as the same network/fabric, even when deployed between two data centers with separate IGP areas and BGP autonomous systems with MP-BGP (as the VXLAN tunnel is end-to-end between VTEPs). Multipod is in effect a single overlay and control plane with single underlay—single replication domain for BUM and single VNI admin domain. As such, multipod would not be suitable for more than two physical locations.

- VXLAN EVPN multisite: Similar to VXLAN multipod, but with additional separation between locations. The VXLAN tunnel is terminated and reestablished between locations in a form of VXLAN stitching, which provides the capability to run VXLAN between more than two physical locations with multiple overlay domains, multiple overlay control-plane domains, multiple underlay domains, multiple replication domains for BUM, and multiple VNI admin domains.

- VRFs and 802.1Q (VRF Lite): This would typically involve a Layer 2 trunk link, with each network's VLANs propagated over the trunk using 802.1Q between locations with a Layer 3 device assigning VLANs to VRFs. It would provide the Layer 2 and 3 separation and scales with the required manual intervention, but it wouldn't be the most flexible technology for use between more than two locations.

- MPLS Layer 3: MPLS Layer 3 is not going to be able to transport Layer 2 without additional protocols, but it will provide the Layer 3 separation between networks with multi-VRF technology.

- H-VPLS: Hierarchical VPLS provides the Layer 2 separation between networks over an MPLS network and overcomes the scale limitation associated with VPLS by use of LDP signaling in the control plane. As this is a point-to-multipoint technology, it would be suitable for more than two locations to propagate Layer 2.

Award yourself half a point per correct row of answers, with a maximum score of three points overall for this question.

Email #7

From: Tim Jacobson

To: CCDE Candidate

Subject: New DC Separation Technology

Hi.

Thanks for the info. I've had time to go through this, but I need you to recommend the right technology for separation of networks that provides us the flexibility to run an additional DC in conjunction to St Helier and Guernsey if we need to in the future. I don't know right now if we want to—I just don't want to limit ourselves to having to change the technology if we do decide to at a later date. The technology would need to provide separation of all of our networks combined on one effective network and should be compatible with what technology we use to actually provision ports in each network. I need you to be confident the technology can also limit our failure domain to a single DC if we have any Layer 2 type issues, even though we still need to propagate Layer 2 between DCs. As mentioned, we have a preference for separation without having to buy additional circuits for BankExt and BankDMZ DCIs. (I've sounded out Security, and they aren't too happy. However, if we can prove physical and logical separation, they said we are compliant with the security policy.)

Rgds,

Tim Jacobson
Network Manager
Bank of Jersey

Question 7

Which of the following technologies is best suited to provide connectivity between St Helier and the new DC location in Guernsey for the Bank based on its requirements for new networks and use of dual 100Gbps circuits? (Choose one.)

Requirements/constraints from supplied documentation:

I need you to recommend the right technology for separation of networks that provides us the flexibility to run an additional DC in conjunction to St Helier and Guernsey if we need to in the future. I don't know right now if we want to, I just don't want to limit ourselves to having to change the technology if we do decide to at a later date. The technology would need to provide separation of all of our networks combined on one effective network and should be compatible with what technology we use to actually provision ports in each network. I need you to be confident the technology can also limit our failure domain to a single DC if we have any Layer 2 type issues even though we still need to propagate Layer 2 between DCs. We have a preference for separation without having to buy additional circuits for BankExt and BankDMZ DCIs. (I've sounded out Security, and they aren't too happy. However, if we can prove physical and logical separation, they said we are compliant with the security policy.)

I'd like you to investigate alternative options so we can run all networks over the dual 100Gbps circuits. There will be a huge amount of capacity with the new circuits and the potential to save a significant amount of shareholders' funds if we can offer separation in a way that will keep the regulators happy.

a. QinQ

This is incorrect. As previously detailed, QinQ would provide the Layer 2 separation, but it would still require a legacy trunked network with associated STP risks between DCs, and without any Layer 3 facility or separation, it would typically only be possible between two locations. Additional technology/infrastructure would also likely be required for the provisioning of each network.

b. H-VPLS

This is incorrect. As previously detailed, H-VPLS would provide the Layer 2 separation, but it wouldn't provide the Layer 3 facility or separation without additional MPLS configuration. The technology could be used between more than two locations, but additional technology/infrastructure would likely be required for the provisioning of each network.

c. VXLAN EVPN Multipod

This is a suboptimal answer. VXLAN EVPN multipod would provide the Layer 2 separation and full Layer 3 capabilities within separate VRFs, but it would only be suitable for a dual-DC topology. The technology facilitates deployment of leaf switches, which could be used to create the different network zones. If you selected this option, award yourself half a point.

d. VXLAN EVPN Multisite

This is the optimal answer. VXLAN EVPN multisite would provide the Layer 2 separation and full Layer 3 capabilities within separate VRFs between dual DCs and would be suitable if an additional DC is required in the future. The technology facilitates deployment of leaf switches, which could be used to create the different network zones. It would be a good design decision to use a multisite configuration from Day 1 to provide additional flexibility and separation between DCs, from a minimal configuration overhead perspective, in comparison to multipod, even in a dual-site deployment.

If you selected Answer D, you scored one point.

Question 8

Bank of Jersey decided to run VXLAN EVPN multisite technology to provide flexibility for the future and to run multiple network overlay instances over a Layer 3 fabric. What is a recommended approach for the deployment to provide separation of legacy network zones to meet the Security department's requirement? (Choose one.)

Requirements/constraints from supplied documentation:

I've sounded out Security, and they aren't too happy. However, if we can prove physical and logical separation, they said we are compliant with the security policy.

a. Provision of separate spines and leaf switches per network zone

This is incorrect. This is effectively a complete network, and combining all three networks would therefore require three sets of spines and leafs in each DC. Similarly, it would be complex to share the dual 100Gbps circuits between each network in this architecture.

b. Provision of separate underlay fabric per network zone

This is incorrect. The underlay fabric can be shared between networks. Having separate underlays would be the same as per the explanation for Answer A.

c. Provision of separate overlay per network zone

This is a suboptimal answer. Separate overlays are required per network zone for logical separation, with each network defining a VRF within VXLAN. However, this doesn't address the physical separation requirement, as detailed in the explanation for Answer D. If you selected this option, award yourself half a point.

d. Provision of separate overlay and leaf switches per network zone

This is the optimal answer. Separate overlays are required, as detailed in the explanation for Answer C, but also having separate leaf switches provides the physical separation that Security requires. Having separate leaf switches would ensure patching issues or deliberate connectivity into specific network zones could be mitigated to the same extent as within the legacy network.

If you selected Answer D, you scored one point.

Email #8

From: Tim Jacobson

To: CCDE Candidate

Subject: VXLAN EVPN Multisite

Hi.

Thanks for your recommendation. Let's go ahead and run an EVPN VXLAN multisite infrastructure to support all of our three network zones between St Helier and Guernsey as separate overlays on one underlay fabric. We are unlikely to need the ability to run more than two data centers, but if we can introduce the flexibility in the initial design, then this would be a real bonus, and I prefer the separation benefits multisite brings. I've been looking at appropriate network hardware (leaf and spine switches) for the new network, including differences between licensing, and can't comment on all the technical features other than we will want to run vPC (virtual port-channel/multi-chassis EtherChannel), as each of our servers will be dual-homed and we have no plans for running multicast in the overlay. If things change, we can always go ahead and pay for a license upgrade in situ, but I need your help in selecting hardware and licensing. So see what you can do to keep costs as low as possible. 100Gbps optics, for example, are running at £2000 vs. £1500 for 40Gbps each. I definitely want the fabric to be non-blocking for the uplinks on the 1Gbps leaf switches, even if we have a single spine switch failure, for example. Don't worry about the costs of the actual switches, as these are fairly standard. Just select what we need to create the network.

Switch types available:

48x 10Gbps-based leaf switches

128x 10Gbps-based leaf switches

48x 1Gbps leaf switches

48x 40/100Gbps spine switches

Spines can support 40Gbps or 100Gbps on each port, depending on optics purchased. The spines are actually from a different vendor than the leafs, as they were significantly cheaper than the leaf vendor's spines, but they are compatible, don't have a license option, and seem to come with an enterprise edition as standard that covers every feature listed on each license type of the leafs.

We will need some border leaf switches dedicated for services for each zone, such as load balancers and zone firewalls. The DCI links can be terminated on border leaf switches also. Border leaf switches can be 48x 10Gbps leaf switches that we purpose as border leafs—I will need you to determine which license is required for them.

All leaf switch options come with six uplink ports onboard and just require the necessary optics purchased to enable the ports (as per the spine ports, they will operate at 40Gbps or 100Gbps, depending on which optics are inserted).

Optics: 40Gbps optics are £1.5K and 100Gbps optics are £2K.

Silver Leaf License Features (included in switch purchase price):

OSPF

IS-IS

MP-BGP

VXLAN

EVPN multipod

EVPN multisite

vPC (multi-chassis EtherChannel)

MACSEC

IPsec

GETVPN

GRE

Multicast

Automation suite (OpenConfig, IETF, native)

Gold Leaf License Features (additional £2K per switch):

OSPF

IS-IS

MP-BGP

VXLAN

EVPN multipod

EVPN multisite

vPC (multi-chassis EtherChannel)

MACSEC

IPsec

GETVPN

GRE

Multicast

vPC (multi-chassis EtherChannel) fabric peering

Tenant routed multicast

Automation suite (OpenConfig, IETF, native)

Streaming telemetry

Here are the latest computer hardware device counts required for Day 1 (per DC):

Network	Servers/devices @ 1Gbps port speed	Servers/devices @ 10Gbps port speed
BankExt	26	—
BankDMZ	32	22
Banknet	92	182

Rgds,

Tim Jacobson
Network Manager
Bank of Jersey

Question 9

Draw out the physical topology of the required EVPN VXLAN network infrastructure for one DC to consolidate the BankExt, BankDMZ, and Banknet networks to support Day 1 services in the most cost-effective manner. Use as many leaf switches, border leaf switches, and spine switches as necessary, based on the requirements provided, and select the most appropriate optic speed and count.

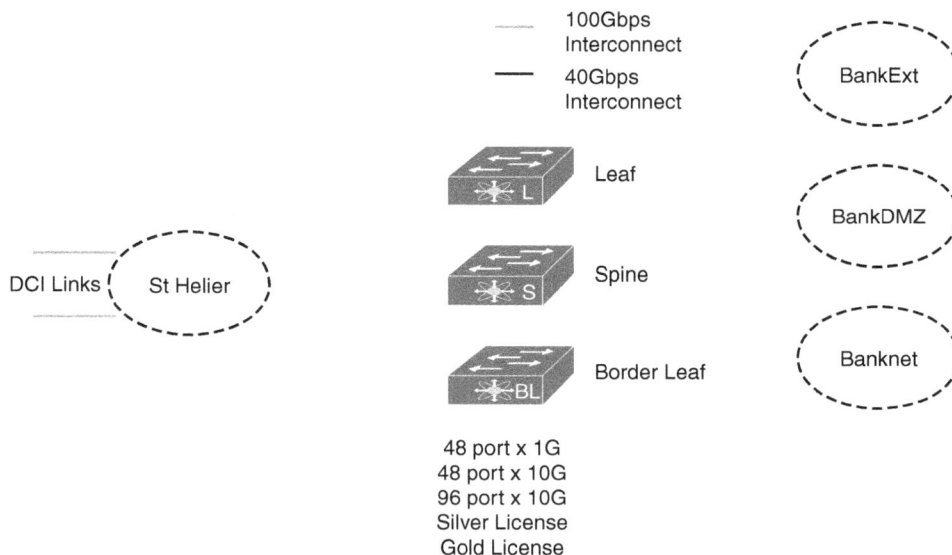

- 100Gbps Interconnect
- 40Gbps Interconnect
- Leaf
- Spine
- Border Leaf
- BankExt
- BankDMZ
- Banknet
- DCI Links — St Helier

48 port x 1G
48 port x 10G
96 port x 10G
Silver License
Gold License

Requirements/constraints from supplied documentation:

We will want to run vPC (multi-chassis EtherChannel) as each of our servers will be dual homed and we have no plans for running multicast in the overlay.

Keep costs as low as possible. 100Gbps optics, for example, are running at £2000 vs. £1500 for 40Gbps each.

I definitely want the fabric to be non-blocking for the uplinks for the 1Gbps leafs, even if we have a spine switch failure, for example.

Spines can support 40Gbps or 100Gbps, depending on the optics purchased.

We will need some border leaf switches dedicated for services for each zone, such as load balancers and zone firewalls. The DCI links can be terminated on border leaf switches also. Border leaf switches can be 48x 10Gbps leaf switches that we purpose as border leafs. I will need you to determine which license is required for them.

All leaf switch options come with six uplink ports onboard and just require the necessary optics purchased to enable the ports (as per the spine ports, they will operate at 40Gbps or 100Gbps, depending on which optics are inserted).

I've sounded out Security, and they aren't too happy. However, if we can prove physical and logical separation, then they said we are compliant with the security policy.

Services are spanned at Layer 2 in all zones, allowing VM migration and dynamic failover of services with a policy of no single points of failure within the network infrastructure.

The most important information you have to begin the design is knowing that you need to create a leaf/spine architecture (with Layer 3 fabric) and that you will need to provide logical and physical separation of the three networks. In order to achieve this, you will simply need separate VRFs within the VXLAN network at the time of configuration for logical separation and separate leaf switches per network zone for physical separation that can share the same underlay and spine but not border leaf switches, as services such as environment firewalls and load balancers would connect into each zone (if all three zones share a single set of border leaf switches, then the physical separation requirement would not be met per network zone). Border leaf switches would need to be deployed in pairs to provide a resilient method of connecting services to ensure there is no single point of failure. Therefore, three sets of border leaf switches will be required, and there is a decision to be made as to which set should contain the physical DCI circuits. In theory, they could go into any zone set, as the DCI links would form part of the underlay, but it makes more sense to deploy them into the Banknet set of border leaf switches, as this zone has the majority of connectivity and traffic (this doesn't breach the physical separation requirement, as BankDMZ traffic flowing over the DCI links, for example, would be logical connectivity as opposed to physical). Another crucial point is that vPCs (multichassis EtherChannels) are required to support dual-homing of each server. This fundamentally means (and easily overlooked in the pressure of the exam) that the compute port count should be doubled, and each server should be dual-homed to different leaf switches to adhere to the requirement of no single points of failure (you were provided with server count as oppose to overall port count). vPC in a leaf switch typically translates to the switches being deployed in pairs, with some form of vPC peer link between them. Normally, this would be a physical vPC peer-link connection, which would allow traffic received on one leaf/VTEP to be sent to the adjacent leaf/VTEP for further forwarding to local connections for that leaf/VTEP. This would mean additional optics (two) per leaf switch to connect to an adjacent leaf for resilience of the peer link. The astute reader may have noticed that the Gold license option for the leaf switches enables a vPC fabric peering feature. This would mean that vPC peer-link capability could be offered across the fabric, a recent neat innovation that would allow you to save the two optics required between leaf switches. If you didn't pick up on this, don't be dismayed, as it is a fairly recent feature. However, it should hopefully point out the need to be aware of innovations in the industry. You are told that cost-effectiveness is important, so you only really need to work out if investing in the Gold license will reduce the overall costs, and which optics to choose. Both licenses provide the basic features required for Day 1 service. When you work out how many leaf switches are required per DC (20), you will see that you can actually reduce the optic count by 40 (spines wouldn't require any vPC peer links between them). If you enable vPC fabric peering with the Gold license (20 switches × 2 optics = 40 optics; 40 optics × £2K = £80K saved), 20 switches with the Gold license equates to an additional £40K cost, so you would actually save £40K based on the use of

100Gbps optics in the fabric by running the Gold license on all leaf switches. Why were costs calculated using 100Gbps optics? Well, you are informed that a non-blocking architecture is required for the 1Gbps leaf switches, even if a spine switch fails. This means that if you are running a 40Gbps optic to a single spine (in the event of one spine failing), then you could be oversubscribed if the switch is fully loaded and all ports are running at maximum speed (48 ports). Running 4x 40Gbps to a leaf from a spine wouldn't be cost-effective, as 100Gbps optics are more cost-effective and the spine would only support 12 leaf switches in this case, so additional spines would also be required, pushing the cost further northward unnecessarily.

You might be tempted to collapse some of the BankDMZ and BankExt functionality into the same leaf switches. Technically, you could make it work, but you have a security dictate stating physical separation is required, and there are some overlapping VLAN numbers between zones, so this should quickly point to the fact that separate switches are required per zone.

Based on the supplied server information, the following switches will be required.

Here are the latest computer hardware device counts required for Day 1 (per DC):

Network	Servers/ devices @ 1Gbps port speed	Servers dual-homed, hence total port count:	Number of 48x 1Gbps leaf switches required per zone:	Servers / devices @ 10Gbps port speed	Servers dual-homed, hence total port count:	Number of 48x or 96x 10Gbps leaf switches required per zone:
BankExt	26	52	2	—	—	—
BankDMZ	32	64	2	22	44	2 (48 port)
Banknet	92	184	4	182	364	4 (96 port)

So this covers the leafs; there will also be two spines in total (per DC) and two border leafs per actual network/zone. A total of 82x 100Gbps optics will be required per DC (two per leaf and border leaf switch to cover the switches themselves and the same number of optics required in the connecting spine switches). The following figure details the resulting design. Partial scoring would be available if you did not create an identical design.

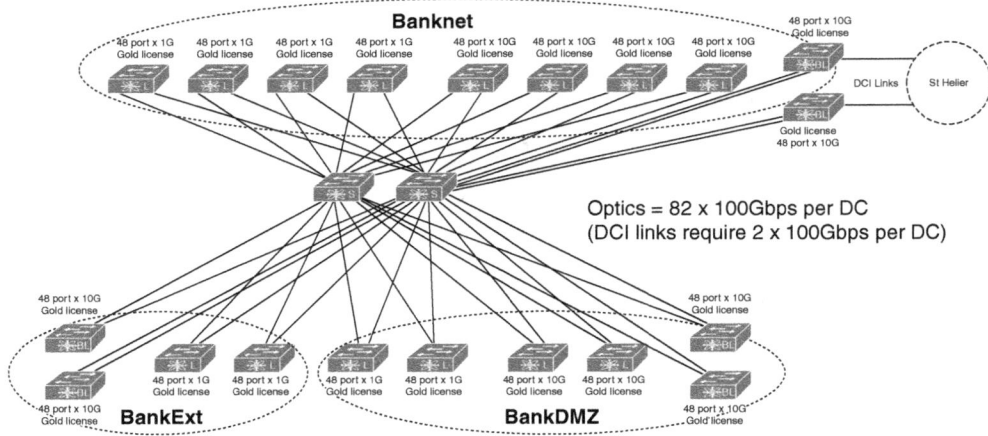

Banknet

48 port x 1G Gold license
48 port x 1G Gold license
48 port x 1G Gold license
48 port x 1G Gold license
48 port x 10G Gold license
48 port x 10G Gold license
48 port x 10G Gold license
48 port x 10G Gold license
48 port x 10G Gold license

DCI Links   St Helier

Gold license
48 port x 10G

Optics = 82 x 100Gbps per DC
(DCI links require 2 x 100Gbps per DC)

48 port x 10G Gold license
48 port x 10G Gold license
48 port x 1G Gold license
48 port x 1G Gold license
48 port x 1G Gold license
48 port x 1G Gold license
48 port x 10G Gold license
48 port x 10G Gold license
48 port x 10G Gold license
48 port x 10G Gold license
48 port x 10G Gold license

BankExt

BankDMZ

If you answered this question correctly, you scored three points.

Question 10

The VXLAN design was submitted to an Architectural Review Board within the bank, and a comment was documented that suggested super-spines would be required within the design in order to provision the BankExt, BankDMZ, and Banknet networks over the same fabric. What would your response be to the comment? (Choose one.)

Requirements/constraints from supplied documentation:

None specifically. This is a general industry best practice item.

Occasionally, you might be fortunate enough to be presented with a simple question that can take seconds to answer. This will do wonders for your motivation, especially if you have just spent 20 minutes on the previous question!

a. Super-spines would be required based on the supplied requirements and can be formed by adding two further spines per DC connecting directly to the planned new spines.

This is incorrect. See the explanation for Answer B—the network is relatively small in switch and port count and would not justify an additional spine layer to increase scale.

b. Super-spines would not be required based on supplied requirements.

This is the correct answer. Super-spines would not be required based on existing requirements. They would typically be required for a hyper-scale environment or if there was a large multisite environment whereby an overall "core" could be created to form a connection module between sites.

If you answered this question correctly, you scored one point.

Email #10

From: Tim Jacobson

To: CCDE Candidate

Subject: New Design

Hi.

Thanks for the design. I've got one of the guys to document it. He initially thought we could reduce leaf count by consolidating some of the BankExt and BankDMZ ports into the same device and allocate ports per VRF, but I told him Security requested physical and logical separation. We can obviously do this if we use distinct switch pairs per environment for physical separation and use the underlay fabric for the logical separation and tunnel VXLAN over the top per environment. The vPC fabric peering enabled by purchase of the Gold license has saved a good sum and reduced the optic and fiber patch requirements between leaf switch pairs considerably in order to provision server resiliency per leaf switch pair. I hadn't realized initially we would need a set of border leaf switches per environment/network zone, but it makes sense if we apply services for each zone such as firewalls or load balancers on a single pair of border leaf switches, then we wouldn't meet our security requirement of providing physical separation between network zones. It seemed to make sense to connect the DCI links into the Banknet border leaf switches, as we have the majority of services running on this network, and this does ensure logical separation between zones, as it's all VXLAN overlay by the time traffic flows over the DCI links.

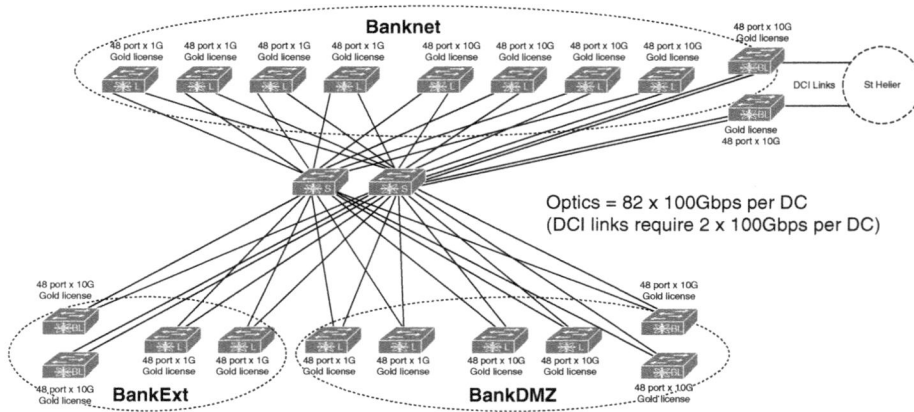

Optics = 82 x 100Gbps per DC
(DCI links require 2 x 100Gbps per DC)

We will connect up the management ports on all of the new switches, which have a dedicated management VRF, and drop these into our dedicated management network that the team has already built out using legacy infrastructure.

We will connect up all circuits and required firewalls for each environment onto the dedicated border leaf switches per zone and assign them to the required VRFs when we build this out.

Rgds,

Tim Jacobson
Network Manager
Bank of Jersey

Question 11

If the Bank of Jersey's Security department changed policy and decided to permit BankExt networks and BankDMZ to share the same physical leaf switches and then applied configuration mitigation for Layer 2 security to block access between networks, is there a further issue that would need to be rectified for this change in policy? (Choose one.)

Requirements/constraints from supplied documentation:

The following VLANs are in use in the BankExt network:

VLAN ID	Description
20	Third-party connectivity
21	ISP connectivity (public range)
22	External firewall state
23	External firewall HA
24	External management

The following VLANs are in use in the BankDMZ network:

VLAN ID	Description
12	RAS VPN
13–20	Public production services – VIP frontend
21–30	Public production services – server VLANs
31–38	Public non-production services VIP frontend
39–50	Public non-production services server VLANs
99	DMZ firewall state
100	DMZ firewall HA
101	DMZ management

a. Yes

This is the correct answer. See the answer to Question 11.1.

b. No

This is incorrect. See the answer to Question 11.2.

Question 11.1

If you chose Yes for Question 11, please validate your answer. (Choose one.)

a. Overlapping VLAN numbers exist between network zones. There would be an issue allocating a VLAN to a unique VNI per network.

This is the correct answer. Overlapping VLAN numbers are not an issue in VXLAN networks when the VLAN resides on different leafs/VTEPs, as the VLANs can be assigned different VNIs, providing different VXLANs per VLAN. The problem arises when the overlapping occurs on the same switch. If this was to happen, without some form of VLAN translation, the VLANs from different networks could not be differentiated throughout the network and would therefore effectively share connectivity bridging networks.

b. Overlapping VLAN numbers exist between network zones. This would mean multi-destination BUM (broadcast unknown multicast) traffic destined from one network would be received on the other network also.

This is incorrect. Overlapping VLAN numbers do exist, but BUM traffic wouldn't be received on multiple networks, as only a single VLAN can be allocated to a VNI, and hence multi-destination BUM traffic is restricted to a single VNI.

If you answered this question correctly by selecting Answer A, you scored one point.

Question 11.2

If you chose No for Question 11, please validate your answer. (Choose one.)

a. Configuring features such as VLAN hopping mitigation would provide sufficient control.

This is incorrect. You can only score a point if you answered Yes to Question 11 and validated your answer correctly by selecting Answer A in Question 11.1.

b. The firewalls required between networks would provide sufficient control.

This is incorrect. You can only score a point if you answered Yes to Question 11 and validated your answer correctly by selecting Answer A in Question 11.1.

Zero points.

Question 12

Complete the following table to assist Bank of Jersey engineers in creating VNIs for the BankExt, BankDMZ, and Banknet networks. Create any VNID using seven digits, with the last four digits used for VLAN numbers.

Requirements/constraints from supplied documentation:

Create any necessary VNID using seven digits, with the last four digits used for VLAN numbers.

Network Zone	VLAN	VNI
BankExt	20	1000020
BankExt	21	1000021
BankDMZ	20	1010020
BankDMZ	21	1010021
Banknet	20	1020020
Banknet	21	1020021

Obviously, there are multiple options available in creating the VNIs. The question is just seeking validation of VNI allocation understanding for overlapping VLANs. The question requires that the last four digits be used for the VLAN ID, so the first three digits must therefore be used for the VRF. The example shows a VRF ID of 100 for the BankExt network, 101 for the BankDMZ network, and 102 for the Banknet network—this means the VLAN IDs can be used within the VNI without fear of overlapping. As long as your answer has a unique VRF prior to the VLAN ID for each network, you have answered the question correctly.

If you answered this question correctly, you scored one point.

Email #11

From: Tim Jacobson

To: CCDE Candidate

Subject: Multi-Destination BUM Traffic

Hi.

As we get closer to implementing the network design, we've been looking into the specifications of how VXLAN will work, and it appears we need a design decision based on the multi-destination BUM (broadcast unknown unicast and multicast) traffic using ingress replication or multicast mode in the underlay. The leaf switches can run either mode, so what do you recommend for our setup?

Rgds,

Tim Jacobson
Network Manager
Bank of Jersey

Question 13

Do you have sufficient information to make a design decision for multi-destination BUM traffic forwarding to run using multicast or ingress replication for the new network? (Choose one.)

Requirements/constraints from supplied documentation:

None. This question is just checking if you are "connected" to the scenario and to ask for information that you don't have and to not ask for information you already have at your disposal.

  a. Yes

   This is incorrect. You would be making an assumption as opposed to an informed decision. You don't have sufficient information, as the appropriate mode would be dependent on the hardware performance.

  b. No

This is correct. See the answer to Question 13.2.

Question 13.1

If you answered Yes for Question 13, which replication mode would you select for multi-destination BUM traffic? (Choose one.)

a. Ingress replication

Possibly. This mode is definitely simpler to implement than multicast in the underlay, but there could be a premium to pay in terms of CPU hit; regardless, there is no correct answer to this question.

b. Multicast replication in the underlay

Multicast is generally the most efficient method for forwarding multi-destination BUM traffic, but it can be more complex to implement and troubleshoot than ingress replication; regardless, there is no correct answer to this question.

Zero points.

Question 13.2

If you answered No for Question 13, what further information do you require? (Choose one.)

a. Additional leaf switch CPU utilization for predicted traffic baseline for ingress replication

This is the correct answer. It's important to know if headend replication is feasible under normal operation. This mode of replication for multi-destination BUM traffic in a VXLAN network does simplify things considerably within the underlay in comparison to multicast (especially between multiple DCs), but it can come at a CPU utilization cost, depending on the hardware in use and levels of BUM traffic. If you are going to make a design decision, it needs to be an informed one with additional information regarding the hardware performance implications of both modes.

b. Which multicast modes are possible for multicast forwarding in the underlay

This is incorrect. Multicast is generally the most efficient method for forwarding multi-destination BUM traffic, but knowing which multicast protocol mode can be used for the BUM traffic replication in the underlay is more of an implementation decision.

If you answered this question correctly by selecting Answer A, you scored one point.

Email #12

From: Tim Jacobson

To: CCDE Candidate

Subject: Multi-Destination Replication Mode Info

Hi.

So the ingress replication mode for multi-destination BUM traffic we are told will increase CPU by only 5% based on our anticipated throughput, and the maximum it could reach is an additional 10%. The multicast mode of replication in the underlay will increase at a fixed additional 3% using BiDir or ASM.

Rgds,

Tim Jacobson
Network Manager
Bank of Jersey

Question 14

The Bank has decided to implement multicast replication for BUM traffic based on a clear CPU reduction in comparison to ingress replication rather than request a design recommendation. When it comes to implementation, however, what would be a benefit of using BiDir as opposed to ASM for the underlay multicast protocol to transport BUM traffic between VTEPs across each DC? (Choose one.)

Requirements/constraints from supplied documentation:

None. This question is just checking multicast knowledge, as a similar question could come up within any of the four labs presented within the exam.

   a. BiDir does not require a rendezvous point.

   This is incorrect. BiDir requires a rendezvous point, and when redundancy is required, a phantom rendezvous point is used between RPs.

   b. BiDir offers native resilience.

   This is incorrect. Resilience would be achieved by configuring multiple RPs and using a phantom RP configuration.

   c. BiDir uses out-of-band signaling between the receiver and the group it requires to join, making it more scalable, and there is no requirement for pruning multicast trees.

   This is incorrect. This is an SSM feature with use of IGMPv3.

   d. BiDir drastically reduces the mroute state in the network.

   This is the correct answer. BiDir uses a shared multicast tree based solely on the (*,G), eliminating any source-specific state (S,G), allowing scale in the multicast domain in terms of resources used and the number of sources.

If you answered this question correctly, you scored one point.

Email #13

From: Tim Jacobson

To: CCDE Candidate

Subject: Pre-Production Banknet Network

Hi.

We've almost fallen down the same hole as before in the legacy network, providing the Banknet as a single network with production and pre-production services as called out by the consultants. I need you to work out how we can provide a pre-production environment within Banknet that can communicate without any policy control to the production environment within Banknet, typically within the same VLAN. Unfortunately, due to legacy reasons, we have some prod and pre-prod compute services running on the same VLANs, and the server guys are telling me it would take six months to re-address and make the required application changes, and that's too long. We want to offer the best possible protection between environments, so a Layer 2 type STP issue or broadcast issue in pre-prod can't affect prod.

Rgds,

Tim Jacobson
Network Manager
Bank of Jersey

Question 15

How can Banknet production and pre-production compute services be provisioned on the new network, providing mitigation from Layer 2 broadcast type events in either network propagating into each other? (Choose one.)

Requirements/constraints from supplied documentation:

I need you to work out how we can provide a pre-production environment within Banknet that can communicate without any policy control to the production environment within Banknet, typically within the same VLAN. Unfortunately, due to legacy reasons, we have some prod and pre-prod compute services running on the same VLANs, and the server guys are telling me it would take six months to readdress and make the required application changes, and that's too long. We want to offer the best possible protection between environments so a Layer 2 type STP issue or broadcast issue in pre-prod can't affect prod.

There is no dedicated test or pre-production network facility. There is a risk to the production network by implementing services without testing them in isolation prior to delivery.

a. Create separate production and pre-production overlay VRFs in VXLAN and use route-leaking between VRFs for communication.

This is incorrect. The services have been implemented within the same VLANs, and you are informed that readdressing isn't an option. This solution would require separate networks in order to function and would break any Layer 2 connectivity previously in use within the VLANs.

b. Create separate production and pre-production overlay VRFs in VXLAN and use route-leaking and NAT between VRFs for communication.

This is incorrect. The services have been implemented within the same VLANs, and you are informed that readdressing isn't an option. This solution would require separate networks in order to function and would break any Layer 2 connectivity previously in use within the VLANs. The NAT would be technically possible if communication was required between different prefixes, however.

c. Create separate production and pre-production overlay VRFs in VXLAN and use a routed firewall between VRFs for communication.

This is incorrect. The services have been implemented within the same VLANs, and you are informed that readdressing isn't an option. You have also been told to allow communication without any policy control, so a firewall that could be positioned for inter-VRF communication can be ruled out.

d. Create separate production and pre-production overlay VRFs in VXLAN and use a transparent firewall between VRFs for communication.

This is incorrect. You have been told to allow communication without any policy control, so a firewall positioned for inter-VRF communication can be ruled out.

e. Group compute production infrastructure onto specific VTEP leaf pairs and pre-production compute onto other pairs with Storm-Control configured on leaf uplinks.

This is the optimal answer. It's not perfect, but based on the constraints of not being able to readdress devices, share VLANs, or use any kind of firewall, the best separation between environments while still allowing full connectivity would be to divide the compute environment into separate leaf/VTEP switches. This, paired with Storm-Control (which could significantly reduce any loop or broadcast storm condition bleeding into multi-destination BUM traffic throughout the network), would ensure that any Layer 2 STP issue only affects the leaf/VTEP where the issue resides, and it would therefore not propagate into the network and affect the production environment if the issue originated in the pre-production environment, for example.

If you answered this question correctly, you scored one point.

Email #14

From: Tim Jacobson

To: CCDE Candidate

Subject: Implementation

Hi.

Thanks for the info. We will create some compute PODs with separate production and pre-production PODs with our leaf pairs. It should look like this:

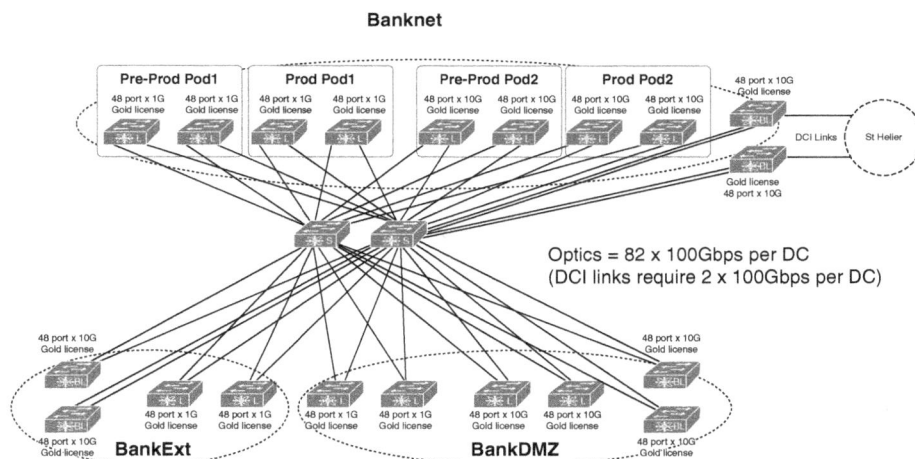

By the way, Jerseytel has informed us the DCI circuits are now in place. Apparently, it was a simple job of splicing in a few locations, as it had fiber in the ground and between Jersey and Guernsey Islands already. We are all tested, error free, and latency is good, so we will have no issues with our replication. We need you to plan the migration of services to the new DC while we wait for the network infrastructure to be delivered from the UK. Internet and WAN circuits have been ordered for the new DC and will be here in time for migration. (We don't need new circuits for St Helier. We can just re-patch these from legacy to new networks at time of migration.)

Rgds,

Tim Jacobson
Network Manager
Bank of Jersey

Question 16

Place the following implementation/migration steps in order to allow the Bank of Jersey to migrate to the new network infrastructure (not all steps are required).

Requirements/constraints from supplied documentation:

Internet and WAN circuits have been ordered for the new DC and will be here in time for migration. (We don't need new circuits for St Helier; we can just repatch these from legacy to new networks at the time of migration.)

Configure VLAN translation for overlapping VLANs on each network on leaf switches.

Connect Layer 2 trunk from legacy Banknet network to new Banknet border leaf switches in St Helier, connect Layer 2 trunk from legacy BankDMZ network to new BankDMZ border leaf switches in St Helier, and connect Layer 2 trunk from legacy BankExt network to new BankExt border leaf switches in St Helier.

Shut down Internet/WAN circuit(s) in Priory Inn.

Enable new Internet/WAN circuit(s) in new Guernsey DC and migrate St Helier Internet/WAN circuit(s) in St Helier.

Connect Layer 3 routing links from legacy Banknet network to new Banknet border leaf switches in St Helier.

Install spine switches in each DC.

Enable Anycast gateways in VXLAN for Banknet VLANs.

Install leaf switches in each DC and configure separate VRFs for BankExt, BankDMZ, and Banknet networks within VXLAN.

Migrate inner and outer FWs and RAS infrastructure to VXLAN network on appropriate border leaf switch.

Shut down HSRP gateways in the legacy Banknet network for each VLAN.

Install border leaf switches and enable DCI circuits in each DC, and test between DCs on the Banknet border leaf switches.

Migrate physical compute environment from St Helier and Priory Inn to new DCs.

This is arguably the hardest question type on the exam. Ask a group of 10 architects the same question and you are likely to get 20 different answers! The simplest way to deal with these questions is to ensure you "make before you break" and that you can leave a period of time, where possible, between steps without an outage of some sort (potentially days or a week, for example). If you can achieve this, you are likely to have achieved the correct sequence. There will, however, always be some steps that cause an outage during a migration, and you just need to sequence steps appropriately to minimize this.

Here is the correct sequence and rationale:

1. Install spine switches in each DC.

   The spines are the logical choice to begin with hardware installation, as they connect to each leaf switch creating the underlay fabric. You could also start with Step 2 and then install the spines to still score effectively.

2. Install leaf switches in each DC and configure separate VRFs for BankExt, BankDMZ, and Banknet networks within VXLAN.

   Next, the leaf switches can be installed and the configuration applied for the separate network zones. This step could be completed after Step 3, but you couldn't run a test between leaf switches in a network zone between DCs without Step 2 being completed first. You could also list this as Step 1 to install the leafs prior to the spines and still score effectively.

3. Install border leaf switches and enable DCI circuits in each DC, and test between DCs on the Banknet border leaf switches.

   Once the sets of borders leaf switches are installed and DCI 100Gbps circuits connected on the Banknet border leafs, then the testing can begin between DC locations to cover all VRFs.

4. Connect Layer 3 routing links from legacy Banknet network to new Banknet border leaf switches in St Helier.

   Layer 3 links would be required between networks to route between VLANs that have been migrated and those that have not. There would be no risk in connecting the Layer 3 routing links, whereas risk would be involved as soon as Layer 2 links are provisioned to the new network, as in Steps 5 and 6. From a project perspective, it would be optimal to provide the risk element (Layer 2) after the minimal risk element (Layer 3).

5. Connect Layer 2 trunk from legacy Banknet network to new Banknet border leaf switches in St Helier, connect Layer 2 trunk from legacy BankDMZ network to new BankDMZ border leaf switches in St Helier, and connect Layer 2 trunk from legacy BankExt network to new BankExt border leaf switches in St Helier.

   This would be required in order to span the network zones into the new environment to allow host migration from legacy networks to new networks. Layer 2 trunk(s) would be provisioned solely into the dedicated border leaf switches per environment. The Layer 2 links would only be required for the duration of the host migration and could be removed once the project has completed. You can only complete this step once Steps 1–4 have been completed.

6. Migrate physical compute environment from St Helier and Priory Inn to new DCs.

   At this point, the physical servers and such could be migrated into the new network, as Layer 2 connectivity would have been provided from the legacy network to the new network. All Layer 3 connectivity would continue to be serviced from the legacy network via firewalls for BankDMZ or BankExt, or the core switches in the case of Banknet. This phase can only be completed after Step 5.

7. Migrate inner and outer FWs and RAS infrastructure to VXLAN network on appropriate border leaf switch.

Once the Layer 2 connectivity of the BankExt and BankDMZ services has been proven on the new network, the Layer 3 element of the networks (firewalls) and RAS infrastructure can be physically migrated to the new network on the dedicated border leaf switches. Typically, the standby appliances would be migrated first, and once proven functional on the new network, these devices could be configured to become active and begin forwarding traffic. Once this functionality has been proven, the standby devices can be migrated and then tested to ensure that there would be no downtime involved for services on these networks.

8. Shut down Internet/WAN circuit(s) in Priory Inn.

The Internet circuit is no longer required in the legacy DC in Priory Inn post Step 7.

9. Enable new Internet/WAN circuit(s) in new Guernsey DC and migrate St Helier Internet/WAN circuit(s) in St Helier.

The new Internet circuit is required in the new DC in Guernsey and in the new network in St Helier. The new Internet circuit can only be enabled after Step 8. Typically, the circuits would be enabled individually per environment but are grouped together here as a single task.

10. Shut down HSRP gateways in the legacy Banknet network for each VLAN.

This step should only be completed after Step 9 to provide an optimal traffic flow. If it was completed prior to Step 9, traffic would be flowing from the new network to the legacy network, and once the HSRP gateways are disabled, there will be an outage for the VLANs being migrated. Typically, groups of VLANs would be migrated or individual VLANs as a test basis, as opposed to the flag-day/big-bang approach depicted in this step.

11. Enable Anycast gateway in VXLAN for Banknet VLANs.

This would be the final step and can only be completed after Step 10. This would allow the Anycast gateway functionality associated to VXLAN EVPN networks to become the Layer 3 gateway for each VLAN (using the original legacy HSRP address per VLAN within each VTEP). Once enabled, the Anycast gateways would send a GARP for the IP address, and connected hosts would update their ARP caches from the legacy HSRP virtual MAC address to that of the Anycast gateway MAC address. Typically, in a large-scale network, this change could be scripted or automated; otherwise, the outage between Steps 10 and 11 would be apparent to users.

The only step not required would be:

Configure VLAN translation for overlapping VLANs on each network.

VLAN translation would be required only if the overlapping VLANs connected into the same leaf switch pair. Because each network will have dedicated leaf switch pairs, there will not be an issue with the overlap, as each VLAN will be assigned a unique VNI within VXLAN.

Clearly, the implementation steps involved have been condensed to make the question more lab friendly. The complexity here is that you need to determine which step(s) are not required, and there are numerous steps involved. It is likely you will have a reduced number of steps in the lab exam (typically around six to seven), but this exercise is designed to challenge you so you are not fazed during the lab exam. (Train hard and race easy!) You should determine that this isn't the kind of question you can realistically study for, and this captures the ethos of the CCDE qualification. You really need to be operating as a CCDE before you can get your number.

If you answered this question correctly, you scored two points.

Email #15

From: Tim Jacobson

To: CCDE Candidate

Subject: Implementation/Migration Update

Hi.

The migration went really well. I got our guys to script the larger number of VLANs we migrated in Banknet in terms of shutting down and re-enabling the Layer 3 side, and we literally had a 1 second blip per VLAN. The users didn't even notice, and we had no related tickets, which was great news. However, good news is usually accompanied with bad, unfortunately. We've had the regulators in post-migration, and we walked them through the new design and what we have accomplished. While their overall impression was positive in regard to the new network and improvements to our business continuity, they have made the following comments:

1. The infrastructure that connects to the production compute environment is not physically protected. We need a cage around it to ensure that nobody who has access to the DC in general can, without restriction, connect devices into the production switches and potentially compromise service.

2. Although not a current legality, we would expect you to encrypt DCI traffic leaving your premises.

3. Also not a current legality, but Banknet WAN and DC are implicitly open. We expect DC services to be protected behind a firewall from the WAN.

Please ensure you are compliant with point number 1 within four weeks and have a plan in place for points 2 and 3, as legislation could change with short notice.

We will need to resolve these matters. For point 2, we are OK on the WAN, as all WAN traffic into the DC uses HTTPS or traffic encrypted at the application layer, but we do know the DCI link will carry some unencrypted traffic.

Rgds,

Tim Jacobson
Network Manager
Bank of Jersey

Question 17

The financial regulator has stated that all of the Banknet network-specific switches that serve the production environment should be placed into a protective caged environment to ensure they are protected from unauthorized access. Highlight on the supplied network diagram where the cage should extend to.

Requirements/constraints from supplied documentation:

The infrastructure that connects to the production compute environment is not physically protected. We need a cage around it to ensure that nobody who has access to the DC in general can, without restriction, connect devices to the production switches and potentially compromise service.

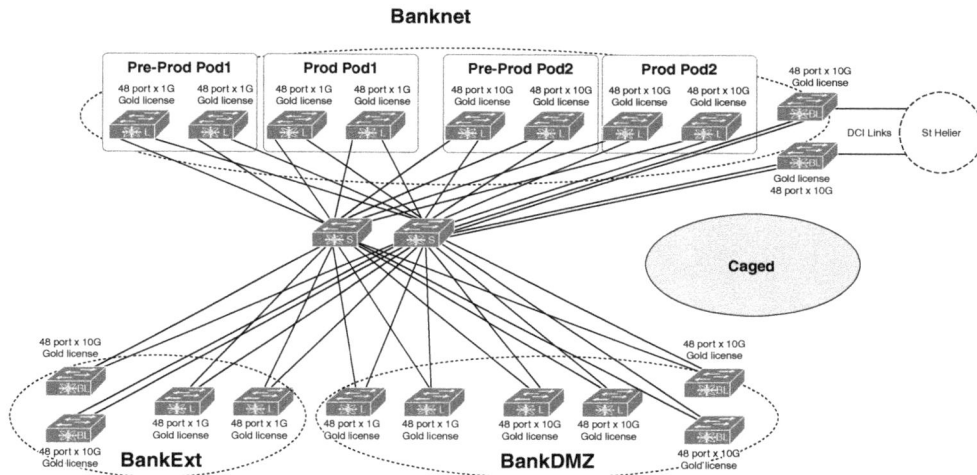

So the only real question to consider here is, do you include spine and DCI links on the Banknet border leaf switches as well as the production-specific Banknet leaf switches? My take on this is usually, "when there is a doubt, there is no doubt." Therefore, it would be safer, in this case, to include the spines and border leaf switches within the cage as if they were unprotected. Somebody could, in theory, access the devices and monitor VXLAN-encapsulated traffic from the production pods via onboard tools or connected sniffers/TAPs or connect into leaf/spine links or DCI circuits. If you only included the production pods within the caged environment, award yourself half a point.

If you answered this question correctly, as illustrated in the following figure, you scored one point.

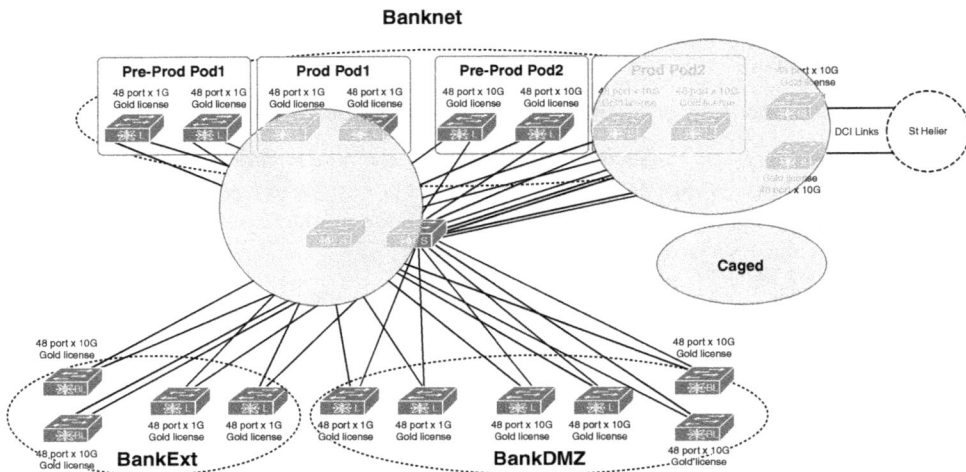

Question 18

If the Bank of Jersey were to encrypt traffic over the DCI links, which technology would you recommend that would be compatible with OSPF if this IGP was used in the underlay fabric? (Choose one.)

Requirements/constraints from supplied documentation:

Although not a current legality, we would expect you to encrypt DCI traffic leaving your premises.

We will need to resolve these matters. For point 2, we are OK on the WAN, as all WAN traffic into the DC uses HTTPS or traffic encrypted at the application layer, but we do know the DCI link will carry some unencrypted traffic.

- **Silver Leaf License Features**
  - MACSEC
  - IPsec
  - GETVPN
  - GRE
- **Gold Leaf License Features**
  - MACSEC
  - IPsec
  - GETVPN
  - GRE

a. GETVPN

This is incorrect. This technology would be better suited to the WAN and would be fully compatible with OSPF. However, there is no requirement to provide encryption within the WAN, as you are informed the protocols traversing the WAN are already encrypted at the application layer.

b. IPsec

This is incorrect. IPsec on its own would not function with OSPF on the DCI links within the underlay.

c. MACSEC

This is correct. MACSEC would be well-suited to this requirement over the DCI links, and due to operating at Layer 2, there would be no compatibility issues with OSPF. Typically deployed in hardware, MACSEC will not have a CPU implication and can generally run at line rate (if there were some limitations with this feature or one in the lab exam, you would be provided with corresponding data).

d. GRE/IPsec

This is a suboptimal answer. While GRE with IPsec would provide encryption that is compatible with OSPF on the DCI underlay links, it would not be as efficient or as simple to deploy as MACSEC. In addition to configuration complexity, there would typically be a performance limitation of throughput or additional CPU hit to run IPsec, which should be considered (unless information has been provided that the feature is deployed in hardware without CPU increase or throughput degradation). You would ultimately be making an assumption if you had assumed that IPsec was available within hardware.

If you answered this question correctly, you scored one point.

Email #16

From: Tim Jacobson

To: CCDE Candidate

Subject: Perimeter FW

Hi.

So, as you are aware, the auditors have raised a concern that the Banknet network is implicitly open once you are connected to the WAN, and they are recommending we place perimeter protection around our applications in the DCs. Ideally, I would like to add a firewall in each branch location, but unfortunately that isn't going to happen. We can get budget for DC/WAN perimeter firewalls (I want to do this with the minimal number possible, as they are expensive) because we want to future-proof it by investing in firewalls with a next-generation feature set. The firewalls we want to use have 10Gbps throughput, so they are fine for the WAN, which connects at 10Gbps into the service provider's network. The firewalls need a dedicated Layer 2 connection between them for state and high availability. They need to support transparent and Layer 3 routed mode. For high availability, they need to support active/standby, where in the event of a failure, the standby device takes over the active IP address and only the active IP address is configured on each firewall. In terms of routing, they can run static routing, OSPF, or iBGP, which is great, as we need the solution to still allow for the dynamic routing from the WAN into the DC. In terms of current setup, we have dual P2P /30 links (on contiguous prefixes) between the WAN CE on each site to the border leafs and eBGP between the borders and the MPLS CEs. I'm told all devices support L2 EtherChannel, and as you know, we can run vPC multi-chassis EtherChannel on the borders if required at L2, but they don't support L3 EtherChannel. In the event of a failure scenario (which could mean failing over between DCs due to a firewall or WAN failure), we need existing sessions to be maintained. We don't have a clue at this point what we should be setting the rule base to initially, so this is more of a tick-in-the-box exercise, and we will come back to define policy once we are able to monitor and baseline flows using some tooling. We can add different prefixes if required into the topology over and above the existing /30s in use, and I have a preference for simplicity with minimal change to the existing environment.

I'll obviously need your help to design this!

Rgds,

Tim Jacobson
Network Manager
Bank of Jersey

Question 19

Which of the following designs would be optimal for the Bank to control north/south flows into the DCs for Banknet services from the WAN? (Choose one.)

Requirements/constraints from supplied documentation:

They are recommending we place perimeter protection around our applications in the DCs.

The firewalls we want to use have 10Gbps throughput, so they are fine for the WAN, which connects at 10Gbps.

The firewalls need a dedicated Layer 2 connection between them for state and high availability. They need to support transparent and Layer 3 routed mode. For high availability, they need to support active/standby, where in the event of a failure, the standby device takes over the active IP address and only the active IP address is configured on each firewall. In terms of routing, they can run static routing, OSPF, or iBGP, which is great, as we need the solution to still allow for the dynamic routing from the WAN into the DC. In terms of current setup, we have dual P2P /30 links (on contiguous prefixes) between the WAN CE on each site to the border leafs and eBGP between the borders and the MPLS CEs.

I'm told all devices support L2 EtherChannel, and as you know we can run vPC multichassis EtherChannel on the borders if required at L2, but they don't support L3 EtherChannel.

In the event of a failure scenario (which could mean failing over between DCs due to a firewall or WAN failure), we need existing sessions to be maintained.

We can add different prefixes if required into the topology over and above the existing /30s in use, and I have a preference for simplicity with minimal change to the existing environment.

a. The firewalls should be deployed in routed mode. The WAN routers should connect directly into a single firewall at each DC location using an L3 EtherChannel for the "outside interfaces." The firewall at each DC location should then connect to the Banknet border leaf switches using an L3 EtherChannel (vPC) for the "inside interfaces." BGP should be configured on the firewalls for routing into and out of the DCs, and a Layer 2 VXLAN should be provisioned between DCs for firewall state connectivity, allowing one firewall in one DC location to be active and one to be standby.

This option can be ruled out because it uses Layer 3 EtherChannel (vPC) between the firewall within a DC to the border leaf switches, and you were informed that Layer 3 EtherChannel is not supported on the border leafs. (This is common on certain DC switches; typically, you would need a Layer 2 EtherChannel with separate Layer 3 IP addresses on each border leaf for a non-VXLAN VLAN or a common Anycast gateway IP for a VXLAN VLAN.)

b. The firewalls should be deployed in routed mode. The WAN routers should connect directly into a single firewall at each DC location using an L3 EtherChannel for the "outside interfaces." The firewall at each DC location should then connect to the Banknet border leaf switches using an L3 EtherChannel (vPC) for the "inside interfaces." BGP should be configured on the firewalls for routing into and out of the DCs, and a Layer 2 VXLAN should be provisioned between DCs for firewall state connectivity, allowing both firewalls to operate in a cluster mode.

This option can also be ruled out because it uses a non-supported L3 EtherChannel on the border leafs and non-supported cluster mode on the firewalls (you were informed they only support an active/standby configuration).

c. The firewalls should be deployed in transparent mode. The WAN routers should connect directly into a single firewall at each DC location using an L2 EtherChannel for the "outside interfaces." The firewall at each DC location should then connect to the Banknet border leaf switches using an L2 EtherChannel (vPC) for the "inside interfaces." A Layer 2 VXLAN should be provisioned between DCs for firewall state connectivity, allowing one firewall in one DC location to be active and one to be standby. eBGP peering between the WAN routers and border leaf switches would remain as is due to the transparent configuration.

This option sounds feasible but does not fully take into consideration the active/standby requirement between DCs to maintain stateful traffic flows in the event of a failure. Only one of the required Layer 2 cross-site connections would be provided with this design (for state). In order to function correctly, the inside firewall interfaces would need to belong on a common VLAN (VXLAN) between DCs, allowing the firewalls to fail over effectively (as would the outside interfaces). Similarly, the WAN routers would actually need to connect into the border leaf switches on one cross-site VLAN (VXLAN) to provide full flexibility in the event of a failure scenario; for example, if the WAN router connected directly into the firewall, there is no way to extend this connectivity between DC locations to allow for a failover event.

d. The firewalls should be deployed in routed mode. The WAN routers should connect into the border leaf switches at each DC location using an L2 EtherChannel. The firewalls at each DC location should then connect to the Banknet border leaf switches using an L2 EtherChannel (vPC) with separate VLANs used for the "inside interfaces" and "outside interfaces." Static routing should be used on the firewalls with DC routes pointing toward the border leafs and WAN routes pointing toward the WAN. Layer 2 VXLANs should be provisioned between DCs for firewall state connectivity—the "inside interface" VLAN and the "outside interface" VLAN allowing one firewall in one DC location to be active and one to be standby in the remote DC. Multihop eBGP should be configured between the WAN routers and border leaf switches.

This is the optimal solution. The topology allows the active and standby firewalls to communicate between DCs for state and on the "inside" and "outside" interfaces to facilitate failover. (The active firewall presents a single IP address, so there is a requirement for VLANs [VXLANs] to span between locations for failover functionality.) For simplicity, static routing is enabled on the firewalls, and the eBGP connections between WAN and LAN are maintained through the firewalls (the peering would need to be multihop now, however). The firewalls simply need to know where the peering destinations are and could have a default route pointing into the LAN via the border leaf switches and WAN for remote WAN prefixes. A real-world application might require the use of loopback interfaces for eBGP peering on the border leaf switches, as traffic directed to an anycast VXLAN could hit either vPC-enabled border leaf switch, so eBGP peering between the WAN and LAN could fail. This solution would not suffer from symmetry issues, as traffic from either DC would be forwarded through the single active firewall due to the firewall operating mode of only presenting a single active IP address via the active device on each interface.

e. The firewalls should be deployed in transparent mode. The WAN routers should connect directly into a single firewall at each DC location using an L2 EtherChannel for the "outside interfaces." The firewall at each DC location should then connect to the Banknet border leaf switches using an L2 EtherChannel (vPC) for the "inside interfaces." A Layer 2 VXLAN should be provisioned between DCs for firewall state connectivity, allowing one firewall in one DC location to be active and one to be standby.

This would not function correctly. You were told a perimeter solution is required, and this solution would see the firewall become the default gateway for each VLAN. The firewall only has a 10G throughput, which is fine for the existing WAN capacity for north/south flows, but wouldn't scale if it was used to be the default gateway for each VLAN, as it wouldn't cater for east/west flows.

If you answered this question correctly, you scored two points.

Email #17

From: Tim Jacobson

To: CCDE Candidate

Subject: Auto m8?

Hi.

You will be glad to hear the firewall implementation has been planned. Thanks for your assistance!

Just when I thought our guys were gaining confidence with the new network, we've had a serious issue. They were making a change on the production network last night, migrating some of the servers responsible for the applications serving the ATM cash machines from the legacy network, and they ended up causing an outage in the entire ATM network. We had some unhappy customers who were unable to withdraw cash, but the damage was limited due to being an early morning change and backing it out quickly when they realized what had happened. The RCA shows some changes missed out on the border leaf switches and some configuration not being accepted correctly. I went through the detail and couldn't believe the amount of configuration required for the actual change for VXLAN parameters. The guys apparently scripted it due to the size and complexity and ended up creating the issue themselves! We simply cannot find ourselves in this position again. I have read that the infrastructure is compatible with network programmability, and I'd like you to look into how we can set up some automation to eliminate human error and introduce efficiencies. We can also enable the telemetry functionality that they have and move away from SNMP possibly. I have a couple of developers I can bring in from the dark side (application developers), when required, who can code. They can work with the network team to define what is required, so maybe we can start our own devops team if this works out. I've got Yin and Yang stuck in my head for some reason after my first conversation with the developers—can you believe one of them is called Jason! Anyway, have a think and let me know how you believe we should begin.

Rgds,

Tim Jacobson
Network Manager
Bank of Jersey

Question 20

In order to initiate automation, the developers need to know which individual YANG model to use for the new infrastructure. Which of the following models would be optimal? (Choose one.)

Requirements/constraints from supplied documentation:

Spines can support 40Gbps or 100Gbps on each port, depending on optics purchased. The spines are actually from a different vendor than the leafs, as they were significantly cheaper than the leaf vendor's spines, but they are compatible. They don't have a license option and seem to come with an enterprise edition as standard that covers every feature listed on each license type for the leafs.

Silver Leaf License Features (included in switch purchase price): Automation suite (OpenConfig, IETF, native)

Gold Leaf License Features (additional £2K per switch): Automation suite (OpenConfig, IETF, native)

a. Native

This is incorrect. You were informed that the spines and leaf switches are from different vendors, and an individual YANG model is required. As such, native would actually require two individual models (one set up for spines and one for leafs).

b. OpenConfig

This is the optimal answer. It really is down to IETF or OpenConfig, given the constraints of not being able to use native or a mix of models. However, OpenConfig models are typically more comprehensive than IETF.

c. IETF

This is a suboptimal answer. IETF would definitely work, but IETF models are generally less comprehensive than OpenConfig models. Award yourself a point if you selected this answer, as it is complex to differentiate between IETF and OpenConfig in this particular case.

d. Mix of models

This is incorrect. The requirements state an individual model. A mix of models (say, native and OpenConfig) can function, and some deployments use them, but this is typically for different features, and unnecessary complexity can be introduced.

Typically, it's considered good practice to begin with non-native models when looking for interoperability and flexibility, but native could be a good choice if there are some features that hadn't been adopted by OpenConfig or IETF when required.

If you answered B or C, you scored one point.

Question 21

In order to deploy the automation, the developers have recommended an OpenDaylight platform to use as a resilient SDN controller and portal for network programmability of the VXLAN infrastructure within the management network. Complete the following table in order that a project task list can be generated to deliver automation for the network infrastructure.

Requirements/constraints from supplied documentation:

We will connect up the management ports on all of the new switches, which have a dedicated management VRF, and drop these into our dedicated management network.

Network management: All management tools that access the infrastructure are sited in a separate Ethernet out-of-band management network that spans both DCs. Firewalls are used between the tools VLAN and multiple VLANs that connect to the management ports of infrastructure. The firewall connects to the production Banknet network in order to provide access to remote WAN sited locations. The Bank has a policy that only management tool hosts can connect to the infrastructure based on IP address and specific management protocols.

Resilient SDN controller and portal for network programmability of the VXLAN infrastructure within the management network.

	OpenDaylight Controller	Spine Switches	Leaf Switches	DC1 Management Network	DC2 Management Network	Management Network Firewall
Task Required	Check the box below if the task is required on the devices/locations above.					
Enable Netconf/ Restconf.	X	X	X	—	—	—
Enable REST API.						
Install SDN controller.	—	—	—	X	X	—
Enable SSH TCP port 22 access from controller.	—	X	X	—	—	X

	OpenDaylight Controller	Spine Switches	Leaf Switches	DC1 Management Network	DC2 Management Network	Management Network Firewall
Enable Netconf TCP port 830 access from controller.	—	X	X	—	—	—
Enable Restconf TCP port 443 access from controller.	—	X	X	—	—	X

This question isn't as complex as it looks initially. You should be able to determine from the supplied information that the controller needs to be resilient and sit in the management network. From this, you could start to build a picture of dual controllers (typically split between sites) that would sit in the tools VLAN and require firewalled access to the new infrastructure, which would have (by policy) restrictions on IP addresses and protocols used for network management. By pairing the supplied information with some high-level automation knowledge, you should be able to complete the table. As a note, you wouldn't be expected to start writing or debugging Python code within the CCDE lab! Partial scoring will be available for this question.

If you answered this question correctly, you scored two points.

Question 22

The Bank of Jersey wants to simplify multiple/recurring API calls from the SDN controller to individual devices for configuration and management purposes while keeping the required authentication as simple and secure as possible. Which authentication method should the Bank choose? (Choose one.)

Requirements/constraints from supplied documentation:

Multiple/recurring API calls from the SDN controller to individual devices should be simple and as secure as possible.

a. Basic Authentication (native)

This is incorrect. Basic Authentication in its native form passes credentials unencrypted, so it wouldn't meet the requirement of being as secure as possible. Generally, this would need to be used in conjunction with SSL or TLS to be a viable authentication method.

b. API Key – String

This is incorrect. A string for an API key is generally used as a one-off method of authentication. This wouldn't scale well with the requirement to handle multiple API calls to the same device, as the string is typically manually entered.

c. API Key – Request Header

This is a suboptimal answer. Request headers are used when making multiple API calls without the need to enter the API key into each API individually, but they are not as simple as a cookie-based approach. If you selected this answer, award yourself half a point.

d. API Key – Cookie

This is the optimum answer and the most common and simple method of authenticating recurring API calls. The API key string is stored as a cookie and reused again and again.

e. Custom token

This is incorrect. A custom token would usually require a username and password combination to receive an encrypted, unique, auto-generated token, which can be stored and used repeatedly, as opposed to entering credentials each time an API is accessed. The token is generally deleted once a session is terminated, so it wouldn't be as efficient as the cookie approach.

If you answered this question correctly, you scored one point.

Question 23

The Bank is wary of atomicity, if one or both of the OpenDaylight controllers fail within the production network. If the controllers fail (under steady state operation and not while performing configuration actions), then which of the following should be viewed as the "source of truth" for the valid configuration of an infrastructure device? (Choose one.)

Requirements/constraints from supplied documentation: None. This is an industry best-knowledge/best-practice item.

a. The primary SDN controller's saved configuration of the infrastructure device

This is incorrect. SDN controllers simply apply configuration changes to the infrastructure, as opposed to saving configurations.

b. The secondary SDN controller's saved configuration of the infrastructure device

This is incorrect. SDN controllers simply apply configuration changes to the infrastructure, as opposed to saving configurations.

c. The infrastructure device itself

This is the correct answer. Atomicity for network configuration means that the intended configuration has been applied to a device without error, or, if errors do exist, there is a method of rectifying those errors. If the programmability capability fails (the SDN controller is simply pushing the configuration in an automated method), then the device itself should be seen as the latest and most valid (source of truth) configuration from the running configuration. For clarity, the question simply states "if the controllers fail" and not "if the controllers fail during a configuration operation." This would be when there needs to be a means of ensuring atomicity.

d. A previous day's backup configuration of the infrastructure device itself

This is a suboptimal answer. If a configuration is restored from a previous day's backup, then any changes made to a device post-backup would be lost. If you did choose this answer, though, award yourself half a point.

If you answered this question correctly, you scored one point.

Question 24

The Bank wants to leverage the new infrastructure's model driven telemetry (MDT) capability. If an existing network management tooling application was limited to XML encoding only and not HTTP for MDT support, which of the following would be compatible on the network infrastructure? (Choose one.)

Requirements/constraints from supplied documentation:

The existing network management tooling application was limited to XML encoding only and not HTTP for MDT support.

a. Dial-out telemetry

This is incorrect. Dial-out telemetry involves the infrastructure device initiating a session to a destination network management device based on a subscription. This approach is not compatible with XML and uses HTTP encoding.

b. Dial-in telemetry

This is correct. XML is compatible with dial-in telemetry, which is where a management system polls an infrastructure device dynamically (similar to SNMP polling to gather statistics).

c. NetFlow

This is incorrect. NetFlow, although considered a form of legacy telemetry, would not be compatible with HTTP, and it uses UDP.

d. IPFIX

This is incorrect. IPFIX, although considered a form of legacy telemetry, would not be considered compatible with HTTP, and it uses UDP.

If you answered this question correctly, you scored one point.

Email #18

From: Tim Jacobson

To: CCDE Candidate

Subject: Cloud Info

Hi.

The automation looks really promising. I have our guys working with the developers to automate some of the scripted tasks they complete on a daily basis and provide a new methodology for troubleshooting. Our guys are learning about Python, and the developers are learning about network operations and configurations, so it really looks mutually beneficial to the teams. The new network is functioning well, and it has allowed us to upgrade our backend compute systems. We've met our obligations with the financial regulators and rectified the majority of previous issues identified by the consultants.

Yesterday I had a long workshop with the CTO and IT department heads. We've been discussing how we are going to host the new Channel account the CEO is so keen to launch. I had originally thought we would spin up the service in each DC on the new network now that we're ready, but we've been discussing cloud and how that may be beneficial depending on if Channel takes off and we struggle to scale the service or if it fails and we have to write off any associated expenditure wasted for running it on-premises. We managed to get a cloud architect from a well-respected cloud provider in the UK (Cloudhop) on a video link for a couple of hours in the afternoon to go over some options, which proved to be really useful. So I need your help to aid the decision-making process to determine if we do go in this direction. From the output of the day, we've put together some information that should help. The CTO stated we have a secured budget of £625K for 12 months of opex for the project, and we have sufficient network firewall and compute infrastructure after the recent upgrade if we need to stand up any services on the premises to support a cloud-based frontend or a complete on-premises hosting without any cloud. Additional capex might not be feasible to aid the project.

Here's what we covered in the session on the technical front:

1. Our on-premises database that we can stand up for Channel in the backend can handle 1000 transactions per second, and the cloud provider we have spoken to (Cloudhop) says it can match that if we need to use its cloud-based database instance. Each transaction is estimated to use approximately 10KB of data, and we want to be able to run at the 1000 transactions-per-second level. We've worked with marketing and calculated for Day 1 service we wouldn't expect any more than 1 million transactions per day, so let's base this as the worst case, but we need the ability to scale communications and compute to grow if this figure is exceeded dynamically, regardless of how the service is provisioned.

2. The service must be highly available, as it's a direct reflection on the Bank and we cannot allow any of the service to be compromised due to being accessible over the Internet. We will need to be able to upgrade available Internet access bandwidth within the space of a couple of days to be able to adjust to the demands of the system.

3. The application developers have stated the Channel service will be a typical load-balanced web frontend protected via a firewall, which is accessible from lightweight Channel apps (typically via a customer's smartphone) over the Internet. The web frontend communicates with the application via load balancers; the application then communicates directly with a database. The web frontend just needs to be accessible for Internet clients so it can be hosted in the cloud or on the BankDMZ network. The middleware with application and database can be either on-premises in Banknet or hosted in the cloud.

4. The replication of the database required for Channel will be handled by a direct SAN connection if running on the premises or handled directly within the cloud if running in the cloud, so we can assume that there is no requirement here for additional network connectivity.

5. Security has dictated for Channel that we want all traffic natively using SSL from the client (which will be offloaded on the load balancers), and we are going to use a host-based firewall system on the Channel compute environment wherever it is hosted so we can provide security in multiple layers.

6. If we do go with cloud, we can host the entire system (web frontend, application servers, and database) in the cloud. If we did host some of the service on the premises, we would need a firewall for access into DC services, and we can provide any on-premises compute equipment into a dedicated Channel VRF to host the service. Note that any link from the cloud would need to be encrypted into our DC(s), and they support only Direct Connect or exchange connections.

7. The latency between the application servers and the database should be <=1ms to provide the best CX journey.

Cloud charges are estimated at £50K per month for private cloud for IaaS network and compute resources and a direct-connect circuit back to each one of our DCs (primary link to St Helier and a backup link to Guernsey). There is a 60% discount available if we wanted to run the service in a public cloud; data transiting the cloud is subject to Direct Connect charges listed below.

Cloudhop Outbound Direct Connect Prices:

First 1GB per month: £10

Over 200GB per month: £5

Cloudhop has stated its private cloud option is its most secure option, with public cloud offering strong levels of security. Packet-scrubbing services prior to entry for DDoS mitigation are offered only with the private cloud option. Cloudhop can run IPsec encryption on the virtual routers and normal routing such as eBGP and even VXLAN multisite to emulate a VTEP, providing Layer EVPN Type 5 routing. RFC1918 addressing can be used on either cloud type. Both cloud offerings include Internet ingress and egress charges, but Direct Connect prices apply to any traffic that is required to be sent back into Banknet from Cloudhop's premises. Internet access speeds and services can be upgraded instantly for the private cloud offering via a portal and within two weeks for the public cloud offering via an online request system.

We're going to treat Channel as a 12-month pilot. Based on the success of the service, we can evaluate our options toward the end of the pilot in terms of scaling the system up or down. We just need to work out where and how to best host it.

Rgds,

Tim Jacobson
Network Manager
Bank of Jersey

Question 25

Complete the following table to allow the Bank to select the optimum hosting method for the Channel system. (Check all required items.)

Requirements/constraints from supplied documentation:

No packet scrubbing is employed on ISP connections. One previous DDoS outage could have been averted.

The service must be highly available, as it's a direct reflection on the Bank, and we cannot allow any of the service to be compromised due to being accessible over the Internet.

We will need to be able to upgrade available Internet access bandwidth within the space of a couple of days to be able to adjust to the demands of the system.

Cloudhop has stated its private cloud option is its most secure option, with public cloud offering strong levels of security. Packet-scrubbing services prior to entry for DDoS mitigation are only offered with the private cloud option.

Cloudhop can run IPsec encryption on the virtual routers and normal routing such as eBGP and even VXLAN multisite to emulate a VTEP providing Layer EVPN Type 5 routing. RFC1918 addressing can be used on either cloud type. Both cloud offerings include Internet ingress and egress charges, but Direct Connect prices apply to any traffic that is required to be sent back into Banknet from Cloudhop's premises. Internet access speeds and services can be upgraded instantly for the private cloud offering.

We've worked with marketing and calculated that for Day 1 service, we wouldn't expect any more than 1 million transactions per day, so let's base this as a worst case, but we need the ability to scale communications and compute to grow if this figure is exceeded dynamically, regardless of how the service is provisioned.

Cloud charges are estimated at £50K per month for private cloud for IaaS network and compute resources and a Direct Connect circuit back to each one of our DCs (primary link to St Helier and a backup link to Guernsey). There is a 60% discount available if we wanted to run the service in a public cloud. Data transiting the cloud is subject to Direct Connect charges.

If we do go with cloud, we can host the entire system (web frontend, application servers, and database) in the cloud, or if we did host some of the service on the premises, we would need a firewall for access into DC services, and we can provide any on-premises compute equipment into a dedicated Channel VRF to host the services. Any link from the cloud would need to be encrypted into our DC(s), and Cloudhop only supports Direct Connect or exchange connections.

Each transaction is estimated to use approximately 10KB of data, and we want to be able to run at the 1000 transaction-per-second level.

Internet access speeds and services can be upgraded instantly for the private cloud offering via a portal and within two weeks for the public cloud offering via an online request system.

Both cloud offerings include Internet ingress and egress charges, but Direct Connect prices apply to any traffic that is required to be sent back into Banknet from Cloudhop's premises.

The latency between the application servers and database should be <=1ms to provide the best CX journey.

Question	Options (place an X in the appropriate cell per question)				
Which is the most suitable hosting platform/location for Channel? (Base your selection on a combination of cost and technical feasibility.)	On-prem Jersey DC	On-prem Guernsey DC	Public cloud all services (Cloudhop)	Private cloud all services (Cloudhop)	Hybrid (private Cloudhop web frontend + Banknet on-prem database)
	—	—	—	X	—

This is a difficult question. You can't simply make an assumption based on gut feel or previous engagement as to optimal hosting location for the Channel service. You have a wealth of information in the email in order to make an informed decision. First, you need to determine what is required to run the service, and then you need to determine which of the possible options provides that capability. For a quick win, however, you can narrow the selection process immediately down to private cloud or hybrid cloud (which incorporated the web frontend element of the private cloud), as you were informed that packet scrubbing and DDoS protection are only available with the private cloud option, and you have a statement regarding high availability of the service and that it cannot be compromised over the Internet (the Bank currently does not have any DDoS or packet-scrubbing facility on its own Internet connections, and this facility is not available within the public cloud offering). The public cloud offering does not also offer the rapid changes that the Bank requires to adjust bandwidth based on system demands. The private cloud offering from Cloudhop, you are told, will be able to accommodate the system requirements in terms of throughput, scale and so on, and will clearly be able to provide the rapid changes to Internet access speeds and DDoS protection. Cost-wise, the service equates to £50K per month, so £600K per annum fits with the defined opex budget of £625K assigned to the project. The hybrid cloud option with the web frontend hosted by Cloudhop also accommodates the system requirements in terms of throughput, scale, and so on, and will clearly be able to provide the rapid changes to Internet access speeds and DDoS protection with the database functionality provided on premises within the Bank over a Direct Connect circuit. This service, however, comes with an additional £2.5K per month charge based on data usage for the Direct Connect circuit to access the on-premises database within the Bank, so at £630K per annum, it is over the budget of £625K opex assigned and is therefore suboptimal in comparison to the private cloud offering. You are also informed that the latency between the application servers and database should be <=1ms to provide the best CX journey. When everything is hosted within the public cloud, this would be achievable; however, if the service is split, the application servers would need to be sited locally to the database in order to meet the latency requirement. (The question, however, does not state where the application servers would be located, so this is purely for informational purposes at this point in time, and it only becomes of real relevance when determining optimum locations for devices in a later question.)

The monthly charge of £2.5K for Direct Connect is calculated as follows:

- Each transaction is estimated to use approximately 10KB of data

- Expect no more than one million transactions per day

- 1M × 10KB = 10GB per day

- 10GB × 30 = 300GB (approx. monthly data rate)

Cloudhop Outbound Direct Connect Prices:

- First 1GB per month: £10

- Over 200GB per month: £5

- 200GB × £10 = £2K

- 100GB × £5 = £500

Total Monthly Direct Connect charges = £2.5K

If you answered this question correctly, assign yourself one point; if you selected the hybrid cloud offering, it was a suboptimal answer based on the information provided, but it's still worthy of a score of half a point.

Question	Options – Select X in the appropriate cell per question				
If a Hybrid solution (private Cloudhop web frontend + Banknet on-premises database) was used, what would the most suitable access method be between Cloud and database infrastructures?	SD WAN Internet connection to Banknet from Cloudhop	Internet VPN to Banknet from Cloudhop	Direct Connect to Banknet to Cloudhop	Exchange connection to Banknet	Jerseytel L3 MPLS VPN to Banknet between Cloudhop and Banknet
	—	—	X	—	—

This appears to be a difficult question, but with the information provided, it is very straightforward. You are informed that the cloud provider supports only Direct Connect or exchange connections. As such, you can just focus on these two options. An exchange connection would be used only when an enterprise connects to multiple cloud providers. The Bank is using a single cloud provider and has no stated requirements to use additional providers. The

Direct Connect facility, where the cloud provider can connect directly to the DC(s)/dedicated Channel VRF with appropriate security controls, is therefore the correct answer.

If you answered this correctly, you scored half a point.

Question	Options – Select X in the appropriate cell per question				
If the database for Channel is located on-premises within the Bank's network, what would be the Day 1 minimum bandwidth required, from cloud provider to the Bank of Jersey DC(s)?	1Mbps	5Mbps	20Mbps	100Mbps	1Gbps
	—	—	—	X	—

This question requires some basic math and will test your understanding of the information provided to you in regard to how the application functions. You are informed that each transaction uses 10KB, and they want to run at up to 1000 transactions per second, so this is simply 10KB × 1000, which equates to 10,000,000, or 10MB. To then calculate the bandwidth required, you would convert the bytes to bits to provide a bps speed (10M × 8 = 80Mbps). The Direct Connect link connecting the cloud provider to the Bank would therefore need to be, at a minimum, 80Mbps if the systems were separated between environments.

If you answered this correctly, you scored half a point.

Question	Options – Select X in the appropriate cell per question				
Day 1 minimum bandwidth required, from cloud provider to Bank of Jersey DC(s), if the web frontend, application servers, and database for Channel are located within the cloud?	0Mbps	5Mbps	20Mbps	100Mbps	1Gbps
	X	—	—	—	—

This is just ensuring you are closely following the scenario in that if the entire service was being run in the cloud, there isn't a specific minimum bandwidth requirement, or indeed even a real need for a Direct Connect circuit between the cloud provider and the Bank. As such, the optimal answer here is 0Mbps.

If you answered this correctly, you scored half a point.

Question 26

The Bank of Jersey decided to use a hybrid cloud model for Channel with the web frontend in a private cloud and the database within a dedicated Channel VRF within the DC VXLAN network in St Helier. Complete the illustrated design that follows by inserting the correct device icons into each environment to show where the individual devices/ functionality should be provisioned for Channel, including where the application servers should be sited (redundancy is not required within the design at this point for the sake of clarity, but do show where load balancers / application delivery controllers would be required).

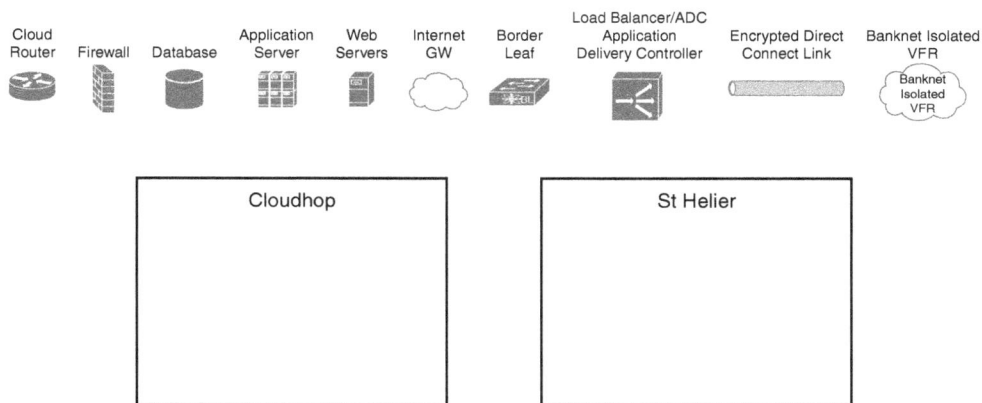

Cloud Router | Firewall | Database | Application Server | Web Servers | Internet GW | Border Leaf | Load Balancer/ADC Application Delivery Controller | Encrypted Direct Connect Link | Banknet Isolated VFR

Cloudhop

St Helier

Requirements/constraints from supplied documentation:

The application developers have stated the Channel service will be a typical load-balanced web frontend protected via a firewall that is accessible from lightweight Channel apps (typically via a customer's smartphone) over the Internet. The web frontend communicates with the application via load balancers. The application then communicates directly with a database. The web frontend just needs to be accessible for Internet clients so it can be hosted in the cloud or in the BankDMZ network, and the middleware with the application and database can be either on-premises in Banknet or hosted in the cloud.

The latency between the application servers and database should be <=1ms to provide the best CX journey.

If we do go with cloud, we can host the entire system (web frontend, application servers, and database) in the cloud, or if we did host some of the service on the premises, we would need a firewall for access into DC services, and we can provide any on-premises compute equipment into a dedicated Channel VRF to host the service.

Any link from the cloud would need to be encrypted into Banknet, and Cloudhop supports Direct Connect or exchange connections.

So the optimal hosting location appeared to be private cloud from Cloudhop, but a customer decision was made to host the backend of the Channel system within the Bank's own network. You are informed that the Channel service will be a typical load-balanced web frontend protected via a firewall that's accessible over the Internet and that the web frontend will be provisioned in the cloud. As such, you will need an Internet connection, firewall, and ADC/load balancer deployed for a web frontend service provisioned in the cloud. You are informed that the database will reside in a dedicated Channel VRF in the VXLAN network in the DC, so you need to make a design decision as to where the application servers need to be sited. There is a requirement that the latency between the application servers and database should be <=1ms to provide the best CX journey. Because the cloud provider is in the UK, you should realize that in order to meet the latency requirement, the servers should be sited alongside the database within the Channel VRF (distances were provided in earlier maps). The communication between the web frontend servers and application servers requires ADCs/load balancers, and the link between the cloud provider and Bank of Jersey (the Direct Connect link) will require a virtual router between the cloud and the border leaf VTEP in St Helier with an encrypted link running over the Direct Connect circuit, which can be terminated either on the border leaf or on-premises firewall. A firewall is required within the Bank of Jersey's DC (from the requirement "if we did host some of the service on the premises, we would need a firewall for access into DC services"). This would connect either directly into the Direct Connect circuit or into the border leaf on the outside in one VRF, and the inside interface of the firewall would be part of the isolated Channel VRF and could then be used as the default gateway service for the application servers and database required for Channel.

This is a question that some will find complex due to the variables in play. You would really need to determine from the information provided that the Internet connections are load balanced to a web frontend, which then communicates with the application servers via load balancers. The application then communicates directly with a database. You are told where the web fronted and database need to reside, so a design decision is required for the application servers and then some basic networking between the environments. This is simple when you have time, but under the pressure of the exam it can become challenging. If you found yourself making assumptions as to which device went where or what devices to use in the design, you must have missed a constraint or requirement, as you will not be forced to make assumptions in the lab exam.

If your design reflects what's shown within the debrief for Question 27, award yourself two points. There would be partial scoring in the lab exam. Placing the application servers with the database would be the most significant item to achieve a score.

Question 27

The Bank of Jersey approved the hybrid cloud design illustrated in the diagram that follows to support Channel. Complete the table to assist in the implementation of the networking functionality in order to host the web frontend within the Cloudhop private cloud and application server and database functionality within the DC on-premises Channel VRF.

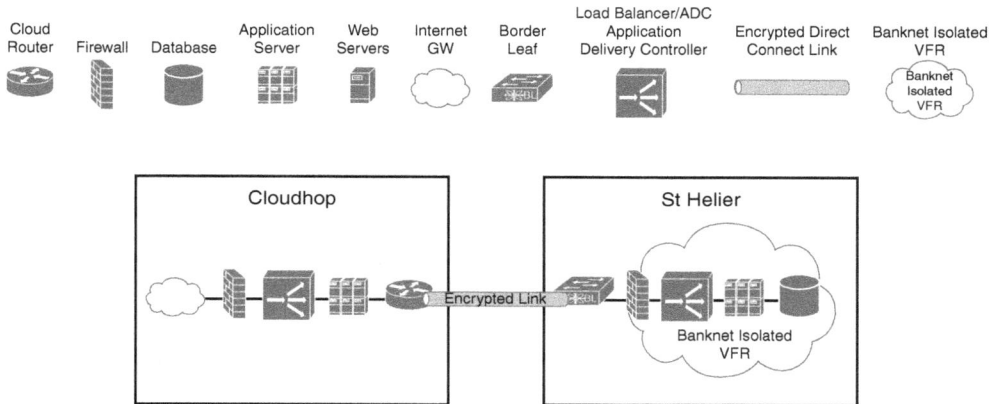

Mark within the table which feature is required for each device/area of the network.

Requirements/constraints from supplied documentation:

Cloudhop can run IPsec encryption on the virtual routers and normal routing such as eBGP and even VXLAN multisite to emulate a VTEP, providing Layer EVPN Type 5 routing. RFC1918 addressing can be used on either cloud type.

Feature	Banknet Border Leafs	Cloudhop Router	Direct Connect Link	Cloudhop VPC
Extend OSPF underlay peering to advertise Banknet isolated VRF prefixes to Cloudhop.	–	–	–	–

OSPF wouldn't be the protocol of choice for advertising the prefixes used to host the application and database servers. There are no specific requirements to extend the VXLAN multisite capability toward the cloud provider (even though this is possible), so you certainly wouldn't extend the underlay peering used to advertise the Bank's VTEPs unless you were running VXLAN toward the cloud provider. If OSPF was to be used to advertise the prefixes between environments, a separate instance within an overlay VRF would be used, as opposed to the underlay OSPF process, which would be reserved for the Bank's fabric.

If you have marked this row correctly, you scored a quarter point.

Feature	Banknet Border Leafs	Cloudhop Router	Direct Connect Link	Cloudhop Virtual Private Cloud
Configure eBGP peering to advertise Banknet isolated VRF prefixes to Cloudhop.	X	X	—	—

eBGP would be the protocol of choice between environments, allowing a magnitude of policy and control. This would be required on the Banknet border leaf switches and the Cloudhop router in order to advertise prefixes between environments.

If you have marked this row correctly, you scored a quarter point.

Feature	Banknet Border Leafs	Cloudhop Router	Direct Connect Link	Cloudhop Virtual Private Cloud
Configure NAT for privately addressed database and application VLANs hosted within the isolated VRF.	—	—	—	—

NAT isn't required for the on-premises infrastructures. You were informed the cloud provider supports RFC1918 addressing, so the traffic inbound from customers would target a public IP address hosted within Cloudhop and then be directed toward the RFC1918-addressed destinations within the Bank's isolated on-premises VRF for the application and database servers. A default route within the isolated VRF and Bank firewall would direct return traffic toward Cloudhop.

If you have marked this row correctly, you scored a quarter point.

Feature	Banknet Border Leafs	Cloudhop Router	Direct Connect Link	Cloudhop Virtual Private Cloud
Enable jumbo MTU support.	X	X	X	—

Typically, you would enable jumbo frames on your underlay fabric to cater for additional VXLAN encapsulation overhead, but there is encryption overhead on the link between

Cloudhop and the Bank on the Direct Connect link due to the requirements of traffic being encrypted. As such, enabling jumbo support on this link would be beneficial to avoid any fragmentation issues. The feature would need to be enabled on the interface of each connecting router and is also marked on the Direct Connect link for clarity, but you would still score a point if you have only selected the Banknet Border Leafs and Cloudhop Router.

If you have marked this row correctly, you scored a quarter point.

Feature	Banknet Border Leafs	Cloudhop Router	Direct Connect Link	Cloudhop Virtual Private Cloud
Enable IPsec.	X	X	X	—

Encryption is required on the Direct Connect link, so you just need to determine if MACSEC or IPsec is required. You were informed that the cloud provider supports IPsec, and previous information stated that both IPsec and MACSEC are supported on the border leaf switches. As such, IPsec would be used as the encryption method and hence why jumbo frame support would be beneficial on the link (MACSEC would still add 32 bytes of overhead to the MTU). The feature would need to be enabled on each connecting router and is also marked on Direct Connect Link for clarity, but you would still score a point if you have only selected the Banknet Border Leafs and Cloudhop Router.

If you have marked this row correctly, you scored a quarter point.

Feature	Banknet Border Leafs	Cloudhop Router	Direct Connect Link	Cloudhop Virtual Private Cloud
Enable MACSEC.	—	—	—	—

MACSEC isn't supported on the Cloudhop router, so this feature would not be enabled.

If you have marked this row correctly, you scored a quarter point.

Feature	Banknet Border Leafs	Cloudhop Router	Direct Connect Link	Cloudhop Virtual Private Cloud
Extend Channel application and database VLANs over VXLAN to Cloudhop.	—	—	—	—

This isn't required. You would just be providing routing information in how to route to the application and database VLANs. If you did want to extend the VLANs, you would need EVPN Type 2 routes over VXLAN multisite to achieve this, which the cloud provider does not support (it does support Type 5 routes, however, which would allow you to run multisite and route prefixes using VXLAN if you needed to). At the time of writing, cloud providers do not support the extension of Layer 2 networks into their environment using VXLAN.

If you have marked this row correctly, you scored a quarter point.

Feature	Banknet Border Leafs	Cloudhop Router	Direct Connect Link	Cloudhop Virtual Private Cloud
Create new VLANs for hosting application servers and database server.	X	—	—	—

This would be required only within the Channel VRF and on the border leaf and VTEPs within the DCs.

If you have marked this row correctly, you scored a quarter point.

Summary

This was a fast-paced scenario that incorporated some recent DC and cloud technology trends and innovations. It's unlikely you would be able to study for everything that came up during this lab, so if you have identified some weaker areas, don't be disheartened. Instead, discuss these areas with colleagues or your study group to gain an insight into rationale or specific technology that they might have more experience with than yourself. If you found the lab straightforward, then congratulations, as it was arguably more challenging than any scenario you might be presented with during your real exam.

Accurate scoring of the lab isn't crucial; neither is completing the lab strictly within two hours. The important factors are that you just experienced the level of complexity you will meet in the real exam, and you have benefited from the exercise of determining the correct answers based on the stipulated requirements. You should realize being successful in the CCDE exam isn't solely about best practice or industry trends; it's about connecting with the scenario and following it, and answering the design-related question based on the constraints and requirements provided to you within the background information, documents, and specific questions. If you found it too hard to select the optimum answer, you likely missed a constraint or requirement and can use this lab as practice to determine which information is worth making a note of and developing a skill to analyze design requirements to aid your design decisions.

If you do want to score yourself, a maximum of 39 points were available in this lab. If you scored over 28 points (approximately 70%), you have a very good chance of being successful on your CCDE exam.

Index

www.ingramcontent.com/pod-product-compliance
Lightning Source LLC
Chambersburg PA
CBHW080138220326
41598CB00032B/5108